:R

Technology Transfers
and Licensing

Technology Transfers and Licensing

John T. Ramsay

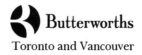 Butterworths

Toronto and Vancouver

Technology Transfers and Licensing

© Butterworths Canada Ltd. 1996
December 1996

The Butterworth Group of Companies

Canada:
75 Clegg Road, MARKHAM, Ontario L6G 1A1
and
1732-808 Nelson St., Box 12148, VANCOUVER, B.C. V6Z 2H2

Australia:
Butterworths Pty Ltd., SYDNEY

Ireland:
Butterworth (Ireland) Ltd., DUBLIN

Malaysia:
Malayan Law Journal Sdn Bhd, KUALA LUMPUR

New Zealand:
Butterworths of New Zealand Ltd., WELLINGTON

Singapore:
Butterworths Asia, SINGAPORE

South Africa:
Butterworth Publishers (Pty.) Ltd., DURBAN

United Kingdom:
Butterworth & Co. (Publishers) Ltd., LONDON

United States:
Michie, CHARLOTTESVILLE, Virginia

Canadian Cataloguing in Publication Data

Ramsay, John T.
    Technology transfers and licensing

Includes bibliographical references and index.
ISBN 0-433-39676-8

1. Technology transfer – Law and legislation – Canada. 2. License agreements – Canada.
3. Software protection – Law and legislation – Canada. 4. Copyright – Computer programs –
Canada. I. Title.

KE2908.R35 1996   346.7104'8   C96-932400-6
KF3145.R35 1996

Printed and bound in Canada.

Cover image supplied by Corel Corporation.

Reprint 1 - 2000

To my partner in law and life,
my wife, Margaret Copithorne Ramsay

ABOUT THE AUTHOR

John T. Ramsay graduated from the University of Western Ontario's Business School in 1963 and from the University of Toronto's Faculty of Law in 1966. He was admitted to the Ontario and Alberta bars in 1968.

John, a partner at Macleod Dixon, represents developers and users of innovative technology (including computer programs), advising them on protecting and transferring (including licensing) their products. He lectures extensively on licensing, legal aspects of computer programs, and structuring the technology company. In the technology area, John has written "Drafting Confidentiality Agreements in Canada", Intellectual Property Journal, Vol. 4, No. 2, December 1988 and the Canadian chapter on "Worldwide Trade Secrets Law", edited by Terrence F. MacLaren and published by Clark Boardman Callaghan, and was a member of the American Bar Association Intellectual Property Subcommittee that wrote the first draft "Model Software Licensing Provisions". He served as Vice President/Canada for the Licensing Executive Society (United States and Canada) Inc., 1992–94, and has served as Chair of the Canadian Bar Association Subcommittee on Computer and Computer-Related Technology. John recently presented "Pirates Beware: The Canadian Copyright Act and Computer Programs" to the 1994 Conference of the Canadian Association of Chemical Engineers; "Dreadful Drafting: The Do's and Don'ts of Licensing Agreements" to the 1992, 1993 and 1994 Licensing Executive Society United States/Canada annual meetings; and "Valuing Technology" to the law professors of the 1994 Learned Societies Conference. He also moderated "Small Dealing with Large: A Negotiating Case Study" at the 1994 and 1995 Licensing Executive Society meetings in Victoria, British Columbia and Toronto, Ontario.

He is presently involved in the American Bar Association's Key Escrow Working Group, a subset of the Digital Signature Working Group, and is leading several Advanced Licensing courses.

John lives outside of Calgary at Jumping Pound with his wife and two daughters.

PREFACE

We are at the dawn of an Age of Networked Intelligence — an age that is giving birth to a new economy, a new politics, and a new society. Businesses will be transformed, governments will be renewed, and individuals will be able to reinvest themselves — all with the help of the new information technology.[1]

Without technology transfers the Age of Networked Intelligence will be delayed. No individual business can separately research and develop technology fast enough to satisfy the seemingly insatiable demand for technological change. Outsourcing and insourcing will become a standard way of doing business, all involving technology transfers. These transfers will not be restricted by international boundaries and may occur electronically without any physical transfer. This revolutionary age will require individuals to reinvent their methods of doing business.

The relevance of the established legal, tax and business principles will be tested by the creativity of the parties, but still must be recognized and respected. Each party must be aware of not only the rules that apply to its position but also rules that apply to the other side's position. These principles must not be allowed to govern the relationship of the parties; they are simply tools to assist the parties to attain their desired goals.

This text is designed to acquaint negotiators of technology transfers (whether the transfers are licences, assignments or some other form of strategic alliance) with some of these principles. The author's intent is to provide these tools to readers who are business-persons, lawyers, accountants or to other advisors who may be involved in the negotiation process. The practical tips or "strategies" that are offered are drawn from lectures, books and articles and from the author's nearly 30 years in the practice of law.

The author frequently represents small- and medium-sized Canadian businesses that are licensing out their technology where, often as not, the other party is based in the United States. In many ways "English" Canada and the United States are similar, but often they have adopted different resolutions of the conflicting social and business philosophies that arise out of these basic principles. Although this text is written from a Canada/U.S. point of view, with a comparison of the rules that apply in each country, the discussion of the principles that give rise to the relevant rules will assist negotiators located in other countries.

---

[1] Don Tapscott, *The Digital Economy: Promise and Peril in the Age of Networked Intelligence* (McGraw-Hill, 1966), p. 2.

Part One of the text reviews methods of commercializing and valuating technology. Some value may come from the protection offered by the relevant intellectual property rights and therefore Part Two provides "primers" on these various rights. Part Three reviews the methods of effecting the technology transfer and recognizes that there may have to be a customization of the technology or a process to establish the acceptability of the technology. The possibility of restrictions on the parties' right to freely contract is the subject-matter of Part Four. Methods of payment and the inevitable tax reach of the governments comprise Part Five. Part Six provides practical guidance on establishing the term of the relationship, ending the relationship, and the consequences of termination. Part Seven provides a primer on the possible ways each party to a technology transfer may incur liability. Warranties and indemnities should not be given lightly and only after reviewing the legal issues discussed in this Part. Legalese is the topic of Part Eight. In this Part the author makes a plea for the use of plain language and also comments on the structure of preliminary matters and legal rules of general application.

This text would not have been possible without the willingness of the author's clients to patiently explain the technology and the type of business environment involved.

This text relies heavily on papers, articles and speeches made by many dedicated and sharing licensing practitioners, particularly in the Licensing Executives Society (United States and Canada) for which group I have had the honour of serving as Vice President–Canada. I am grateful to all those who have generously granted permission to reproduce from their works. I am deeply indebted to my colleague Jim Hassett, who has spent many hours of energy researching, editing and offering constructive suggestions. Likewise, my firm of Macleod Dixon has been very supportive, especially the librarians and those who have spent so much time typing and retyping the material — Bev Davis, Louise Gorski and Theda Offereins. In addition I owe a great debt to those who reviewed my material — Shawn Abbott, Melissa Ramsay and Margaret Ramsay.

Albert Einstein was monitoring an exam for graduate physics students and was told that there was problem because the questions on the exam were the same as on the previous year's test. "That's okay," he replied, "The answers are different this year."[2]

Calgary, Alberta   John T. Ramsay
December 1996

---

[2] *Ibid.*

TABLE OF CONTENTS

PART II — INTELLECTUAL PROPERTY PROTECTION

PART IV — RESTRICTIONS ON ABILITY TO CONTRACT

PART V — CONSIDERATION

PART VII — LIABILITY

PART VIII — LEGALESE

Part I

COMMERCIALIZING METHODS AND VALUATION

Chapter 1

METHODS OF COMMERCIALIZATION

Nor do men light a lamp and put it under a bushel, but on a stand, and it gives light to all in the house.[1]

1.1 Methods

Technology and the related intellectual property rights by themselves bring no value to either society as a whole or the individual innovator. The technology must be made available in some manner. It may be released to the general public for all to use, the innovator (whether an individual or a company) may keep the technology for its own business use or the technology may be made available to others for their use in exchange for valuable consideration. The innovator who keeps the technology for itself or who allows others to commercialize it will gain the maximum economic advantage only if the innovator has a method of excluding others from freely duplicating the technology. This chapter will discuss the various ways innovators may benefit from the development of technology.

1.1.1 Release to the Public

The innovator may release the technology to the world for the benefit of humankind. For example, a professor who has developed a method of purifying water in rural areas may altruistically publish his or her findings and, thus, freely permit everyone to use his or her technology. The reward would come from the prestige and honour of publishing those findings. Less idealistically, an innovator who publishes may also receive an indirect economic reward by satisfying the scholastic "publish or perish" requirements of many colleges and universities. Some commercially oriented innovators choose to publish their innovations because they do not wish to patent them but do want to prevent others from gaining a patent on similar technology. For example, IBM produces its monthly *Technical Disclosure Bulletin*, in which it publishes its own innovations and those of others who wish to publish anonymously. Apparently this is "one of the most frequently cited prior art sources by the USPTO" (United States Patent and Trademark Office).[2] The Software Patent Institute

---

[1]   Matthew 5:15, R.S.V.
[2]   See advertisement in Vol. 38, No. 1, January 1995.

has developed a database that can be used by inventors wishing to make "defensive disclosures",[3] which also can be made anonymously.[4] An innovator may release to the public details of technology that it wants to be accepted as a standard for all to use. This practice is adopted by some of the developers of software usable on the Internet. More frequently, however, technology offered freely to everyone is not used in practice; most business entities are not prepared to make any investment to improve or to commercialize technology so readily available to all of its competitors. Unfortunately, considerable amounts of promising technology developed in universities or in government research laboratories remain unused because no one is prepared to make the investment to commercialize it.

1.1.2 Keep the Technology for Itself

The innovator may decide to keep the innovation for itself and exclude others from using it. This may give the business an edge that sets it apart in a highly competitive market. To keep the competitive advantage, the business entity will have to find a way to prevent its competitors from legally cloning its technology. An innovator may decide to keep the technology to itself if (a) it can afford to complete further stages of the research and development, (b) it can commercialize the technology itself in the ordinary course of its business, (c) the technology is essentially know-how of a type that is difficult to pass on to others, or (d) the product or process resulting from the exploitation of the technology is highly volatile and the innovator could suffer from an adverse product liability claim or adverse publicity.

1.1.3 Selling All the Rights to the Technology

The innovator may decide that it will not commercialize the technology itself but rather will transfer all its rights to someone else. This decision could result from:

(a) the market-place being controlled by a few large business entities who will make the innovator's entry into the market-place extremely expensive;

(b) the innovation being usable only in conjunction with other technology;

(c) the innovator's immediate need for cash not allowing it to wait for royalties under a licence agreement to flow in to cover its continuing expenses and research. In the early stages of some technology ventures, even though a licence with a running royalty would produce more money in the long run, an outright sale might be necessary to fund the business' short-term future;

---

[3] See American Bar Association, Section on Intellectual Property Law, *Annual Report* 1994/95, p. 328.

[4] Although the inventor may wish to make the disclosure, it may have good business reasons not to let others know that it is even working in the area of the disclosure.

(d)   the innovation being outside the innovator's business altogether and the innovator not wanting any further involvement with it; or

(e)   the innovator's unwillingness or inability to fund foreseeable infringement or product liability suits.

1.1.4 Transfer Only a Portion of the Rights

The innovator may be able to transfer or assign a portion of its rights to the intellectual property related to the innovation. For example, the innovator could partially transfer its copyright for a specified application (a "field of use"). The same principles that apply to a full assignment of its rights will have general application to a partial assignment (protection, value, payment and allocation of risks) in addition to principles that apply to co-ownership,[5] all of which will be discussed later in this text.

1.1.5 License or Establish an Alliance

The innovator may decide to transfer only a right of use reserving to itself certain rights ("licence"). The licence could exclude everyone, including the transferor, from using the licensed technology ("exclusive licence"), could exclude all others but not the innovator ("sole licence") or could be non-exclusive.[6] Exclusivity could relate to fields of use,[7] time periods or geographic territories.[8] Instead of continuing to develop or market the technology independently, the innovator may decide to enter into some sort of an alliance (*e.g.*, strategic alliance, joint venture, industry consortium) to further develop or market the innovation jointly. Each party may have technology desired by the other party. Then there could be cross-licences whereby each party licenses to the other either all or only part of its intellectual property, perhaps restricted to a particular application. A variation of a cross-licence is a pooling arrangement where holders of intellectual property "pool" their intellectual property either for their own benefit or to offer the package to third parties in a common marketing effort. The advantages of cross-licensing and pooling include integrating complementary techniques, reduction of transaction costs and removal of patent "blocking" positions.[9]

1.2 Common Elements

Although the methods of commercializing technology are diverse, there are many common elements that will apply to each of them and that will be discussed further in this text. In each case, the extent of the reward to the innovator that chooses to commercialize its technology may depend on its ability to exclude others from replicating and using the technology without

---

[5]   See §4.39 of this text.
[6]   See §7.15 of this text.
[7]   See §7.5 of this text.
[8]   See §7.8 of this text.
[9]   See §3.21(c) of this text but anti-trust rules must be kept in mind; see Chapter 10 of this text.

compensation,[10] the extent of the rights transferred and those retained,[11] the continuing contributions of each party,[12] the tax effect on those contributions[13] and the allocation of risks of liability.[14]

---

[10]   See Chapters 3, 4, 5 and 6 of this text.
[11]   Generally, see Chapter 7 of this text.
[12]   See §2.11 of this text.
[13]   See Chapter 12 of this text.
[14]   See Chapters 14, 15 and 16 of this text.

Chapter 2

VALUATION

There is a risk of profit and loss in everything involved in a license. No matter how the license is structured, the most intelligent price is a balance between the risks of profit and loss — a risk balance.[1]

2.1 Introduction

There is no one "right way" to value technology. Each party to a transaction must examine a number of factors and come to a balance of risk and profit that endeavours to produce a fair result for all concerned. The extent of risk involved will influence the discount rate to be applied to anticipated future cash flow; the higher the risk, the higher the discount rate. The actual allocation of these risks will also influence price. The factors outlined below may assist in determining a fair "risk" balance.

2.2 Strength of Intellectual Property Protection[2]

Patents are not always the best form of protection. Some technologies may be protected in a number of ways, including patent, copyright and trade secrecy. The innovator of the technology may have to choose among the various protections. Patent protection requires disclosure and loss of trade secrecy.[3] Copyright and trade secrecy do not prevent independent development,[4] as do patents, but the ability to maintain secrecy[5] may successfully delay a competitor from "cloning" the technology, perhaps providing an adequate competitive advantage especially with rapidly evolving technologies. The type of protection chosen will depend on the type of technology involved and its economic life. The strength of the chosen intellectual property protection to exclude competitors will affect the value of the technology.

---

[1] Tom Arnold, "100 Factors Involved in Pricing the Technology Licensing", in Licensing Law Library, *1988 Licensing Law Handbook* (New York: Clark Boardman Co. Ltd.) (hereinafter "Arnold, '100 Factors'").

[2] The various forms of intellectual property protection will be reviewed in Chapters 3, 4, 5 and 6 of this text.

[3] See §§3.15 to 3.17 of this text.

[4] See §§4.12 and 6.3 of this text.

[5] For copyright see §4.10.1 of this text.

2.2.1 Strength of a Patent

When evaluating the strength of the protection offered by a patent,[6] consider:

(a)   has the patent been previously litigated?

(b)   has the patent been subject to re-examination?

(c)   have other sophisticated parties licensed the patent?

(d)   does the patent apply to the entire product, or merely to a feature of the product?

(e)   the effect on the target transferee's ability to manufacture if it could not obtain a licence for the protected technology;

(f)   the ability to detect infringement;

(g)   the ease of working around the patented claims;

(h)   has competent patent counsel provided an opinion on the validity of the patent taking into account the credibility of the claims, their application to the intended use and any potential for a claim of "patent abuse";[7] and

(i)   efforts made by patent owner to develop the market-place for the patented technology?[8]

2.3 Stage of Development

The stage of development of the innovation is very material in determining its value. A transferee will pay more if the certainty of profits is increased and the risk of loss is decreased.[9] The more certain the qualities of the product are, the better will be the profit/risk ratio. The value of technology increases in the following order of development:

(a)   The *undeveloped idea* has the least value.[10] Although it may require the greatest level of genius, capturing its value is difficult without further development. How does one disclose the idea without losing all value? Ideas cannot be protected by copyright or patent but only by trade secrecy. The potential transferee will be very reluctant to even receive a disclosure of an undeveloped, unpatentable idea because the transferee's independent development may become tainted. It will not want to risk any suggestion of misappropriation of the idea.

(b)   The development of the idea to the *research stage* has more value, particularly if the research data confirms the inherent hypothesis or the author of the research is highly reputable. The research process gives credibility to the researcher/innovator and encourages further participation.

---

6   See §3.2 of this text.

7   See §3.2 of this text.

8   The above points were adapted from the American Bar Association, Section on Intellectual Property Law Chicago, Illinois, *Annual Report* 1994/95, pp. 487–8 (hereinafter "ABA *Annual Report* 94/95").

9   See Arnold, "100 Factors", p. 297.

10   See §§3.5, 3.15, 4.3 and 6.4 of this text.

(c)   When the resulting product becomes ready for market even though still unproven, market value is added. The strategic partner does not have to perform the research to see whether or not a product can even be produced.

(d)   Once the product is proven to perform as anticipated, more value is added.

(e)   When the product, proven as to performance, is shown to have strong market appeal, more value is added.

(f)   Provision of not only a proven product, both as to performance and market appeal, but also the financial strength to allow a credible and supportable performance guarantee gives further value.[11]

2.4 Cost

Although frequently referred to, the cost of development is generally the most irrelevant factor to a transferee.[12] Costs that are likely to be irrelevant are those expended on

(a)   the inventor who is wasteful of time and resources in developing the technology in contrast to the inventor who is highly productive;

(b)   eliminating unworkable variables that will not be incurred by competitors;

(c)   development that may have produced a well-researched product, but the benefit offered by that product may have little correlation to the cost expended;

(d)   an invention with features the market does not need; or

(e)   a very narrow market.

Richard Razgaitis in his excellent article, "Pricing Intellectual Property",[13] points out that the cost to Picasso of oils, brushes and canvas had no correlation to the market value of his resulting paintings.

2.5 Relevant Costs

The following costs are likely relevant:

(a)   reproducing or working around the invention, especially in a tight time frame;

(b)   acquiring in the market-place a competitive/displaced product — this cost may set an upper limit on the value and on the extent of the competitive advantage;

(c)   reproducing clinical studies for a pharmaceutical product;

---

[11]   See Arnold, "100 Factors", pp. 297–98.

[12]   See Association of University Technology Managers, Inc., *Technology Transfer Manual 1993*, VII–Chapter 4, p. 1, at 9 (hereinafter called "AUTM *Manual*").

[13]   AUTM *Manual*, VII- Chapter 4, p. 1, at 10.

(d)   obtaining governmental approvals;

(e)   savings to the user resulting from the innovative technology; and

(f)   policing the licence agreement:

  (i)   availability and cost of performing a meaningful audit of a "running royalty", especially in a foreign country;

  (ii)   ease of access to a suitable court on a cost-effective basis to enforce payment;

  (iii) availability of an effective court order to restrain continued breach of contract or infringement.

2.6 Comparable Rates

If they can be located, comparable royalties or royalty rates can be very helpful. What the transferor may have received from other licensees, what the licensee may have paid for a licence of substitute technology and what is the customary rate, if any, in the particular industry are all very relevant factors.[14] There are two significant challenges: first, finding any material that is useful and, second, seeing how it compares to your situation. All variables must be compared, not just the resulting royalty rate. For example, a royalty could be lower in one case than in another if the licensee contributes more in the first case, such as contributing material improvements or complementary technology.[15]

2.6.1 Sources of Comparable Rates

Ashley J. Stevens suggests that the licensor look first to its own in-house data base for comparable deals.[16] These deals will provide guidance as to techniques previously used, with both good and bad results. In a rapidly changing market, however, what worked in the past may not be appropriate in the future. Stevens' second source of material is surveys, but Stevens points out that "There aren't many good surveys on average or comparable royalty rates. This is difficult information to obtain on a wide and consistent basis."[17]

2.6.2 Difficulty in Making Comparisons

Goldscheider cautions us to review precedents carefully for the "many distinguishing circumstances that could effectively negate [their] relevance". As examples, he recommends watching for "differences in market conditions for any

---

[14] See items 1, 2 and 11 of the list of classic valuation factors in *Georgia Pacific Corp. v. United States Plywood-Champion Papers Inc.*, 318 F. Supp. 1116 (1970), as placed in a software patent context in ABA, 94/95, pp. 488-89.

[15] Ashley J. Stevens has contributed a useful chapter entitled "Finding Comparable Licensing Terms" in the AUTM *Manual*, VII–Chapter 5, p. 1.

[16] AUTM *Manual*, VII–Chapter 5, p. 2.

[17] *Ibid.* See also Patrick H. Sullivan, "Royalty Rates Conform to 'Industry Norm'", in Les Nouvelles, the Journal of the Licensing Executive Society, Vol. XXIX, No. 3, September 1994, p. 140, at 145 (hereinafter "Sullivan, 'Royalty Rates', Les Nouvelles, September 1994").

reason, variations in the competitive strengths of the parties at different points and times, or whether a particular license was part of the broader transaction, where other conditions may have been paramount".[18] Other authors point out that

> statistically significant "industry rates" are generally not available; even if they were, they more than likely would neglect many of the economic conditions that should be factored into any specific royalty negotiation. In order to facilitate successful licensing programs, organizations need to understand and prioritize their own strategic, economic and legal motivations as well as those of prospective licensing partners.[19]

2.6.3 Publications

A number of periodicals on licensing economics and valuation are published on a regular basis, and material is becoming available on the Internet. Another source is material that becomes publicly available through security/corporate disclosure requirements, such as the Toronto Stock Exchange or the U.S. Security and Exchange Commission (SEC)[20] and published court cases. Unfortunately, even with the SEC, when agreements are filed "the specific dollar figures as well as percentage rate data" are usually deleted.[21]

2.6.4 Networks

One study showed that although lawyers and licensing executives were "slow to reveal specific examples of running [royalty] rates from their own experience"[22] and "although royalty rate information is held highly confidential, lawyers and executives involved in this activity have an informal network of communication that keeps them advised of the results of recent agreements".[23] Networks can be built through active memberships in industry associations such as the Licensing Executives Society and the Association of University Technology Managers and their various committees.

2.7 Profit to Licensor

The profits to the licensor are one of the most relevant valuation factors.[24] Consider the following:

---

[18] Robert Goldscheider, "Litigation Backgrounder for Licensing", in Les Nouvelles, the Journal of the Licensing Executive Society, Vol. XXIX, No.1, March 1994, p. 20, at 24 (hereinafter "Goldscheider, 'Litigation Backgrounder', Les Nouvelles, March 1994").

[19] Daniel M. McGavock, David A. Haas and Michael P. Patin, "Factors Affecting Royalty Rates", in Les Nouvelles, the Journal of the Licensing Executive Society, Vol. XXVII, No. 2, June 1992, p. 107, at 107 (hereinafter "McGavock et al., 'Factors', Les Nouvelles, June 1992").

[20] Stevens, AUTM *Manual*, VII–Chapter 5, p. 5.

[21] Sullivan, "Royalty Rates", Les Nouvelles, September 1994, p. 140, at 144.

[22] *Ibid.*

[23] *Ibid.*, p. 145.

[24] See for example item 12 of the *Georgia-Pacific* classic valuation factors placed in the context of software patents, ABA *Annual Report* 94/95, pp. 488–89.

(a)   savings that may be expected by the licensee as a result of the use of the licensor's innovation;

(b)   economic life of the technology — how soon obsolescence will occur (particularly rapid in the computer/software industries);

(c)   costs that the licensee will save by not having to independently develop the subject technology, including the costs of:

    (i)   completing the research and development;

    (ii)   obtaining the requisite governmental approvals;

    (iii)   intellectual property protection: obtaining, maintaining and protecting;

    (iv)   manufacture/reproduction;

    (v)   packaging;

    (vi)   advertising; and

    (vii)   distribution.

2.7.1 *"The 25% Rule*

There is a widely cited tool of pricing known as the "25% Rule"; it is appealing in its apparent simplicity. In the appropriate circumstances, it will provide a fair risk balance. The AUTM *Manual* provides a summary of the "25% Rule":[25]

4.8.A. The 25% Rule

One of the most widely cited tools of pricing is the infamous "25% Rule". It has various manifestations, but when most managers invoke it they usually mean either of the following:

(1)   The royalty in $ should be 1/4th of the *savings* in $ to the licensee by the use of the license subject matter, or

(2)   The royalty in % of the net sales price should be 1/4th of the *profit* before taxes enjoyed by the licensee as a result of selling products made by the licensed subject matter.

Although this looks simple, it is not. One of the key issues is the degree the licensed subject matter accomplishes the savings or produces the profit. For example, an invention incorporated into a process may produce a savings of $1 a unit. However, when one examines in detail how such savings are attained, it may be that there are several other technologies that already belong to the licensee and that will need to be exploited in order to realize the full $1. In such a case is the licensor deserving of 25 cents, or should the savings be discounted in some way before the 1/4th fraction is computed? The issue seems to hinge on whether the invention opens the door to an otherwise locked room called "I can save you $1" or whether it is a link in a multi-link chain that together combine to save $1. [When using a savings approach, the technology transfer manager should build in some inflation factor to avoid collecting 25 cents a unit over a 15-year period when inflation eats into the real value of the royalty. Remember the $1 savings is $1 in the currency of the year that the royalty is calculated (in this example). Ten years later, with inflation or increasing costs of electricity or a particular raw

---

[25]   AUTM *Manual*, VII–Chapter 4, p. 28.

material, the savings could be $8 in the currency of that 10th year; the agreement should have some provision for the calculation of royalty to similarly inflate in $ so that, as in this example, it would yield $2 in the 10th year.]

In the second (profit) manifestation of the rule, things get even more complicated. Although "net sales" is generally a straightforward term to apply, profit before tax is subject to many interpretations. Normally, the royalty rate is applied to the royalty basis defined by "net sales" as follows:

> Net sales price is the gross invoice price charged less all allowances for returns, and less cash and other discounts granted, charges for packaging and shipping, and sales and excise taxes included. [This particular form of the definition is adapted from an article by Evelyn M. Sommer, "Patent and Technology License Agreements Explained", The Licensing Journal, August 1993, p. 3 ff. This article and other similar sources also deal with an important but complicated issue of transfer pricing: that is, when a licensee "sells" or transfers the product made by the practice of the technology to another division or a subsidiary of the licensee.]

There is no comparable generally accepted definition of "profit before tax". One of the basic problems is determining an appropriate income. . . .

2.7.2 25% of What

The rule loses its appealing simplicity as you try to apply it. How do you calculate the savings for the user? At what point on the revenue statement do you calculate profit? How do you allocate overhead and amortize fixed costs? Is this profit calculated before or after research and development costs? Robert Goldscheider suggests that one start with a "25% split to the licensor and then either 'tune' this figure up or down, depending on the peculiar circumstances of each case, including the significance of the intellectual property portfolio and the location of the principal burden of risk".[26] Goldscheider states that with "the benefit of considerable experience", the 25% Rule has been useful. This experience perhaps allows the evaluator to move the 25% factor to a fair allocation of the risk of profit and loss.

2.7.3 "The 50% Rule

Again, the AUTM *Manual* provides a useful summary:[27]

4.8.B. The 50% Rule

4.8.B.1 The 50% Rule, Version I

A related version of the 25% rule has been stated by Duke Leahey in approximately the following fashion:

(1)   At the point of product introduction, approximately 50% of the total risk of product failure remains;

---

[26]   Goldscheider, "Litigation Backgrounder", Les Nouvelles, March 1994, p. 25.
[27]   AUTM *Manual*, VII–Chapter 4, p. 28.

(2)   If the inventing organization brings the technology to the state of product introduction, it is entitled to 50% of the total reward (profit);

(3)   If the commercializing organization participates in the pre-market development costs and risks, it is entitled to more than 50% of the total reward.

From this perspective, the 25% rule represents a 50:50 participation in the pre-market risk. Accordingly, the 50% Rule suggests that the way to determine a fair apportionment of profit is to assess the extent to which all the pre-market risks and costs will have been borne by the licensor and licensee when the product finally gets to the market. Unfortunately, this is not easy to do.

All the variations of the 25% or 50% Rules are useful; they all must be considered in the valuation of any technology. The exercise is helpful even if the principles are rejected because they do not apply to the particular fact situation. In conclusion, however, it must be noted that the premise that a fair share of profit should belong to a licensor has been accepted by the leading U.S. case *Georgia-Pacific Corp. v. United States Plywood-Champion Papers, Inc.*[28]

2.8 Controlled Greed

If the price is established so that it produces a very high profit margin for the commercialization of the technology, others will be encouraged to replicate the technology. High profit margins may have to be limited to the time period in which it would take others to get to market with competing technology, or, perhaps, even a shorter time to discourage others from continuing research on clones or substitutes. High royalty rates may also encourage competitors to infringe or challenge the validity of the intellectual property protection rather than concede to licensing. The risk of future litigation may be more attractive than the present certainty of high license fees.

2.9 Market Characterization

The characteristics of the market will influence the overall value of the innovation. This requires consideration of:

(a)   the market for the technology — leading edge technology may not be needed and may be characterized as technology that "was, is, and always will be the technology of the future";[29]

---

[28]   318 F. Supp. 1116 (1970). For a further discussion on the valuation principles set out in this case, see §17.5 of this text. This case discussed the methods of calculating damages from infringement and lists as its 13th factor:

13. The portion of the realizable profit that should be credited to the invention, as distinguished from the non-patented elements, the manufacturing process, business risk, or significant features or improvements added by the infringer.

[29]   John T. Preston, "Success Factors in Technology Development", An Entrepreneurial Approach to the Commercialization of Technology, March 7 and 8, 1995, Edmonton, Alberta, Canada, Workshop Sponsored by PACT (Partnership/Alberta for the Commercialization of Technology) (unpublished) (hereinafter "Preston, 'Success Factors', in Edmonton").

(b)   the distinctiveness of the market niche;

(c)   the size of the market;

(d)   the extent of competition;

(e)   the size and nature of competitors;

(f)   the lead time before technology is "cloned":

    (i)   ease of design around;

    (ii)   the lead time compared to the economic life;

(g)   access to alternate and competing technology;

(h)   effect of restraint of trade rules;

(i)   availability of cross-licensing to avoid intellectual property infringement suits;

(j)   difficulties in repatriating money from a country that has currency controls; and

(k)   local market requirements:

    (i)   local agent required;

    (ii)   need to adapt technology to local market (*e.g.*, electrical device);

    (iii)   inflation (*e.g.*, Brazil/Russia); and

    (iv)   currency devaluations.

2.10 Spin-off Potential

Some technologies are more valuable than others due to their "spin-off" potential. Technology that has many uses in different industries may have more enduring value than technology that can be used only one way in one industry.

2.10.1 Trickle-down/ Trickle-up Spin-off

Some technology may have a "trickle-down" spin-off effect.[30] If the technology has a high performance and will be sold in low volumes at a high cost with a high margin, the entity commercializing the technology may gain the opportunity to learn about cost reduction techniques before it introduces the technology to a much larger mass market. On the other hand, technology could be introduced to a market-place that is already well served by competitive products, where the product introduced has low incremental performance and a high volume sold at low cost with low margins. In that case, the commercializing entity may decide to introduce the product into that market to learn more about the manufacturing and marketing and then to use that knowledge in areas with higher incremental performance and higher margins. For example, a company may decide to market liquid displays in digital watches (a well established, perhaps even saturated market) to learn more about producing liquid displays for

---

[30]   Lewis M. Branscomb, "Building Capacity to Create, Share, and Use Technology: Civil and Military Models", An Entrepreneurial Approach to the Commercialization of Technology, March 7 and 8, 1995, Edmonton, Alberta, Canada, Workshop Sponsored by PACT (Partnership/Alberta for the Commercialization of Technology) (unpublished).

lap-top computers or, perhaps, even television monitors (a low-volume higher margin market).[31]

2.10.2 Sell, Design, Build

A company may use the "sell-design-build" business model to its advantage. It may enter into a contract for the development of technology for a particular customer on a cost recovery basis, but may retain the rights to market the technology to others. The company may give the customer exclusivity for certain specified uses, reserving other uses for itself; this exclusivity may be forever or for only a limited period of time.

2.10.3 Convoyed Sales

Another spin-off is "convoyed" sales.[32] Although the convoyed sales must be included as part of the overall value, different royalty rates may be applicable to the convoyed sales than to sales on the basic technology.[33] One study ranked the value of convoyed sales fairly low in relation to other valuation factors. The authors, expressing caution as to the validity of their study, state that "it is possible that convoyed sales relationships are very difficult to identify, especially for new technology, and therefore do not carry much weight in negotiations".[34]

2.11 Contribution of the Parties

The contribution of each party to the development and commercialization of the technology will affect the amount it will have to pay to participate. Some of the factors to consider are:

(a) who will significantly contribute to future enhancements:[35]
  (i) continued contributions of the inventor in research and development;
  (ii) expertise of licensee and its presently developed improvements that can be easily integrated;
(b) corporate reputation of either party, which will ease the opening of markets;
(c) access to markets:
  (i) established distribution network;
  (ii) complementary products being distributed — tag-along or derivative sales;

---

[31] *Ibid.*

[32] See Goldscheider, "Litigation Backgrounder", Les Nouvelles, March 1994, p. 20, at 24. See also McGavock et al., "Factors", Les Nouvelles, June 1992, p. 107, at 109. See also item 6 of the *Georgia Pacific* classic valuation factors, as placed in a software patent context in ABA, 94/95, p. 489.

[33] See Goldscheider, "Litigation Backgrounder", Les Nouvelles, March 1994, p. 20, at 24.

[34] McGavock et al., "Factors", Les Nouvelles, June 1992, p. 107, at 110.

[35] For a discussion on improvements generally, see Chapter 9 of this text.

(d)   insight that recognizes a significant pending shift in the market;

(e)   network of connections — ability to introduce strategically placed individuals to the innovator's technology for continued research and development, additional funding or market entry is highly valuable.

2.12 Unique Attributes of the Team: Preston's Four Non-technical Components for Success

It is not only the quality of the technology that produces commercial success. The attributes of the various members of the commercializing team will also contribute to the success or failure. Preston sets out four non-technical components for success.[36]

(1)   Quality of Management:

management gets high quality ratings if it maintains a healthy balance sheet; has a clearly focused strategy; and is realistic about marketing;[37]

(2)   Quality of the Investor:

there are a number of factors that influence the quality of the investors: first, the track record in building successful businesses; second, the network of connections with potential partners or customers; third, the level of personal involvement the investor is willing to devote to the business; and fourth, their access to money and long-term vision.[38]

(3)   Passion for Success:

the passion of the various players is a key deterrent of success. Worded differently, any new business will encounter hundreds of barriers before it succeeds. People with no passion will use the first barrier as excuse for failure, while people with high passion will do whatever it takes to overcome the barriers. . . . Should any of these three groups be indifferent about success, the future of the company will be greatly impacted. Some companies succeed despite low marks in one or more areas, but as competitive pressures increase, it becomes more important that the start-up company have dedicated personnel. People with high passion will achieve spectacular results, and do whatever is necessary to reach their goals. As a result, it is important to evaluate and modify, if possible, the strength, determination and commitment (or 'passion') of the technologists, the managers and the investors.

There are many ways to kill passion, but greed takes first place.[39]

(4)   Image:

The image factor is the way the company is perceived by potential strategic partners, investors, customers, employees . . . for example, a biotech company

---

[36]   Preston, "Success Factors", in Edmonton.

[37]   *Ibid.*, p. 6.

[38]   *Ibid.*

[39]   *Ibid.*, p. 7.

with a Nobel Laureate on its Board of Directors will have more credibility in presenting a joint venture plan to a large pharmaceutical company than a company with unknown scientists. Similarly, a computer company in partnership with IBM will have an easier time selling its next product than a company without such an endorsement. Also, a company deriving its technology from Stanford, Harvard, or MIT will have a higher image rating than technology from a lesser known university.[40]

2.13 Type of Licence

The more security the licensee has to attain desired profits, the more it should be expected to pay. Some of the features of a licence that will influence value are:

    (a)   exclusivity:[41]
        (i)   excluding all future licensees;
        (ii) excluding all licensees, including the present ones;
        (iii) excluding you, the licensor;
    (b)   field of use restrictions;
    (c)   territorial restrictions;
    (d)   value added restrictions; and
    (e)   duration of the licence: the shorter the term, the less may be the value.[42]

2.14 Type of Consideration to be Paid

There are many types of considerations that are payable and the method of selection may very well influence value. The more paid up front, the more the risk to the transferee increases and the greater the discount rate for anticipated cash flow can become. The type of consideration may significantly affect value, whether such consideration be a running royalty, one or more lump sum payments, equity shares issued by the licensee, lending of continued research, fees for support, appointment to advisory boards, consulting/employment fees, certain first rights, most favoured licensee rights, grant backs and settlement of outstanding litigation.

2.15 Warranties

The extent of credible and supportable warranties against product defects and infringement will also influence value. Consider the following:

    (a)   product warranties,[43] their scope and limitations, the track record of the licensor in remedying defects, the service record of the transferor, such as providing support, training on methods of use

---

[40] *Ibid.*, p. 8. Note that Preston is from MIT.
[41] For a further discussion of these topics, see Chapter 7.
[42] See, for example, item 7 of the *Georgia-Pacific* classic valuation factors, as placed in a software patent context, ABA *Annual Report* 94/95, pp. 488–89. These factors are set out in §2.13 of this text.
[43] For further discussion on warranties against product defects, see Chapter 14 of this text.

and the provision of seminars to enhance general knowledge that
will encourage use;

(b)   infringement warranties,[44] their scope and limitation as to type of
infringement, amount of damages and territory covered;

(c)   risk of bankruptcy of the transferor and its effect on the technology
transfer agreement.

---

[44]   For further discussion on infringement and its consequences, see Chapter 16 of this text.

Part II

INTELLECTUAL PROPERTY PROTECTION

Chapter 3

PATENTS

The primary goal of the patent system is to encourage innovation and commercialization of technological advances. To this end, the patent system offers an incentive to inventors to publicly disclose their inventions in exchange for the exclusive right to prevent others from making, using, offering for sale or selling the inventions throughout the [country that issues the patent] or importing the inventions into the [country that issues the patent].[1]

3.1 Applicable Legislation

Patent rights, which are restricted to the country that issues the relevant patent, come only from the legislation of that country.[2] There are no common-law rights to a patent in Canada or the United States. If the legislation does not cover the subject-matter, then a patent is not available.

Strategy: What you see is what you get. If the subject-matter of your invention is not covered by the applicable Patent Act, your invention is not patentable under that Act. Consider another form of intellectual property protection.

PATENTS VERSUS RESTRAINT OF TRADE

3.2 Patents Give Right to Prevent

In practice, the Canadian and U.S. *Patent Acts* do not give the patentee the right to exploit any technology; they give only the right to prevent others from doing certain things. The patentee may need the consent, or a "licence", from the holder of another patent or intellectual property right if the making, using or

---

[1]   United States, Intellectual Property in the National Information Infrastructure, the report of the Working Group on Intellectual Property Rights, Bruce A. Lehman, Assistant Secretary of Commerce and Commissioner of Patents and Trademarks, Chair, September 1995 (hereinafter "NII"). This report is available on the Internet by pointing the Gopher Client to IITF. DOC.GOV and is located on many other sites on the Internet.

[2]   In Canada, this is the Patent Act, R.S.C 1985, c. P-4 (hereinafter "Patent Act (Canada)"). In the United States, this is Title 35 of the United States Code (U.S.C.), 1952 (hereinafter "U.S. Patent Act").

selling of the patented invention infringes that other person's intellectual property right.[3] The right to make, use or sell a patented invention may be regulated by federal, provincial, state or local law.[4]

3.2.1 Patents as Monopolies

Patents are often referred to as "monopolies"; this is a misnomer arising out of the title to the first patent legislation in England — the *Statute of Monopolies*.[5] Patent protection is better described as an exclusionary right, particularly in the United States where the word "monopolies" has profound antitrust ramifications.[6]

Strategy: Patents are exclusionary not monopolistic.

3.2.2 Constitutional Protection Versus Restraint of Trade

In the United States patents and copyrights are constitutionally protected and therefore prevail over government policies such as the federal anti-restraint of trade policy — policy that otherwise opposes monopolies. Thus, the courts are forced to reconcile these competing policies: the courts and technology transfer agreements that involve an American party must "walk a thin line" between these two bodies of law. On the one hand, they must protect, as broadly as possible, the rights of the intellectual property holder and its licensees; on the other hand, they must avoid protecting these rights so broadly that they cross the line between the legitimate exercise of intellectual property rights and the violation of competition law. This gives rise "to the 'rule of necessity', which seeks to limit patentees to exercising their rights in a manner least restrictive of competition".[7]

---

[3]   It is not the holding of the patent that gives rise to the infringement; it is the making, using or selling of the invention covered by the patent.

[4]   See Art. 28 of The Agreement on Trade-Related Aspects of Intellectual Property Rights (hereinafter "TRIPPS") where it identifies the difference between "product" patent rights and "process" patent rights, stating:

    1. A patent shall confer on its owner the following exclusive rights:

        (a) where the subject matter of a patent is a product, to prevent third parties not having his consent from the acts of: making, using, offering for sale, selling, or importing for these purposes that product;

        (b) where the subject matter of a patent is a process, to prevent third parties not having his consent from the act of using the process, and from the acts of: using, offering for sale, selling, or importing for these purposes at least the product obtained directly by that process.

    2. Patent owners shall also have the right to assign, or transfer by succession, the patent and to conclude licensing contracts.

[5]   1623, 21 Jac. I, c. 3.

[6]   R.M. Milgrim, *Milgrim On Licensing*, rev. ed. (New York: Matthew Bender, 1995), §2.28 (hereinafter "Milgrim, *On Licensing*").

[7]   R.J. Roberts, "Technology Transfer Agreements and North American Competition" in M. Goudreau, G. Bisson, N. Lacasse and L. Perret, eds., *Exporting our Technology: International Protection and Transfers of Industrial Innovations* (Montreal: Wilson & Lafleur, 1995), p. 151, at 158; also printed in Intellectual Property Journal, December 1995, Vol. 9, No. 3, p. 247.

3.3 Civil Remedy for Restraint of Trade Violation

Although anti-restraint of trade rules could have been restricted to criminal actions, in the United States they have given rise to civil remedies, including damages, that may be sought by competitors.

3.3.1 Unique to the United States?

This protection versus competition tension does not exist in other countries. In agreements where all parties are Canadian, one must be careful not to expect anti-restraint of trade policy to have the same restrictive effect on patents and copyrights as it would on American parties. Yet,

> U.S. antitrust jurisprudence must . . . be borne in mind when drafting and reviewing Canadian technology transfer agreements that might affect in some way commerce or consumers in the United States. Where the effect of such agreement is deemed substantial enough, the courts in the United States will assert jurisdiction extraterritorially and review the agreement for conformity to the requirements of U.S. antitrust law.[8]

Strategy: In the United States, patents may not be abused to unduly restrain trade.[9]

PATENTABLE SUBJECT-MATTER

3.4 Works Covered

The Canadian *Patent Act* provides protection to any "new and useful art, process, machine, manufacture or composition of matter, or any new and useful improvement in any art, process, machine, manufacture or composition of matter".[10] The U.S. *Patent Act* is substantially similar, speaking in terms of "processes, machines, manufactures or compositions of matter".[11] The latter three categories define "things" while the process category defines inventions that consist of "actions" (*i.e.*, a series of steps or acts to be performed).[12] The scope of the subject-matter of a patent may be summarized as follows:

  (a)   An art is abstract in that it is capable of contemplation, but concrete in that it involves applying physical forces to physical objects to change the character or condition of material objects; it is broader than a method or process.[13]

---

[8]   *Ibid.*, p. 155.
[9]   See Chapter 10 of this text.
[10]   *Patent Act* (Canada), s. 2.
[11]   35 U.S.C. §101. See also TRIPPS, Art. 27.
[12]   *Legal Analysis to Support Proposed Examination Guidelines for Computer-implemented Inventions*, October 3, 1995, Patent and Trademark Office, United States Department of Commerce, Section III.A (hereinafter "*Legal Analysis*"). In the U.S. *Patent Act* "the term 'process' means process, art or method, and includes a new use of a known process, machine, manufacturer, composition of matter, or material".
[13]   George Francis Takach, *Patents: A Canadian compendium of law and practice* (Edmonton: Juriliber, 1993), p. 18, Section 2.2 (hereinafter "Takach, *Patents*").

(b)   Process is a method involving the application of materials to produce a result. Although the method and materials may be known, combining them to produce something new may be patentable.[14]

A statutory process (*i.e.*, one within the scope of the U.S. *Patent Act*)

> is a series of one or more acts that manipulate physical matter or energy resulting in some form of a physical transformation. Accordingly, a claimed process is statutory if it:
> (i)   manipulates some form of physical matter or energy; and
> (ii)   results in a transformation or reduction of the subject matter manipulated into a different state or into a different thing to achieve a practical application.[15]

(c)   A machine is any instrument used to transmit force and modify its application.[16]

(d)   'A manufacture' may mean either a completed machine or the mode of constructing it. It is a principle connected with or embodied in tangible substances to produce a practical effect, whether manually or with instruments.[17]

Strategy: An invention must be within the scope of "art, process, machine, manufacture or composition of matter" to be protected by a patent.

3.4.1 Industrial Designs

In Canada, industrial designs are protected under the *Industrial Design Act*;[18] in the United States they are protected as "design" patents under the U.S. *Patent Act*.[19] Industrial designs are aesthetic and not utilitarian. They appeal to and are judged by the eye alone[20] and are protected for their "ornamental qualities".[21] This text will not further discuss industrial design or design patents, and the word "patent" will refer to a utility patent.

3.4.2 Plants

Reproduction of plants is covered in Canada by the *Plant Breeders' Rights Act*[22] and in the United States by the *Plant Variety Protection Act*.[23] In addition, in the United States, "plant patents" are available for a "distinct and new variety of a plant which asexually reproduces".[24] This text will not further discuss "plant patents".

---

[14]   *Ibid.*, Section 2.3.
[15]   *Legal Analysis*, Section III.B.2.(b).
[16]   Takach, *Patents*, p. 19, Section 2.4.
[17]   *Ibid.*, p. 19, Section 2.5.
[18]   R.S.C. 1985, c. I-9, as amended
[19]   U.S. *Patent Act*, 35 U.S.C.
[20]   Takach, *Patents*, p. 161, citing *Industrial Design Act*, R.S.C. 1985, c. I-9, s. 2 as amended.
[21]   Milgrim, *On Licensing*, §219.
[22]   S.C. 1990, c. 20.
[23]   35 U.S.C. §§1562, 1611, 2321, as *per* Milgrim, *On Licensing*, §2.18.
[24]   Milgrim, *On Licensing*, §2.18. See U.S. *Patent Act*, 35 U.S.C. §§161–64.

3.4.3 Patents for Micro-organisms

The Canadian patent system currently does not offer patent protection for life forms other than plants.[25] In the United States, the law is different. The United States Supreme Court has "decided that a new, human-made single-celled organism can be patentable subject matter under Section 101".[26] In 1980, the U.S. Supreme Court, ruling that certain micro-organisms could be patented,[27] wrote "[the inventor's] discovery is not nature's handiwork, but his own. Accordingly, it is patentable subject matter under 101".[28] By 1988, U.S. Patent and Trademark Office (USPTO) had issued its first animal patent (a transgenic mouse).[29]

3.4.4 Patent Protection Varies From Country to Country

Not all countries, even those with patent systems that appear to be similar to the Canadian or United States systems, provide the same scope of protection from independent development. Some countries may have adopted narrower doctrines of equivalents "in order to stimulate local efforts to work around issued patents".[30]

3.5 Works Not Covered: Scientific Principles

A Canadian patent will not be granted "for any mere scientific principle or abstract theorem".[31] Although the U.S. Supreme Court has held that "anything under the sun that is made by man" is patentable,[32] that is an overstatement even for the United States. The U.S. *Patent Act* cites four categories of appropriate statutory material for patents, processes, machines, manufactures or compositions of matter.[33] These four categories do not include "mental processes as such", which are "not afforded patent protection".[34] The issue of non-patentability comes to the forefront when dealing with the area of patentability of computer programs, as illustrated by the following review of the principles involved:

---

[25] *Pioneer Hi-Bred Ltd. v. Canada (Commr. of Patents)*, [1989] 1 S.C.R. 1623, 60 D.L.R. (4th) 223, 97 N.R. 185, 25 C.P.R. (3d) 257, 25 C.I.P.R. 1.

[26] Phillip B.C. Jones "Overview of United States Patent Law", Foley & Lardner home page: http://biotechlaw.ari.net (hereinafter "Jones, 'Overview'").

[27] *Diamond v. Chakrabarty*, 447 U.S. 303, 206 U.S.P.Q. 193 (1980) .

[28] *Ibid.*, at 197.

[29] For further discussion on this topic see Jones, "Overview".

[30] Jerome H. Reichman, "GATT, TRIPS and NAFTA, the TRIPS component of the GATT's Uruguay Round: Competitive Prospects for Intellectual Property Owners in an Integrated World Market", Fordham Intellectual Property, Media and Entertainment Law Journal, Vol. 14, Summer 1993, No. 1, p. 1, at 17 (hereinafter "Reichman, 'GATT'"). Also printed in M. Goudreau et al., *Exporting our Technology*, p. 3.

[31] *Patent Act* (Canada), s. 27(3) (rep. & sub. S.C. 1993, c. 44, s. 192).

[32] Section III. A of *Legal Analysis*, citing *Diamond v. Chakrabarty*, pp. 308-09 (U.S.), pp. 196–97 (U.S.P.Q.)

[33] 35 U.S.C. §101.

[34] Milgrim, *On Licensing*, §2.22.

Subject matter *not* within one of the four statutory invention categories or which is not "useful" in a patent sense, accordingly, is not eligible to and cannot be patented.

The subject matter courts have found to be outside the four statutory categories of invention is limited to abstract ideas, laws of nature and natural phenomena. While this is easily stated, determining whether an applicant is seeking to patent an abstract idea, a law of nature or a natural phenomena has proven to be challenging. These three exclusions recognize that subject matter that is not a *practical application or use* of an idea, a law of nature or a natural phenomena is not patentable.

Courts have expressed a concern over "preemption" of ideas, law of natures [sic] or natural phenomena. The concern over preemption serves to bolster and justify the prohibition against the patenting of subject matter. Such concerns are only relevant to claiming a scientific truth or principle. Thus, a claim to an "abstract" idea is non-statutory because it does not represent a practical application of the idea, not because it would preempt the idea.[35]

. . .

A process that consists solely of mathematical operations is non-statutory. Mathematical algorithms do not manipulate physical matter and cannot cause a physical effect. Courts have, however, recognized a distinction between types of mathematical algorithms, namely, some define a "law of nature" in mathematical terms and others merely describe an "abstract idea".

Certain mathematical algorithms have been held non-statutory because they represent a mathematical definition of a law of nature or a natural phenomenon. For example the formula $E=mc^2$ is a "law of nature" — it defines a "fundamental scientific truth" (*i.e.*, the relationship between energy and mass). To comprehend how the law of nature relates to any object, one invariably has to perform certain steps (*e.g.*, multiplying a number representing the mass of an object by the square of a number representing the speed of light). If an applicant defines a process to consist solely of those steps that one must follow to solve the mathematical representation of the law of nature, the "process" is indistinguishable from the law of nature and would "preempt the law of nature". A patent cannot be granted on such a process.

Other mathematical algorithms have been held non-statutory because they merely describe an abstract idea. An "abstract idea" may simply be any sequence of mathematical operations that are combined to solve a mathematical problem. The concern addressed by holding such subject matter non-statutory is that the mathematical operations merely describe an idea and do not define a process that represents a practical application of the idea.[36]

3.6 Computer Programs

Until recently, the exclusion of scientific principles was considered sufficient to deny patent protection for computer programs because they were made up of algorithms (*i.e.*, mathematical formulae). In 1994, the Canadian Patent Office released new rules that will broaden its previous position concerning the patentability of

---

[35] *Legal Analysis*, Section III.
[36] *Ibid.*, Section III-3(a).

computer programs and will now allow patent protection for computer programs to the extent that the claims of the patent are not "unapplied mathematical formulae" that are "considered equivalent to mere scientific principles or abstract theorems which are not patentable . . .".[37]

3.6.1 Patentability Neutral

The presence of a computer program in the invention will not add to or detract from patentability in the United States. In the U.S. case *In re Meyer*[38] it is stated:

> The presence of a mathematical algorithm or formula in a claim is merely an indication that a scientific principle, law of nature, idea or mental process may be the subject matter claimed and, thus, justify a rejection of that claim under 35 USC 101; but the presence of a mathematical algorithm or formula is only a signpost for further analysis.[39]

Legal Analysis states that as a matter of policy of the USPTO ". . . [Its] Office personnel will no longer begin examination [of a patent application for a computer program] by determining if a claim recites 'mathematical algorithm'".[40] In essence, applications for patents of computer programs, even though they include mathematical algorithms will be treated like patent applications for other inventions. All the principles of general application must be examined to see how they apply to the particular patent application. *Legal Analysis* usefully sets out the process the patent examiners will use for U.S. applications and can be expected to influence the examinations in other jurisdictions.

3.6.2 Increased Sophistication May Provide Appropriate Protection

It is to be hoped that as a result of the increased hiring by the USPTO of computer science graduates,[41] the efforts of organizations, such as the Software Patent Institute, to collect and make available prior art,[42] and the new U.S. and Canadian guidelines,[43] the software patents that issue will give appropriate protection and no more.

ESSENTIALS FOR PROTECTION

3.7 New, Useful and Unobvious

To be protected by a Canadian or U.S. patent, the invention must be new, useful and unobvious.[44]

---

[37] The January 1995 Newsletter of The Patent and Trademark Institute of Canada.
[38] 688 F.2d 789, at 794–95, 215 U.S.P.Q. 193, at 197 (C.C.P.A. 1982).
[39] Quoted in *Legal Analysis*, note 32.
[40] *Legal Analysis*, Part II, "Determine what applicant has invented and is seeking to patent".
[41] American Bar Association, Section on Intellectual Property Law, Chicago, Illinois, *Annual Report*, 1994/95, p. 331 (hereinafter "ABA, *Annual Report*, 94/95").
[42] ABA *Annual Report*, 94/95, p. 328.
[43] See §3.4 of this text.
[44] See the *Patent Act* (Canada), ss. 2 and 28.3 (re-en. S.C. 1993, c. 15, s. 33) and the U.S. *Patent Act*, 35 U.S.C. §§101–103.

3.8 The Invention Must Be New

For an invention to be "new" for the purposes of a Canadian patent, the invention must not have been disclosed to the public in Canada or anywhere else in the world by anyone other than the inventor before the patent application is filed, subject to patent treaties.[45] Such a disclosure will include any patent application that has been laid open for inspection by the public or that has issued anywhere in the world.

3.8.1 Extra — U.S. Inventive Act: Prior Act

Prior to recent changes, an "applicant for a [U.S.] patent was not able to establish a date of invention by reference to activity in a foreign country except as provided in 35 U.S.C. 119 and 365. Thus, applicants who made their invention outside the territorial limits of the United States were able to rely only on the filing date of a foreign priority application or the filing date of an international application filed under the Patent Cooperation Treaty to establish a date of invention before the U.S. filing date of their application."[46] In other words, the United States had a first-to-file system for inventions made outside the United States and a first-to-invent system for inventions made in the United States. The U.S. Act has now been amended to provide that:

> [i]n proceedings in the Patent and Trademark Office, in the courts, and before any other competent authority an application for a patent, or a patentee, may not establish a date of invention by reference to knowledge or use thereof, or other activity with respect thereto, in a foreign country, *other than a NAFTA country or a WTO member country*, except as provided in sections 119 and 365 of this title.[47]
>
> [Emphasis added.]

As a result, inventors in The North American Free Trade Agreement (NAFTA) or in the World Trade Organization (WTO) member countries will be entitled to rely on the first-to-invent criterion.[48] Additionally, the Patent Acts of other member countries can be expected to permit a reference to prior art[49] disclosed in other WTO member countries.

3.8.2 Grace Period in Canada and the United States

The inventor can generally file a patent application in Canada even if the inventor (but not someone else) has disclosed details of it within the previous year, since Canada allows a one-year grace period.[50] The United States also offers a

---

[45] *Patent Act* (Canada), s. 27(1) (rep. & sub. R.S.C. 1985, c. 33 (3rd Supp.), s. 8). For disclosures made voluntarily to the public see Chapter 1, §1.1.1.

[46] *Effects of GATT and NAFTA on PTO Practices*, http://www.uspto.gov/web/uruguay/URPA-PER.html (hereinafter "*Effects of GATT*").

[47] *Effects of GATT*, p. 2.

[48] See §3.8.3 of this chapter.

[49] For further discussion of "prior art", see §3.41 of this chapter.

[50] *Patent Act* (Canada), s. 28.3(a) (re-en. S.C. 1993, c. 15. s. 33).

grace period.[51] Relying on this grace period, however, may be dangerous because most countries, other than Canada and the United States, require "absolute novelty". No grace period is allowed, and a patent will be denied if any public disclosure has been made anywhere before the application is filed. It is to be hoped that the movement towards global harmonization of the patent system will result in other countries adopting this attractive feature of the U.S. and Canadian patent systems.[52] Thus, if a professor invents a process and publishes details of that process in a learned journal, application for a patent may be made in Canada or the United States during the "grace period". Application, however, cannot be made for a patent in many other countries, including those in the European Community, because of this disclosure: the invention is deemed to have lost its novelty due to the disclosure. The professor may also be prevented from relying on a Canadian or U.S. application to file later in those countries if absolute novelty was lost by disclosure prior to filing.

3.8.3 First-to-File Versus First-to-Invent

On October 1, 1989, Canada developed a "first-to-file" system[53] that brought its system into line with the patent systems of most of the industrialized countries other than the United States. If two people independently develop an invention, the first person to file a patent application at the Canadian Patent Office will have priority. This provides more certainty than the "first-to-invent" criterion previously used in Canada and still used in the United States. The benefits of a "first-to-file" system are certainty and encouragement to inventors to file their applications at the earliest opportunity. On the other hand, the necessity to file early under this "first-to-file" system, to avoid being displaced by another invention independently developed, may discourage a thorough examination of the demand in the market-place prior to filing the patent application. As a result, patents may be filed for inventions that have no commercial application or that may be incorrectly structured due to the lack of time to do the proper business research. The "first-to-invent" system may produce fairer treatment to the inventor; the first one to the patent office does not necessarily win, but this advantage must be balanced against an increased likelihood for litigation to determine who, in fact, was the first to invent.

3.8.4 Supporting Documentation

Documentation to establish an invention is important to establish the identity of the inventors and, in the United States particularly, which inventors were the first to conceive the invention. Each party to a technology transfer agreement

---

[51] U.S. *Patent Act*, 35 U.S.C. §102.
[52] For a further discussion on this harmonization, see American Intellectual Property Law Association *A Guide to Patent Law Harmonization: Towards a More Inventor-Friendly Worldwide Patent System*, 1994, 1995, p. 4 (hereinafter "AIPLA"). Copies are available from American Intellectual Property Law Assoc., 2001 Jefferson Davis Highway, Suite 203, Arlington VA, 22202, Ph. (703) 415-0780.
[53] *Patent Act* (Canada), s. 28.2 (re-en. S.C. 1993, c. 15, s. 33).

will wish to perform due diligence to satisfy itself that the claims to the invention (ownership and timing) are supportable. Proper documentation often consists of notebooks and documents generated during the inventive process. Patricia D. Granados writes:[54]

> The following guidelines are offered for purposes of ensuring that a notebook practice produces the quality of evidence needed for establishing inventorship and date of invention:
>
> (1)   Keep bound notebooks or journals for purposes of recording ideas and experiments. Loose papers get lost and are subject to challenge if they are not properly dated.
>
> (2)   Use permanent ink. Remember, you don't want someone to challenge the authenticity or dates of your recordations.
>
> (3)   Record experiments contemporaneously with the actual work.
>
> (4)   Date each experiment on the first and each subsequent day. All too often, scientists forget to date each page of their notebook. It is not uncommon to see a date followed by a subsequent date two or three weeks later. If the important work occurred in between those dates, only the later date would be relevant. If the notebook isn't bound, you have an even more serious problem.
>
> (5)   Define the objective of the experiment. This eliminates subsequent speculation as to why you were conducting the experiment.
>
> (6)   Record all relevant facts, *e.g.*, type of equipment used, conditions, times, materials, including sources and data, etc. If standard procedures are used and not discussed in the notebook in detail, note where full descriptions of such standard procedures can be found. Use only well-known or defined abbreviations and codes. This type of information is probably what is most valuable to the scientist anyway. It explains exactly what was done and why and what the results were. Subsequent work may be based upon such facts. If possible, state a conclusion but do not make derogatory remarks about the results.
>
> (7)   Attach or copy into the notebook equipment generated data or note where such data can be found. Cross-reference the notebook and the data that is not actually in the notebook.
>
> (8)   Have a non-inventor who understands the work being recorded sign and date the relevant recordation.

3.9 Novelty

Since the Canadian and U.S. rules concerning novelty have been changing over the past several years, it is recommended that the legislation that was in effect on the date of filing for a particular patent be checked. In Canada, novelty is a question of fact, is presumed and is established as of the filing date.[55] In Canada and the United States, prior art (or what is previously known about the subject-matter of the patent application) is examined to see if the invention disclosed within the application was previously anticipated. If a claim set out in a patent application

---

[54]   "How to prove that you are an Inventor or were the first to Invent", Foley and Lardner home page: http://biotechlaw.ari.net.

[55]   Takach, *Patents*, p. 29, Section 3.5.

was anticipated in a single source or piece of prior art, it will be invalid.[56] It may not matter that the possessor of the prior art did not realize that an invention had a particular application, so long as the prior art sufficiently described the subject-matter of the claim.

3.10 The Invention Must Not Be Obvious

"The subject-matter defined by a claim in an application for a patent in Canada must be subject-matter that would not have been obvious on the claim date to a person skilled in the art or science to which it pertains."[57] "An invention satisfies the non-obviousness requirement if a 'person of ordinary skill in the art' would not have viewed the invention as having been obvious in view of the prior art at the time the invention was made."[58] A Canadian case offers the following test for obviousness:

> The test for obviousness is not to ask what competent inventors did or would have done to solve the problem. Inventors are by definition inventive. The classical touchstone for obviousness is the technician skilled in the art but having no scintilla of inventiveness or imagination; a paragon of deduction and dexterity, wholly devoid of intuition; a triumph of the left hemisphere over the right. The question to be asked is whether this mythical creature (the man in the Clapham omnibus of patent law) would, in the light of the state of the art and of common knowledge as at the claimed date of invention, have come directly and without difficulty to the solution taught by the patent. It is a very difficult test to satisfy.[59]

In contrast, a U.S. judge wrote:

> Invention is not always the offspring of genius; more frequently it is the product of plain hard work; not infrequently it arises from accident or carelessness; occasionally it is a happy thought of an ordinary mind; and there have been instances where it is the result of sheer stupidity. It is with the inventive concept, the thing achieved, not with the manner of its achievement or the quality of the mind which gave it birth, that the patent law concerns itself.[60]

3.10.1 When Obviousness Exists

Milgrim writes that obviousness exists where

> there has been [i] exercise of only ordinary mechanical skill; [ii] mere perfecting a quality or workmanship; [iii] mere logical extensions from the teachings of the

[56] Takach, p. 29, Section 3.6.
[57] *Patent Act* (Canada), s. 28.3 (re-en. S.C. 1993, c. 15, s. 33).
[58] NII, pp. 157–58.
[59] Hugessen J. in *Beloit Can. Ltée/Ltd. v. Valmet Oy* (1986), 7 C.I.P.R. 205, at 211, 8 C.P.R. (3d) 289, 64 N.R. 287 (Fed. C.A.); leave to appeal refused (1986), 69 N.R. 80n, 8 C.I.P.R. xlviin (S.C.C.).
[60] *88 Specialty Co. v. H.W. Buhot*, 4 U.S.P.Q. 205, at 209 (3rd Cir. 1930), quoted in "*Resolving Inventorship*" by Sandra M. Nolan, in *Blast*, The Bulletin of Law/Science and Technology, American Bar Association Section of Science and Technology, October 1995, No. 95, p. 5, at 9.

prior art, [iv] substitution or alteration or modification of known elements, or dimensions, or form; or [v] application of an existing machine or process to an analogous use.[61]

3.11 The Invention Must Be Useful

In Canada "useful" means "having industrial or commercial value in a manner that benefits the public".[62] The appropriate test will be "whether the invention will be practically fit for the purpose described in the specification in the hands of a competent person".[63] To satisfy the "useful" requirement, the invention must be reduced to practice; it must be more advanced than mere research.[64]

> The purpose of this requirement [as to usefulness] is to limit patent protection to inventions that possess a certain level of "real world" (value), as opposed to subject matter that represents nothing more than an idea or concept, or is simply a starting point for future investigation or research.[65]

PROVISIONAL APPLICATIONS

3.12 Provisional Patent Applications

As a result of the recently concluded General Agreement on Tariffs and Trade (GATT) negotiations, the U.S. *Patent Act* has been amended to establish "a new type of patent application called a provisional application . . . designed to be a simple inexpensive patent application that will not be examined except for certain formal requirements". A provisional application can be filed in the U.S. on or after December 8, 1995.[66] The benefits of filing a provisional application are:

(a)   a provisional application acts as an internal priority document that is followed by another application within 12 months of the filing of the provisional application;[67]

(b)   a provisional application helps "an applicant to establish a filing date for inventions that may be useful in establishing senior party status in an interference proceeding (in the U.S.) or establishing a date of invention in almost every other country in the world that follows a first-to-file principle. The filing date of an application in the U.S. also establishes a prior art date effective under the provisions of 35 U.S.C.(E)";[68] and

---

[61] Milgrim, *On Licensing*, §2.11.

[62] Takach, *Patents*, p. 31, Section 4.1.

[63] *Ibid.*, p. 34, Section 4.2.

[64] See Association of University Technology Managers, Inc., *Technology Transfer Manual 1993*, IV-2.1, p. 12, s. 2.1.5. (hereinafter called "AUTM *Manual*").

[65] Section III.A of *Legal Analysis*.

[66] *Effects of GATT*, http: //www.uspto.gov/web/uruguay/URPAPER.html, p. 3.

[67] *Ibid.*, at 3-4.

[68] *Ibid.*, at 4.

(c)   a provisional application is an "effective tool in deferring examination of an invention for a period of a year. This tool will be useful to
those applicants who may want to seek financial assistance from third
parties before the cost of prosecution begins, or the applicant who
updates the content of an application within one year of the original
filing before presenting a C-I-P application for examination".[69]

3.12.1 No Examination for Provisionals

Unlike patent applications in the United States, which are set up for automatic
examination on filing,[70] provisional applications are not examined. All that hap-
pens is that provisional applications are given a filing date which, in itself, is an
"essential critical achievement for the protection of rights in the U.S. and every
foreign country".[71] Filing gives the inventor one year in which to file an application that meets the standards of a formal application.

3.12.2 Provisionals and First-to-File

The provisional filing option may overcome some of the perceived difficulties of
a first-to-file system because it may avoid loss of priority, as further and necessary development is done before filing a formal application.[72] The provisional
application, however, still requires a disclosure of the invention, and this disclosure "must be complete enough to enable a person skilled in that particular field
to be able to understand how to make and use the invention without having to
resort to experimentation to do so".[73]

WHERE TO FILE

3.13 Where to File: Generally

The inventor must initially decide in which jurisdiction(s) to file a patent application to obtain appropriate protection. An inventor based in Canada need not file in
Canada first. Many countries belong to the Paris Convention for the Protection of
Industrial Property, a treaty that allows for "convention priority". Thus, an inventor's filing date in one country will be recognized in other countries if the inventor files in those countries within one year of the original filing.[74]

---

[69]   *Ibid.*
[70]   This is not the case under the revised Canadian Patent System — a separate application must be
       made for examination. If an application for examination is not made within seven years, the
       application will be deemed abandoned. For further discussion on this topic, see Canadian Intel-
       lectual Property Office, "Patent Guide", available on the Internet at http://www.nlc-bnc.ca/open-
       gov/cipo/home_e.html.
[71]   AIPLA, p. 4.
[72]   *Ibid.*
[73]   *Ibid.*
[74]   Canadian Intellectual Property Office, "Patent Guide", S.B.8.2.

3.13.1 *Where to File: Patent Cooperation Treaty (PCT)*

Often, in the early stages of the development of technology, it is difficult to determine how successful the innovation will be. If the technology proves to be more successful than initially expected, to avoid losing out in some countries, the patent application can be made pursuant to the PCT. At the time of making the first application "[i]nstead of the multiplicity of foreign applications, only one initial application has to be filed. This means that only one set of documents is required instead of several. . . ."[75] The PCT "offers [the inventor] an improved basis for taking decisions, permits time to be gained before making additional commitments, provides an improved possibility for checking the appropriateness of the international application and of the country coverage, and gives the opportunity for cost saving".[76] For example, rather than incurring the cost of translations, official fees and foreign representatives that the inventor would incur with separate applications, only the cost of one application need be initially expended.[77] Making a PCT application allows more time for the inventor to choose in what countries he or she wishes to pursue patent protection.[78]

TERRITORY

3.14 Territorial Limitations

A patent prohibits infringement only within the country that issues the patent. Thus, a patent issued in the United States has no exclusionary effect in Canada, unless a comparable patent has been issued by the Canadian authorities. Indeed, in Canada there would be free access to the details of the U.S. invention, because these details were disclosed to the public world-wide once the U.S. patent issued.[79] Moreover, the holder of a U.S. patent may not be able to contractually prohibit its licensee from exploiting the patented technology outside the United States if that would be considered an antitrust violation.[80]

DISCLOSURE

3.15 Full Disclosure

In exchange for the exclusionary rights provided by a patent, the patentee must disclose sufficient details of a patent in "full, clear, concise and exact terms"

---

[75] Albert Tramposch, "Harmonization of Industrial Property Laws" in M. Goudreau et al., *Exporting our Technology*, p. 101.

[76] *Ibid.*

[77] *Ibid.*, at 105.

[78] *Ibid.*, at 104.

[79] Since November 1995 patents are available for partial review on USPTO's site on the Internet: http://www.uspto.gov/; also available is the U.S. Patent Classification Database at http://patents.cnidr.org:4242/access/access.html.

[80] See Reichman, "GATT", p. 38.

sufficient to permit a person experienced in the relevant art or science to implement the protected innovation.[81]

3.15.1 Best Mode

In the case of a process patent, in both Canada and the United States, the applicant must explain the necessary sequence of the various steps involved.[82] For a machine, the applicant must explain its principle and the best mode in which the application of that principle has been contemplated.[83] This description of the best mode is in addition to disclosure adequate to enable one skilled in the art to practise the invention.[84] The purpose of the disclosure is to "teach a person in each art [for each field of technology involved in the claimed invention] how to make and use the relevant aspect of the invention without undue experimentation".[85] The U.S. guidelines for patenting computer programs state: "Applicants should be encouraged to functionally define the steps the computer will perform rather than simply providing the source or object code."[86]

3.15.2 Disclosure of Prior Art

Prior art relating to an invention must be disclosed in an application for patenting that invention. As *Legal Analysis* states: "The written description will provide the clearest explanation of the applicant's invention by exemplifying the invention, explaining how it relates to the prior art and by explaining the relative significance of various features of the invention."[87] A U.S. applicant and anyone involved in a re-examination of a U.S. patent "has a duty of candor and good faith in dealing with the [USPTO], which includes a duty to disclose to the Office all information known to that individual to be material to patentability . . .".[88] If the patent applicant is not sufficiently candid, the applicant may have committed fraud on the patent office. Milgrim writes:

(a)   there are numerous ways of not fulfilling one's duty of candor with the Patent Office; one obvious way is not to disclose matter known to be material, with the intent to deceive; another way of doing it is burying that which is plainly material in a welter of other citations;

(b)   a district court must determine, but need not make explicit findings on, whether undisclosed art in fact anticipated or rendered the claimed invention

---

[81]   *Patent Act* (Canada), s. 34(1)(b); U.S. *Patent Act*, 35 U.S.C. §112.

[82]   *Patent Act* (Canada), s. 34(1)(d) (am. S.C. 1992, c. 1, s. 113; rep. S.C. 1993, c. 15, s. 36); U.S. *Patent Act*, 35 U.S.C. §112.

[83]   *Patent Act* (Canada), s. 34(1)(c) (am. S.C. 1992, c. 1, s. 113; rep. S.C. 1993, c. 15, s. 36); U.S. *Patent Act*, 35 U.S.C. §112. See also Milgrim, *On Licensing*, §53.

[84]   Milgrim, *On Licensing*, §2.53.

[85]   *Legal Analysis*, Section IV.A.

[86]   *Ibid.*, Section IV.E.

[87]   *Ibid.*, Section II.B.

[88]   *Rules of Practice in Patent Cases; Reexamination Proceedings*, Department of Commerce, USPTO, p. 23, located at http://www/uspto/gov/.

obvious in order for the district court to assess the requirement that the omission be sufficiently material to constitute inequitable conduct;

(c)   in essence, where conduct before the [US]PTO has resulted in an infirmity, such as failure to disclose best mode, a court must scrutinize all the evidence to determine whether the omission was merely negligence or whether there was an absence of good faith;

(d)   fraud on the [USPTO] turns on the materiality of the material not disclosed and intent.[89]

3.15.3 Licensing Risks as a Result of "Best Mode" Requirement

A U.S. patent may be challenged and invalidated on the basis of failure to describe the invention using the "best mode". Problems arising out of the "best mode" requirement are:

(a)   it is "difficult to understand and apply in many cases";[90]
(b)   it frequently causes litigation;
(c)   it leads to extensive litigation expenses; and
(d)   it can result in patent invalidation by a district court judge or jury with little understanding of the "inventive or patenting process".[91]

It "is difficult or impossible for patent practitioners to avoid all best mode issues".[92]

Strategy:

(1)   Determine who will have control over the conduct of defending a challenge.

(2)   Allocate fairly between the parties the cost of defending a challenge to the validity of a licensed patent, based on failure to disclose the best mode.

3.16 Disclosure 18 Months After Filing

In Canada, since October 1, 1989, and in the United States, since June 8, 1995, the details of a patent application will be "laid open" to public inspection at the relevant patent office 18 months after the filing date of the application.[93] The issuance of a Canadian patent, for infringement purposes, will have a retroactive effect to the date the application was laid open for public inspection.[94] This disclosure will occur even though it may be likely that at the expiry of that 18-month period the patent will not have issued and may not issue for some considerable time thereafter. The United States has undertaken

---

[89] *On Licensing*, §256.
[90] ABA *Annual Report*, 94/95, p. 84.
[91] Summarized from ABA *Annual Report*, 94/95, p. 142.
[92] ABA, *Annual Report*, 94/95, p. 142.
[93] *Patent Act* (Canada), s. 10(1) (rep. & sub. R.S.C. 1985, c. 33 (3rd Supp.), s. 2; re-en. S.C. 1993, c. 15, s. 28).
[94] *Patent Act (Canada)*, s. 55(1)(b) (rep. & sub. R.S.C. 1985, c. 33 (3rd Supp.), s. 21; re-en. S.C. 1993, c. 15, s. 48).

to publish patent applications 18 months after applications but the enabling legislation is still pending.[95]

3.16.1 Trade Secrecy and "Laying Open" Patent Application

Everyone is entitled to review the application and to study the disclosure after the patent application is "laid open". Because a Canadian and U.S. patent application must disclose the "best mode" of applying the principles of the invention covered by the patent application, the underlying trade secrets will likely be disclosed. These secrets become part of the public domain even if, subsequently to the laying open, the patent application is rejected or withdrawn. Thus, the applicant must decide prior to the 18-month disclosure whether he or she wants to rely on trade secrecy or patents; after that date these protections are mutually exclusive as to the technology disclosed by the application.[96] The applicant may wish to speed up the examination process or to obtain opinions of patentability and defensibility from a reputable patent counsel before the 18-month period expires.[97]

Strategy: In a technology transfer agreement, agree which party will decide to continue or to withdraw the application prior to it being "laid open".

3.17 Disclosure Benefits Business in Other Countries

Reichman emphasizes the beneficial effect of the best mode disclosure to users of the disclosed technology who are located in countries where no patent application has been made:

> The lack of a grace period enables alert entrepreneurs in countries where no timely application has been filed to exploit technical disclosures published in other countries . . . . In effect, the disclosure requirements constitute a vehicle for direct acquisition of foreign technological knowledge. Potential competitors in developing countries who monitor information flowing from the international patent system will find it easier to work around or improve foreign inventions.[98]

Because of this, some innovators will increasingly choose to rely on trade secrecy as the selected intellectual property production.[99]

3.17.1 Cost of European Patent Office (EPO) May Give Europeans a Free Ride

Some writers have complained that the costs of seeking patent protection in the EPO is becoming prohibitive and, thus, inventors may not pursue patent

---

[95] John C. Todara, "Potential Changes in U.S. Patent Laws: The Publication of Patent Applications", in Canadian Intellectual Property Rev., Patent and Trademark Institute of Canada, August 1996, Vol. 12, No. 2, p. 227, at 230.

[96] See E. Robert Yoches, "Strategies for Patent Protection", in *Corporate Counsel's Guide to Intellectual Property* (Chestertand, Ohio: Business Laws Inc., 1996), p. 1.205 (hereinafter "Yoches 'Strategies'").

[97] AIPLA, p. 7.

[98] Reichman, "GATT", p. 18.

[99] *Ibid.*

protection in Europe. This allows exploitation of technology disclosed by a U.S. or Canadian patent application by permitting a free ride in Europe without reward to the U.S. or Canadian inventor.[100]

Strategy: When negotiating who will pay the cost of prosecuting patent applications in which countries, consider the benefit that the disclosure of the technology through the patent application will have for competitors in unprotected territories.

TERM

3.18 Duration

If an application for a patent is filed in Canada after October 1, 1989, or in the United States after June 8, 1995, the term of the patent is for 20 years from the filing date.[101] Patents filed before those dates have a term of 17 years from the date of issue.

Strategy: When licensing rights under any patent, determine the remaining duration of the patent protection.

3.19 Maintenance Fees

To maintain issued patents, many jurisdictions require the payment of maintenance fees. In Canada, these fees must be paid annually and cannot be prepaid;[102] a reduction in fees is available for small entities.[103] No advance notice is given requiring payment.[104] The United States also imposes maintenance fees[105] and has reduced rates for small entities.[106] The Canadian and U.S. maintenance fees are modest in comparison with those charged by some other countries.[107] Failure to pay the maintenance fee will result in the termination of the patent.[108]

Strategy:

    (1)   In a technology transfer agreement, negotiate which party will pay the fees necessary to maintain a patent. Do not assume that the obligation is implicitly the licensor's.

    (2)   Establish controls to ensure the payment of fees.

---

[100] ABA *Annual Report*, 94/95, p. 166.

[101] *Patent Act* (Canada), s. 44 (rep. & sub. R.S.C. 1985, c. 33 (3rd Supp.), s. 16; re-en. S.C. 1993, c. 15, s. 42).

[102] Section 76.1 of the Rules under the Canadian *Patent Act*.

[103] *Ibid.*, s. 77.1 and Schedule 2.

[104] Takach, *Patents*, p. 89, Section 7.64.

[105] U.S. *Patent Act*, 35 U.S.C. §41(b).

[106] U.S. *Patent Rules*, 37 C.F.R. §1.9.

[107] Milgrim, *On Licensing*, §2.61.

[108] *Patent Act* (Canada), s. 46(2) (re-en. S.C. 1993, c. 15, s. 43).

3.19.1 Submarine Patents Under Old System

Under the system that prevailed before the adoption of the patent term of 20 years from the date of filing, rather than 17 years from the date of issue,[109] and the requirement to lay open to the public the patent application 18 months after filing[110] (which system still applies to patents filed before the applicable date of the reform), a patent application could be processed very slowly and could issue once the technology was well established in its use by competitors, to the surprise of many unauthorized users of the patented technology. The move to protection starting 20 years from the date of filing is viewed by some as "an effective weapon against these 'submarine' patents",[111] thus limiting the "submarine" to a more reasonable duration and giving more certainty to other innovators and their marketing entities.[112] Under the former Canadian and United States patent systems, the term of the patent was calculated from the date of issue. This created the risk that applications filed many years back could issue. This risk continues for applications filed prior to the revised systems becoming effective. "When these hidden or submerged applications are issued as patents, existing products or industrial processes can suddenly become infringements."[113] Under the new Canadian system, the "submarine" period in which non-disclosure continues is only 18 months after filing.

Strategy: Determine which party bears the risk, especially in trade secret licences, of a submarine patent issuing after execution of the licence and precluding continued use of the licensed technology. The licensee will not want to continue paying royalties to the transferor if it has to pay a royalty to the patent holder.

EFFECT ON INDEPENDENT DEVELOPMENT

3.20 Patents May Preclude Independent Development

A valid Canadian or U.S. patent excludes the possibility that another entity can legally practise in Canada or the United States the art covered by that patent during its term, even if the other entity independently developed the subject-matter of the patent or if its infringement was innocent. This broad protection is not available under copyright or trade secrecy. This strong exclusionary power makes patents "potent licensing tools".[114] The stronger the patent, the more valuable it will be.

---

[109] See §3.18 of this text.
[110] See §3.16.1 of this text.
[111] ABA *Annual Report*, 94/95, p. 84. See also AIPLA.
[112] For further discussion on this topic see AIPLA.
[113] AIPLA, p. 5.
[114] Milgrim, *On Licensing*, §2.27.

PATENT STRATEGIES

3.21 Reasons for Obtaining Patents

Not all patents are obtained for the same reasons. The following are some of the reasons for obtaining patents.

(a) Some are commercialized in their own right. The patentee may hold the patent with the intention of licensing it to others to produce revenue, or to keep it for use in the patentee's own business to acquire an advantage over competitors.[115]

(b) Some serve as a shield, *i.e.*, as a defence against someone else independently developing and patenting the technology. If a company is secretly developing technology and, prior to it commercializing that technology, another company, which also has been independently developing that technology, applies for a patent, the first-to-file rule may take the first company out of the market-place.

(c) "Some companies build up large patent portfolios to protect themselves from patent lawsuits from other patent owners. This strategy is akin to the 'mutually assured destruction' theory for avoiding nuclear war: both sides will refrain from suing for fear of countersuits."[116]

(d) Some are used as a sword. Some companies take out patents that, in an economic sense, encircle a competitor's patent like a picket fence and prevent further enhancements of the competitor's technology. They may thus be able to force the competitor to license to them some of its patentable technology that would not otherwise be available, in exchange for licences of the constraining encircling patents. This strategy may be used to maintain or to capture market position.

(e) In some industries, such as the electronic industry, cross-licensing exists as a matter of course, particularly where the exclusivity offered by patents is not economic to maintain. In other industries, such as the pharmaceutical industry where the cost to enter a market is so high, cross-licensing is seldom done.

(f) Reputable patent attorneys will prosecute weaker patents that will be used only as a sword or a shield and will push the validity to the limit (or past the limit?). With the cutbacks of government budgets, the patent offices will not always have the opportunity to properly review patent applications, and patents with weak claims may be issued more and more frequently.[117]

Strategy: When licensing, be sure that the patent claims have been carefully reviewed on their inherent strength. Not all patents are created equal.

---

[115] Yoches, "Strategies", p. 1.202.

[116] *Ibid.* An alternative to this strategy is to publish innovations to establish prior art and, thus, prevent a patent being applied for the same subject-matter because the material is then prior art. See §3.15.2 of this text.

[117] Newsletter from American Bar Association, Intellectual Property Section, Winter 1995.

MARKING

3.22 Requirement to Mark

In Canada and the United States there is no longer a requirement to mark a patented product to give public notice of the patented status. "Phrases such as "patent pending" and "patent applied for" have no legal effect and serve to inform only."[118]

3.22.1 Should You Mark?

Although there is no legal obligation in the United States to mark products protected by a patent, there is still good reason to mark. The amount of damages awarded in the case of infringement of a U.S. patent will increase if the product is marked with a notice concerning the patent.[119] Damages are recoverable for unmarked products only if it can be proven that the infringer had actual notice.[120] If marking starts part way through the infringement, damages are recoverable without proving actual notice for the period after the marking started.[121] Lack of marking does not render the patent protection unenforceable, it merely limits the damages that are recoverable; a restraining order would still be available.

Strategy: The licensor should insist on patent marking by the licensee. Appropriate marking will vary according to the particular product.[122]

SHOULD YOU PATENT?

3.23 Factors to Consider

Some of the factors to consider when one is deciding whether to patent are:[123]

(a) the strengths of alternate protections (copyright, trade secrecy, technical protection) and the ability to commercialize the invention without patent protection;

(b) the benefits to be obtained by the patent, which are obtained at the cost of disclosing the trade secrets. The more costly it is to enter a market (such as with a new drug), the more important it is to obtain patent protection — keeping in mind that the technology may be free for the using in any country where a patent is not obtained;[124]

---

[118] Takach, *Patents*, Section 7.63, p. 89, and U.S. *Patent Act*, 35 U.S.C. §207.

[119] U.S. *Patent Act*, 35 U.S.C. §287.

[120] *Ibid.*

[121] *Ibid.*

[122] See Carl Oppedahl, "Patent Marking of Systems", Santa Clara Computer and High Technology Law Journal (1995), Vol. 11, No. 2, p. 205 on the Internet at HTTP: //www.patents.com/lrl.htm.

[123] See Yoches, "Strategies", p. 1.201.

[124] See §3.14 of this text.

(c)   the monetary cost of obtaining and maintaining patents in each of the jurisdictions where the technology will be marketed;[125]

(d)   the non-monetary cost of obtaining and maintaining patents, for example, the time consumed by the inventors that could be used in a technically productive fashion. What would be otherwise productive time can be consumed: (i) educating the "attorney about technology and the 'state of the art' so that the attorney can properly distinguish the invention from what was done before",[126] and (ii) developing a sufficiently detailed disclosure needed for a patent application, together with a review and analysis of the prior art;

(e)   the ability to detect infringement. Total inability to detect infringement often is sufficient reason to reject patenting, but not always. The patent may be useful for defensive reasons;[127]

(f)   the reluctance to prosecute infringement, particularly if infringers are likely to be customers;[128] and

(g)   the possibility of publishing to prevent others from obtaining a patent.[129]

3.23.1 Assess Merits of Patent Protection for Each Invention

The reasons for seeking a patent should be assessed separately for each invention because the business goals of an enterprise may differ according to the invention. For example, an enterprise with a well-established position in one market which has successfully competed on a marketing or technological basis may well use patents on its main product line defensively. That same enterprise, however, may plan an offensive use for patents in a market that it is just entering. On the other hand, a small enterprise competing against relative giants may need to protect its market position by offensively using patents to protect its main products. On the other hand, the enterprise might decide to license its patents on processes and secondary products to obtain needed revenue.[130]

DUE DILIGENCE BY LICENSEE

3.24 Matters to Review

Prior to entering into a technology transfer agreement, the prudent transferee may want to take the following steps prior to being contractually bound to unwanted obligations:

(a)   examine the scope of the patent claims to satisfy itself that the claims are broad enough to cover the transferee's proposed activities (one or more of "making, using or selling" some product or using some process);

---

[125]   Yoches, "Strategies", p. 1.204.
[126]   *Ibid.*
[127]   *Ibid.*, p. 1.206.
[128]   *Ibid.*
[129]   *Ibid.*
[130]   *Ibid.*, p. 1.203.

(b)   examine any opinion of patent validity that the transferor has and is prepared to make available — a transferee may want to obtain independent opinions of validity and strength;

(c)   obtain assurance from the transferor that

　　(i)   the subject patent is the only patent that the transferor holds that the transferee will need to authorize its proposed activity. This is particularly relevant if a licence results from a settlement of allegations of infringement; the transferee does not want to sign the agreement and then immediately find out that the transferor holds more patents that prohibit the transferee's proposed activity, and

　　(ii)   the transferor is the rightful owner of the patent and that no employees, contractors or other third parties have a (potential) interest in that patent;

(d)   examine the applicable law to determine the term of the patent (for example, 17 years from date of issue versus 20 years from the date of filing);

(e)   examine the patent application in the same way a patent examiner would to check that:

　　(i)   the claims are credible,

　　(ii)   the invention is useful,

　　(iii)   the claim is within one of the statutory categories and not merely scientific principle,

　　(iv)   the application does clearly explain the invention and how it relates to the prior art and the relative significance of the various features of the invention,

　　(v)   there are no "forced" definitions in the patent application that give meanings different from normal usage of the defined words,[131]

　　(vi)   the claims have been amended to "better reflect the intended scope of the claim",[132]

　　(vii)   the effect of every limitation set out in the claims being made for the invention is clear,

　　(viii) the details are disclosed sufficient to permit a person normally skilled in the art to reproduce the invention,

　　(ix)   the claims are precise, clear, correct and unambiguous,[133]

　　(x)   all prior art has been disclosed; and

　　(xi)   there is no other potential for allegation of patent misuse.

---

[131] For a discussion on "forced definitions", see §18.6.3 of this text.

[132] *Legal Analysis*, Section II.C.

[133] *Legal Analysis*, footnote 11.

Chapter 4

COPYRIGHT

The primary objective of copyright is not to reward the labor of authors, but [t]o promote the Progress of Science and useful Arts. To this end, copyright assures authors the right in their original expression, but encourages others to build freely upon the ideas and information conveyed by a work. [1]

INTRODUCTION

4.1 Where Copyright Exists

Copyright exists by virtue of legislation but is afforded protection only in that country offering the copyright protection, unless there is some arrangement that extends the rights to another territory, such as the Berne Convention,[2] the Universal Copyright Convention (UCC)[3] and agreements between World Trade Organization (WTO) members.[4]

4.1.1 Berne Convention

Most of the industrialized countries of the world are long-time parties to the Berne Convention.[5] This Convention establishes the minimum protection that must be given to creators of works that are within the scope of copyright. Canada and the United States are members of this Convention. The United States became a party effective only on March 1, 1989. American works created before that date may therefore have different treatment. This extra-territorial protection for copyright through the Berne Convention is unlike protection for patents, which is restricted to the country where the patents issue. Even though a country

---

[1] United States, Intellectual Property in the National Information Infrastructure, the report of the Working Group on Intellectual Property Rights, Bruce A. Lehman, Assistant Secretary of Commerce and Commissioner of Patents and Trademarks, Chair, September 1995, p. 20 (hereinafter "NII"), quoting from *Feist Publications, Inc. v. Rural Telephone Service Co.*, see *infra*, note 11, at 349–50 (L. Ed.). This report is available on the Internet by pointing the Gopher Client to IITF.DOC.GOV and is located on many other sites on the Internet. All page references are to the page numbers as printed using Adobe Acrobat Reader.

[2] Convention for the Protection of Literary and Artistic Works concluded at Berne on September 9, 1886 and includes revisions such as the Paris Act of 1971.

[3] Adopted on September 6, 1952 in Geneva, Switzerland and revised in Paris on July 24, 1971.

[4] See the General Agreement on Tariffs and Trade (GATT), specifically the Agreement on Trade-Related Aspects of Intellectual Property Rights (TRIPPS).

[5] Convention for the Protection of Literary and Artistic Works concluded at Berne on September 9, 1886.

is party to the Berne Convention, this does not necessarily mean that there are appropriate courts and remedies available in that country.

Strategy: A review of any licensing situation in a foreign country must include an examination of the ability to enforce contractual and intellectual property rights.

4.1.2 Universal Copyright Convention (UCC)

The UCC operates separately from the Berne Convention; however, countries may be parties to both conventions. The underlying protection offered through the UCC is that certain minimum levels of copyright protection will be offered to individuals of the other signatory countries, through the portion of the General Agreement on Tariffs and Trades (GATT) known as the Agreement on Trade-related Aspects of Intellecual Property Rights (TRIPPS).

4.1.3 World Trade Organization (WTO)

Member countries of GATT have also identified certain minimum protections that will be offered to copyrights of other signatory countries.

ESSENTIALS OF COPYRIGHT: WORKS COVERED

4.2 Categories

Canada offers copyright protection to "every original literary, dramatic, musical and artistic work"[6] if the appropriate conditions are met. The U.S. *Copyright Act* lists essentially the same categories in eight parts:

    (1)   literary works;
    (2)   musical works, including any accompanying words;
    (3)   dramatic works, including any accompanying music;
    (4)   pantomimes and choreographic works;
    (5)   pictorial, graphic and sculptural works;
    (6)   motion pictures and other audiovisual works;
    (7)   sound recordings; and
    (8)   architectural works.[7]

4.2.1 Expanding Coverage

In either case, the list of covered works is intended to expand with changing technology. For example, the Canadian definition of "every original literary, dramatic, musical and artistic work" is defined to *include* specific types of works, *i.e.*, it is not intended to be restricted to those works. These works are "every original production in the literary, scientific or artistic domain, whatever may be the mode or form of its

---

[6]   *Copyright Act*, R.S.C. 1985, c. C-42, s. 5 (rep. & sub. S.C. 1993, c. 44, s. 57(1) (hereinafter *Copyright Act* (Canada)).

[7]   NII, pp. 35–36, quoting 17 U.S.C. §102(a) (1988 and Supp. V 1993).

expression, such as compilations, books, pamphlets and other writings, lectures, dramatic or dramatic-musical works, musical works, translations, illustrations, sketches and plastic works relative to geography, topography, architecture or science".[8] In Canada and the United States the "literary work" classification includes books and other ways of recording textual material, and includes computer programs.

4.2.2 Effect of Separate Classifications

For technology licensing, the separate classifications for "literary, dramatic, musical and artistic works" become very important for multimedia use. Each classification gives rise to different ownership and use rights that may be held by different people.[9]

4.3 Eligibility for Protection

There are "three basic requirements for copyright protection — originality, creativity and fixation".[10] Substantial effort alone is not sufficient to qualify a work for copyright protection; it must be coupled with an original form of expression. The extent of the effort, often referred to as "sweat of the brow" or "industrious collection," is not, by itself, relevant.[11] The method of recording the work is irrelevant. The work must merely be "fixed in some fashion for more than a "transitory duration";[12] *i.e.*, its fixation must have some "permanent endurance".[13] "The form of fixation and the manner, method or medium used are virtually unlimited."[14]

4.3.1 What is Not Protected

In both Canada and the United States "an author has no copyright in ideas or information, but only in his expression of them".[15] As the U.S. Supreme Court has ruled: "the most fundamental axiom of copyright law is that 'no author may copyright his ideas or the facts he narrates'".[16] This gives rise to the "idea/expression or fact/expression dichotomy" that applies to all works of authorship.[17]

---

[8]   Section 2 of *Copyright Act* (Canada), definition of "every original literary, dramatic, musical and artistic work" (rep. & sub. S.C. 1993, c. 44, s. 53 (2)).
[9]   For further discussion, see §4.28 in "Multimedia; The Information Highway" later in this chapter.
[10] NII, at 24. See R.T. Hughes, S.J. Peacock, N. Armstrong, and D. Smith, *Hughes on Copyright and Industrial Design*, rev. ed. (Markham: Butterworths, 1984) at §7, p. 351 (hereinafter "Hughes, *On Copyright*". See also TRIPPS Art. 14 respecting fixation and performers, producers of Phonograms and Broadcasting and Art. 14, Section 5 for the 50-year term applying from the date of fixation.
[11] See, for example, the leading U.S. Supreme Court case on this point, *Feist Publications, Inc. v. Rural Telephone Service Co.*, 113 L. Ed. 2d 35A, 113, S. Ct. 1282, at 1290 (U.S. 1991).
[12] See 17 U.S.C. §101 (1988) (definition of "fixed").
[13] See Hughes, *On Copyright*, §8, p. 353, and cases cited in the footnotes.
[14] NII, p. 26.
[15] Hughes, *On Copyright*, §16, pp. 383–84 quoting *Delrina Corp. v. Triolet Systems Inc.* (1993), 9 B.L.R. (2d) 140, 47 C.P.R. (3d) 1 (Ont. Ct. (Gen. Div.)). Also see NII, pp. 20 and 33.
[16] *Feist Publications, supra* note 11, pp. 344–45. The U.S. Supreme Court has stated the principle: "copyright assures authors the right to the original expression, but encourages others to build freely upon the ideas and information conveyed by a work". See also TRIPPS, Art. 9, Section 2.
[17] *Ibid.*, at 350.

4.4 Derivative Works

A derivative work is one "based upon one or more pre-existing works".[18] A derivative work is specifically covered by the U.S. *Copyright Act*, but there is no equivalent provision in the Canadian Act. In Canada, derivative works are controlled, if at all, by the basic prohibition against copying of "any substantial part" of a work.

Strategy:

  (1)   *In Canada, do not use the phrase "derivative work" assuming it has statutory meaning; define it, perhaps using the U.S. statutory definition.*

  (2)   *In a contract involving a Canadian, consider specifically controlling the creation of a derivative work because that is not expressly covered by the Canadian Copyright Act.*

4.5 Rights Granted

There is an extensive list or "bundle"[19] of exclusive rights granted to the holder of copyright. For technology licences that do not involve multimedia or the information highway,[20] the following are the most relevant rights, using the Canadian wording which expresses essentially the same ideas as the U.S. wording (except as to publishing unpublished works):

> For the purposes of this Act, "copyright" means the sole right to produce or reproduce the work or any substantial part thereof in any material form whatever, to perform, or in the case of a lecture to deliver, the work or any substantial part thereof in public or, if the work is unpublished, to publish the work or any substantial part thereof, and includes the sole right
>
> (a)   to produce, reproduce, perform or publish any translation of the work,
>
> . . .
>
> and to authorize any such acts.[21]

Additional rules relating to computer programs will be discussed at §4.18 and following later in this chapter.

FAIR DEALING/USE

4.6 Introduction

Both the Canadian and U.S. *Copyright Acts* list activities that do not constitute an infringement of copyright; in Canada, these are referred to as "fair dealings" and in the United States as "fair uses".

---

[18]   NII, p. 40, quoting in part from 17 U.S.C. §101 (1988) (definition of "derivative work").
[19]   *Ibid.*, p. 63.
[20]   See §4.28 of this chapter for further discussion.
[21]   Section 3(1) of the *Copyright Act* (Canada).

The most significant and, perhaps, murky of the limitations on a copyright owner's exclusive rights is the doctrine of fair use. Fair use [dealing] is an affirmative defence to an action for copyright infringement. It is potentially available with respect to all manners of unauthorized use of all types of works in all media. When it exists, the user is not required to seek permission from the copyright owner or to pay a license fee for the use.[22]

4.6.1 Canadian Fair Dealing

The Canadian rules specify limited acts that fit within the "fair dealing" exception.[23] This list appears to be finite and is not given as examples of fair dealing. To fit within the Canadian exception from copyright infringement, the dealing must be both fair and fit within the specifically stated activities.

4.6.2 American Fair Use

The American rules are different; the items listed for "fair use" are only examples of acts that are thought to be appropriate for consideration. The main difference between the two lists is the American exemption for "teaching (including multiple copies for classroom use), scholarship or research,"[24] whereas the Canadian exemptions cover only "private study or research".[25]

4.7 What is Fair

The U.S. *Copyright Act* gives some guidance that may be helpful in determining what is fair. The Canadian Act has no equivalent provisions,[26] but the U.S. rules may be of persuasive value. Section 107 provides:

> In determining whether the use made of a work in any particular case is a fair use, the factors to be considered shall include
>
> (1) the purpose and character of the use, including whether such use is of a commercial nature or is for non profit educational purposes;
>
> (2) the nature of the copyrighted work;

---

[22] NII, p. 73.

[23] *Copyright Act* (Canada), s. 27(2) (am. R.S.C. 1985, c. 1 (3rd Supp.), s. 13; R.S.C. 1985, c. 10 (4th Supp.), s. 5; S.C. 1993, c. 44, s. 64 (1) and (2)).

[24] U.S. *Copyright Act*, 17 U.S.C. §107.

[25] *Copyright Act* (Canada), s. 27(2) (am. R.S.C. 1985, c. 1 (3rd Supp.), s. 13; R.S.C. 1985, c. 10 (4th Supp.), s. 5; S.C. 1993, c. 44, s. 64(1) and (2)).

[26] Sheldon Burshtein in "Surfing the Internet: Canadian Intellectual Property Issues", presented at the 1996 McGill University Meredith Lectures, May 1996, writes at §3.2.9:
   Whether activity in respect of a work is 'fair' is left to judicial interpretation upon the facts of each case. The courts have determined that the factors which are relevant in determining the fairness of the dealings include (1) the length of the excerpts which have been appropriated from the works; (2) the relative importance of the excerpts in relation to the critic's or journalist's own comments; (3) the use made of the work; and (4) the nature of the use, be it criticism, review or summary . . . even though the criteria as to what constitutes fairness set out in the United States legislation are appealing, it is only with great caution that they may be considered to determine whether an activity constitutes fair dealing in Canada.

(3)   the amount and substantiality of the portion used in relation to the copyright work as a whole; and

(4)   the effect of the use upon the potential market for or value of the copyrighted work.[27]

Strategy: Before copying a work without permission of the author, review the fair dealing/use exceptions to the enforcement of copyright protection to determine if the copying is permissible.

4.7.1 Unpublished Works

There is one other material difference between the Canadian and U.S. rules. The U.S. *Copyright Act* goes on to provide that "The fact that a work is unpublished shall not itself bar a finding of fair use if such finding is made upon consideration of all of the above factors."[28] In Canada, copying unpublished works is not included in the list of defences; copying of copyrighted works in Canada will be permissible only if it is for "private study, research" or one of the other activities specifically listed as fair dealing, and, in any event, if such copying is "fair".

Strategy: In a technology licence of a copyrighted work, consider contractual prohibitions on activities that otherwise would be permitted as fair dealing/use, after determining whether these prohibitions would violate public policy or be unlawful restraints of trade.[29]

DURATION

4.8 Duration

In Canada and the United States, for most works the term for which copyrights exist is the life of the author plus 50 years.[30] Under the European Directive,[31] the duration is the life of the author plus 50 years. In Canada, where the identity of the author is unknown, copyrighted works subsist for 50 years in the case of a published work, and for 75 years in the case of an unpublished work.[32]

---

[27]   NII, pp. 74–75.

[28]   17 U.S.C. §107.

[29]   See NII, p. 49, which says "limitations on exclusive rights, such as the first sale, fair use, or library exemptions, may be overridden by contract. However, such contract terms can be enforced only under state law. . . . Licenses and other contracts cannot transform non-infringing uses (such as fair uses) into infringement. They can, however, make such uses violations of the terms and conditions of the agreements."

[30]   *Copyright Act* (Canada), s. 6 (rep. & sub. S.C. 1993, c. 44, s. 58); U.S. *Copyright Act*, 17 U.S.C. §302.

[31]   European Communities Council Directive on the Legal Protection of Computer Programs, 14 May 1991, No. L 122/42 . (Hereinafter "European Software Directive").

[32]   *Copyright Act* (Canada), s. 6.1 (S.C. 1993, c. 44, s. 58). See also TRIPPS Art. 12, where it states: Whenever the term of protection of a work, other than a photographic work or a work of applied art, is calculated on a basis other than the life of a natural person, such term shall be no less than fifty years from the end of the calendar year of authorized publication, or, failing such authorised publication within fifty years from the making of the work, fifty years from the end of the calendar year of making.

Strategy: If the duration of the licence is the term of the copyright, clarify the applicable term. It may vary with the date of the creation of the work (as a result of changes to the relevant Copyright Act), with the country where it was created and with the country where the restricted activity is done.

4.9 Reversion of Assigned Rights

If an author assigns copyright, both Canada and the United States have rules relating to the reversion (*i.e.*, assignment back) of the copyright to the author. In Canada, the copyright will revert to the author's estate 25 years after the author's death.[33] In the United States, the reversion occurs 35 years after the transfer, at the option of the author.[34] Therefore, reversion is not automatic in the United States. "This right to terminate, intended to protect authors, cannot be waived by contract or other agreement. However, termination is not automatic; an author must assert his or her termination rights and comply with certain statutory requirements to regain copyright ownership."[35]

Strategy: Be cautious when dealing with the owner of a copyrighted work who has derived his or her rights as a result of an assignment because that owner, by assignment, could lose the rights as a result of a reversion.

REGISTRATION AND DISCLOSURE

4.10 Registration and Disclosure Not Necessary

In Canada, neither disclosure nor registration has ever been required to obtain copyright protection. Registration of the work in Canada may be made by registering the title to the work. The work itself is not delivered for registration. In the United States, registration was required prior to March 1, 1989, and the registration notice had to comply with the format required by the then prevailing U.S. *Copyright Act*. Failure to register or to place the proper copyright notice resulted in a forfeiture of copyright protection. After March 1, 1989, registration is no longer required in the United States for copyright to exist, but it may be necessary to register before an action is brought to enforce copyright in court.[36] With a work that has been evolving for many years and has material parts that were copied from works publicly distributed before March 1, 1989 in the United States, out of prudence, keep registering the work and affixing the proper copyright notice to avoid loss of copyright for those works.

Strategy: Do not risk forfeiting copyright to works that were publicly distributed in the United States prior to March 1, 1989 by failing to place the requisite copyright notice.

---

[33] *Copyright Act*, s. 14(1). This reversion does not occur with collective works.
[34] U.S. *Copyright Act*, 17 U.S.C. §203(a) (1988).
[35] NII, pp. 48–49.
[36] *Ibid.*, at 61, referring to 17 U.S.C. §41(a).

4.10.1 Trade Secrecy Versus Registration of Copyright

Milgrim discusses the issue "whether use of a copyright notice might evidence publication denying trade secret confidentiality, and uncertainty whether widespread commercial exploitation of copyrighted software might be deemed 'publication' despite confidentiality restrictions imposed by licensing terms".[37] Since he concludes that this issue is "arguably still unsettled", he recommends "use of a form of notice which preserves both trade secret confidentiality and copyright".[38]

4.10.2 Place a Copyright Notice Anyway

It may be prudent practice to place a copyright notice on works even though there is no statutory requirement. In Canada, this registration gives the benefit of the presumption of ownership and notice to others that there is a copyright. In the United States, timely registration may entitle the copyright holder to gain statutory damages and legal fees.[39]

The NII suggests:

> If a copyright notice is used, generally it must consist of three elements:
> - the letter "c" in a circle © or the word "Copyright" or the abbreviation "Copr." (in the case of sound recordings embodied in phonorecords, the letter "P" in a circle);
> - the year of first publication of the work; and
> - the name of the owner of copyright in the work.[40]

Strategy: The giving of notice may be very relevant depending on where you may seek protection. A suggestion may be to use "© [Date] [Name of Copyright Owner], All Rights Reserved" to obtain maximum international protection; but a prudent licensor will verify the local and current requirements.

4.11 Netiquette

Users of the Internet ("Netizens") have developed their own protocol ("netiquette") and freedom in copying appears to be an accepted netiquette. This freedom does not exist in law; copying anything from the Internet may violate copyright and may be defensible only if it fits within one of the fair dealing/use defences. Indeed, "browsing" on the Internet may be copyright infringement;[41] with present technology, browsing involves downloading the work (*i.e.*, copying it onto a computer's memory), even if only temporarily.

---

[37]   R.M. Milgrim, *Milgrim On Licensing*, rev. ed. (New York: Matthew Bender, 1995), §5.51, pp. 5–175 (hereinafter "Milgrim, *On Licensing*").

[38]   *Ibid.*

[39]   NII, p. 62.

[40]   *Ibid.*, p. 61, referring to 17 U.S.C. §§401(b) and 402(b) (1988).

[41]   See Canada: Information Highway Advisory Council, *Subcommittee Report on Copyright and the Information Highway* (March 1995), Chapter 3 in the Section: "Should 'browsing' be permitted as a use of works in the Information Highway" (hereinafter "Browsing NII").

4.11.1 Waiver Versus Reservation of Copyright on the Internet

On the Internet, a user may find a work that he or she wishes to copy. Practically, the user may not be able to tell if the author has waived all rights to copyright, has consented to the work being posted for specific purposes only, or has not consented at all to someone else misappropriating the work and improperly placing it at that site. By placing a work on the Internet, will an author be considered to have given an implied licence for specific uses? The law remains undeveloped.

4.11.2 Liability of Bulletin Board Operator

In *Playboy Enterprises Inc. v. Freena*,[42] someone uploaded photographs that had originally appeared in *Playboy* magazine and, as you would expect, many of its other subscribers downloaded those photographs. The bulletin board operator was held liable for copyright infringement. Although the case itself involved an action against the operator of the bulletin board, the case also illustrates infringement by the person who uploaded and by those who downloaded the photographs.

4.11.3 Playboy, Morphing and Moral Rights

With the ability to manipulate digital data and the possibility of photographs being manipulated, consider the potential of the "moral rights"[43] of the *Playboy* photographer being infringed, assuming that this photographer had sufficient reputation to be dishonoured by the manipulation.

Strategy: For works that can be formatted for electronic transmission, consider placing a copyright notice and specifying what uses (e.g., copying and modification) are permitted. Perhaps place a notice that discloses the address where copyright consent may be obtained.

EFFECT ON INDEPENDENT DEVELOPMENT

4.12 Copyright Does Not Give Coverage Offered by a Patent

Generally, copyright does not prevent independent development of a copyrighted work.

> [B]asic copyright norms recognized by all developed legal systems protect only an author's original expression, not his ideas, and independent creation constitutes a perfect defence to any charge of copying. These limitations promote competition by a built-in process of "reverse engineering" that permits third parties to freely use the facts and ideas underlying clusters of related expression.[44]

---

[42] 839 F.Supp. 1552 (M.D. Fla. 1993).

[43] For further discussion see §4.13 below.

[44] Jerome H. Reichman, "Intellectual Property In International Trade and the GATT", in M. Goudreau, G. Bisson, N. Lacasse and L. Perret., eds., *Exporting our Technology: International Protection and Transfers of Industrial Innovations* (Montreal: Wilson & Lafleur, 1995), p. 3, at 49.

Anyone who legitimately discovers the underlying ideas of one computer program can create another that implements those ideas in a different manner. Thus, copyright protection generally is much weaker than patent protection.

MORAL RIGHTS

4.13 Economic Rights Versus Moral Rights

In many countries, the copyright legislation distinguishes between an author's economic rights (the right to prevent copying, publishing, performance, public display, etc.) and moral rights (the right of "paternity" and the right of "integrity"). To this point, we have been discussing the author's economic rights. "Moral rights" is somewhat of a misnomer; these rights do not have anything to do with morality or ethics. Waiving "moral" rights does not mean that the author has thrown off all propriety and will now engage in immoral or licentious behaviour. Canada has adopted a broad variety of moral rights; the United States has adopted a narrow variety in its *Visual Artist Rights Act* of 1991.[45]

4.13.1 Paternity Rights

In Canada, the moral rights of paternity are the "right . . . to be associated with the work as its author by name or under a pseudonym and the right to remain anonymous".[46] The rights of integrity are infringed "only if the work is, to the prejudice of the honour or reputation of the author, (a) distorted, mutilated or otherwise modified, or (b) used in association with a product, service, cause or institution".[47] In the case of a painting, sculpture or engraving, the prejudice is "deemed to have occurred as a result of any distortion, mutilation or other modification of the work".[48]

4.14 Multimedia and Moral Rights

With the ability to manipulate artistic works, copies of which have been scanned in a digital format, moral rights become a realistic problem, particularly in the multimedia area. In Canada, unless moral rights have been waived, the author of any textual material can require that his or her name be used in connection with the reproduction of work, even if copyright has been assigned. Conversely, the author(s) of a book can require that his or her name not be used in connection with that book (joining that great group of authors known as "Anon"). As a result of the Canadian rules, even though a creator of a formation of flying geese on display in a Toronto shopping centre had assigned copyright, he required the removal of red ribbons that had been placed around the necks of the geese by an over-exuberant Christmas decorator. (Rudolph may have a red nose, but geese may not have red ribbons.)[49]

---

[45]   17 U.S.C. §106A.
[46]   *Copyright Act* (Canada), s. 14.1 (en. R.S.C. 1985, c. 10 (4th Supp.), s. 4).
[47]   *Ibid.*, s. 28.2(1) (en. R.S.C. 1985, c. 10 (4th Supp.), s. 6).
[48]   *Ibid.*, s. 28.2(2) (en. R.S.C. 1985, c. 10 (4th Supp.), s. 6).
[49]   *Snow v. Eaton Centre Ltd.* (1982), 70 C.P.R. (2d) 105 (Ont. H.C.J.).

4.15 U.S. Variety of Moral Rights

The United States has adopted a modest variation of "moral rights" by the *Visual Artist Rights Act*, "which created certain rights of integrity and attribution to works of visual art".[50] The right of integrity is the right "to prevent any intentional distortion, mutilation, or other modification of [a work of visual art] which would be prejudicial to his or her honour or reputation"[51] if a work of visual art is

> (1) a painting, drawing, print or sculpture existing in a single copy, in a limited edition of 200 copies or fewer that are signed or consecutively numbered by the author, or, in the case of a sculpture, in a multiple cast, carved, or fabricated sculptures of 200 or fewer that are consecutively numbered by the author and bear the signature or other identifying mark of the author; or (2) a still photographic image produced for exhibition purposes only, existing in a single copy that is signed by the author, or in a limited edition of 200 copies or fewer that are signed and consecutively numbered by the author.[52]

4.16 Waiver of Moral Rights

Traditional moral rights cannot be assigned. In some countries, such as Canada, they can be waived. In Canada, moral rights apply to all types of works without limitation.[53]

Strategies:
(1)   Assess the impact of moral rights on source code of software and other digitized works.
(2)   Require all employees/consultants to waive their moral rights in addition to assigning their copyrights.

COPYRIGHT FOR GOVERNMENT-CREATED WORK

4.17 U.S. Versus Canadian Government-created Works

There is a material difference between Canada and the United States in the treatment of government-created works. Canada reserves copyright to the government for most works. The United States denies protection for most (but not necessarily all) government-created works. This denial of protection, however, may apply only within the United States; copyright may exist extra-territorially.

4.17.1 Canadian Rule

Under the Canadian rule, if "any work is, or has been, prepared or published by or under the direction or control of Her Majesty or any government department, the

---

[50]   D. Bender and D.A. Jarvis, "Multimedia Licensing" (address to the U.S. and Canada Licensing Executive Society's Annual Meeting, Advanced Software Licensing Issues Seminar, Thursday, October 20, 1994 (unpublished) (hereinafter "Bender and Jarvis, 'Multimedia Licensing'").
[51]   17 U.S.C. §106A.
[52]   *Ibid.*, §101.
[53]   *Copyright Act* (Canada), s. 14.1(1) (en. R.S.C. 1985, c. 10 (4th Supp.), s. 4).

copyright in the work shall, subject to any agreement with the author, belong to Her Majesty . . . ".[54] Her Majesty includes the federal and provincial governments and any of their agencies. In an ostensibly democratic country, this has startling implications: some works, such as statutes, regulations, court decisions, parliamentary proceedings and the like should be readily available. On the other hand, the Canadian governments, both federal and provincial, have engaged in creating works that often would be produced for commercialization and, thus, are recognized as deserving protection.[55] As s. 12 of the Canadian *Copyright Act* indicates, an author entering into a relationship with a Canadian government or one of its agencies for the preparation or publication of a work by, or under control of, that government or agency will lose copyright to the government, unless there is an agreement to the contrary. In September 1991, the federal government, through its Treasury Board, adopted a new policy for intellectual property arising in federal government contracts. Unfortunately, it appears that this policy is not uniformly applied.[56] Intellectual property resulting from the performance of the contract is now presumed to vest in the contractor, unless the contract determines that the Crown ownership of resulting intellectual property is justified. Note that this policy applies only to the federal government and not to the provinces. In any event, the policy of any Canadian government can be changed without public consultation.[57] In the United States the general rule is that copyright protection is "not extended . . . to works of the U.S. Government",[58] subject to limited exceptions. "Therefore, nearly all works of the U.S. government . . . may be reproduced, distributed, adapted, publicly performed and publicly displayed [in the U.S.] without infringement . . . under its copyright laws."[59] Engaging in these activities in a country outside the United States may not be lawful. It is noted that "while the Copyright Act leaves most works created by the U.S. Government unprotected under U.S. copyright laws, Congress did not intend for the section to have any effect on the protection of U.S. government works abroad".[60]

Strategies:

(1)   *When dealing with the Canadian federal government, the government of its provinces or territories or any of their agencies, in the contract clarify the ownership of copyright.*

(2)   *When licensing a work that was produced or published by, or under, the control of the Canadian federal government, the government of the provinces or territories, or any of their agencies, check the relevant contract; silence on the issue is not a good thing.*

(3)   *Watch out for the copyright of Her Majesty and of Uncle Sam!*

---

[54] *Ibid.*, s. 12 (rep. & sub. S.C. 1993, c. 44, s. 60(1)).

[55] Canada: Information Highway Advisory Council, *Subcommittee Report on Copyright and the Information Highway* (March 1995), Chapter 6.

[56] *Ibid.*

[57] *Ibid.*

[58] NII, pp. 34–35, citing 17 U.S.C. §105 (1988).

[59] *Ibid.*, p. 35.

[60] *Ibid.*

COMPUTER PROGRAMS

4.18 Computer Programs are Literary Works

In both Canada and the United States, computer programs are a subset of "literary works" that are protected by their *Copyright Acts.*[61] By amendments enacted in 1976, the United States protected computer programs in this manner, and on June 8, 1988, somewhat similar amendments were made to the *Copyright Act* (Canada).

4.18.1 Debate over Type of Protection for Computer Programs

Prior to each country deciding to expressly protect computer programs by copyright, there was considerable debate over the proper form of intellectual property protection that is appropriate for software, and this debate now continues into the courts. Computer programs do not fit easily into any of the traditional categories of copyright or patent. Copyright, traditionally, covers artistic works (paintings, sculptures), dramatic works (plays) and music and literary works (books). Patents, traditionally, protect utilitarian items, such as machinery or other kinds of hardware. Software usually achieves a utilitarian result, but operates as a result of a written work, *i.e.*, source code. Types of software range from software on chips that directs hardware, such as a vehicle's fuel system, to software that directs other software, such as operating systems, to software that interacts with people (word processing packages) or entertains them (video games). The debates on whether copyright should be applied to software may be summarized as follows:

1. Copyright was not intended to protect essentially utilitarian tools.
2. Software is derived from written works (source codes) and, therefore, should be protected by copyright.
3. The term of protection for copyrighted works (life of the author plus 50 years) was too long for software; even the term of protection for patents was too long (formerly 17 years after issuance, now 20 years after filing). Software should have its own shorter term of protection.
4. Software should be protected only if it shows novelty or inventiveness as required for patent protection; copyright law requires only that the work be the original work of the author.
5. The grant of patent protection requires disclosure of the invention; copyright protection does not require disclosure. Software, being essentially utilitarian, should be protected only if disclosure is made, it is wrong to provide a term of protection almost three times as long as the term of patent protection when there is no disclosure required to obtain copyright protection.

---

[61] See also TRIPPS, Art. 10, Section 1.

4.19 Canadian Definition of "Computer Programs"

The following is the definition of a "computer program" that was adopted in the *Copyright Act* (Canada):

> "computer program" means a set of instructions or statements, expressed, fixed, embodied or stored in any manner, that is to be used directly or indirectly in a computer in order to bring about a specific result.[62]

4.19.1 Comparable American Provision

The Canadian and U.S. statutory definitions of computer programs are very similar.[63] This similarity will be very helpful for creators that license their software both in Canada and the United States and will be helpful to courts in Canada (the less litigious country) as they will be able to look to American decisions for guidance.[64]

4.19.2 Program on a Disk Versus Program on a Chip

It should not matter whether the program is stored on a disk or a chip or any other kind of media that may be developed in the future, so long as it is "expressed, fixed, embodied or stored *in any manner*".[65] The definition appears to be broad enough to include the screen display that has been described as an exact reflection "and is a visual reproduction of the instructions that a creator of the program embodied on the tape or disk".[66] Thus "[i]f someone else copies the screen display . . . for use in another program, he infringes any copyright the owner of the work held in it"[67] unless he or she has the consent of the copyright owner. However, this issue remains in doubt pending clarification by the courts.

4.19.3 Result Related

It is hard to contemplate a computer program that does not produce any results. The result does not have to be economically beneficial.

RIGHTS IN SOFTWARE PROTECTED BY COPYRIGHT

4.20 Copyright Protection

To understand the implications of copyright protection for computer programs, one must review the basic copyright protection for literary works. The owner of

---

[62] Section 2 (en. R.S.C. 1985, c. 10 (4th Supp.), s. 1(3)).

[63] The U.S. equivalent is 17 U.S.C. §102 which states "A 'computer program' is a set of statements or instructions to be used directly or indirectly in a computer in order to bring about a certain result".

[64] For example, *Delrina Corp v. Triolet, supra* note 15, drew heavily on U.S. decisions.

[65] *Copyright Act* (Canada), s. 2 (en. R.S.C. 1985, c. 10 (4th Supp.), s. 1 (3)), definition of "computer program".

[66] *Delrina Corp. v. Triolet, supra* note 15, at p. 28 (C.P.R.).

[67] *Ibid.* However, the owner of the work copied still has to prove he or she has copyright in the work under the abstraction, filtration and comparison analysis, discussed further in *Delrina* and in this material.

the copyright has the sole right to "to produce or reproduce the work, or any substantial part thereof in any material form whatever, to perform, if the work is unpublished, to publish the work or any substantial part thereof",[68] and also has the sole right to "produce, reproduce, perform or publish any *translation* of the work",[69] "make any record . . . or other contrivance by means of which the work may be mechanically performed or delivered",[70] import a copy of the work into Canada; or rent out a computer program that can be reproduced in the ordinary course of its use, other than by a reproduction during its execution in conjunction with a machine, device or computer;[71] and to authorize any of these acts. Other exclusive rights are discussed in this chapter in "Multimedia: The Information Highway" starting at §4.28.

4.20.1 *"Produce or Reproduce"*

In software terms, this means to:

(a)   copy onto a hard drive;[72]
(b)   copy onto a floppy disk to be put away for archival purposes;
(c)   copy onto storage tapes to be kept at a remote site for disaster recovery;
(d)   copy onto a floppy disk to give to friends;
(e)   copy onto a floppy disk for use on a home computer;
(f)   copy onto a bulletin board for distribution to other subscribers;[73]
(g)   copy (download) from a bulletin board for personal use;[74]
(h)   scan a printed work (*e.g.*, a text or photograph) into a digital file (which file is the "copy");[75] and
(i)   browse on the Internet.[76]

4.20.2 *"Perform"*

This is a broad definition and could, for example, include the display of a computer game in a public place.

4.20.3 *"The Work or Any Substantial Part Thereof"*

As we will see later in this chapter,[77] there is an ongoing dispute about what is a "substantial part" of a computer program. Does this mean its structure,

---

[68]   *Copyright Act* (Canada), s. 3(1).
[69]   *Ibid.*, s. 3(1)(a).
[70]   *Ibid.*, s. 3(1)(d).
[71]   Transmission rights are discussed in this chapter at §4.28.5.
[72]   Note that this is likely a fair dealing/use. Copying from a "floppy" disk to a hard drive may be essential for the compatibility of the computer program with a particular computer.
[73]   See NII, pp. 66 and 81.
[74]   See *Sega Enterprises and Sega of America v. Maphia et al.*, summarized in the Software Law Bulletin July/August 1994, pp. 1–2. See also NII, pp. 66 and 81.
[75]   NII, p. 65.
[76]   See, generally, Browsing NII.
[77]   See §4.28.1 and following.

sequence, or organization? Or does it mean the essential components that any program of this nature must have?

4.20.4 "Publishing an Unpublished Computer Program"

This can include the publication of the source code, but this is rarely released as it contains the trade secrets.

4.20.5 "Translation"

The word is defined broadly. Translation is not restricted to translation into another spoken language (such as English to French), but may include translations from one platform to another (for example, DOS to Windows or Macintosh).[78]

4.20.6 "Record or a Contrivance"

This term includes transferral of software stored on floppy disks to compact discs or transferral of a computer program to a bulletin board.

4.20.7 "Authorize"

You need not do the infringing act yourself; you need only to authorize the act. It is sometimes difficult to tell when acquiescence could be considered authorization.[79]

4.20.8 "Rentals"

This section was required as a result of the North American Free Trade Agreement (NAFTA) and was designed to overcome the invitation to copy that was promoted by the rental of software. The Canadian prohibition on rentals applies to any "computer program that can be reproduced in the ordinary course of its use, other than by a reproduction during its execution in conjunction with a machine, device or computer".[80] The prohibition also covers commercial rental-like transactions.[81] There are industry sponsored associations that take steps to enforce the copyrights of their members (illegal copying and illegal renting), and a visit from them can be a very discomforting experience.

---

[78] This would seem to be the implication of the Supreme Court's affirmation of the decisions at trial and on appeal in *Apple Computer Inc. v. Mackintosh Computers Ltd.* [1987] 1 F.C. 173, 3 F.T.R. 118, 28 D.L.R. (4th) 178, 8 C.I.L.R. 153, 10, C.P.R. (3d) 1; additional reasons 12 F.T.R. 287, 43 D.L.R. (4th), 184, 14 C.I.P.R. 315; vard [1988] 1 F.C. 673, 44 D.L.R. (4th) 74, 81 N.R. 3, 16 C.I.P.R. 15, 18 C.P.R. (3d) 129 (C.A.); affd [1990] 2 S.C.R. 209, 36 F.T.R. 159n, 71 D.L.R. (4th) 95, 110 N.R. 66, 30 C.P.R. (3d) 257. Specifically, see the appeal decision at p. 29 (16 C.I.P.R.).

[79] For example, a librarian who is custodian of a university copy of a computer program should not give guidance about methods of copying, but should not be responsible under the *Copyright Act* if a user independently copies even though the library has notices prohibiting copying.

[80] *Copyright Act* (Canada), s. 3(1)(h) (en. S.C. 1993, c. 44, s. 55 (2)).

[81] *Ibid.*, s. 3(2) (rep. & sub. S.C. 1993, c. 44, s. 55) and (3) (en. S.C. 1993, c. 44, s. 55).

4.20.9 *"Import"*

By court application, an order can be obtained to require the Canadian customs officials to prohibit the importation of illegal copies into Canada. This is a very strong and cost-effective weapon.

SPECIAL FAIR DEALING/USE RULES FOR COMPUTER PROGRAMS

4.21 Fair Dealing/Use for Software

Because computer programs were not placed in a separate category for copyright purposes, the traditional exception of an infringement for "fair dealing" or "fair use" applies (*i.e.*, any fair dealings with, or fair use of, any work is a defence to infringement).[82] In addition, the revised *Copyright Act* (Canada) provides that the following do not constitute an infringement of copyright of a computer program (note that the word "person" refers to individuals, businesses, universities, governments and other entities):[83]

(a) A person who *owns* a copy of a program may make a *"single reproduction for backup purposes* . . . if the person proves that the reproduction . . . is destroyed forthwith when the person ceases to be the owner of the computer program" [emphasis added].[84]

(b) A person who *owns* a copy of a computer program, which copy is authorized by the owner of the copyright, may make a single reproduction of the copy, by adapting, modifying or converting the computer program, or translating it into another computer language [IF] the person proves all of the following three things: "(i) the reproduction is essential for the compatibility of the computer program with a particular *computer*,[85] (ii) the reproduction is solely for the person's own use, and (iii) the reproduction is

---

[82] For a further discussion of what is fair and what dealing/uses are listed, see §4.6 and following in this chapter.

[83] *Interpretation Act*, R.S.C. 1985, c. I-21, s. 35.

[84] *Copyright Act* (Canada), s. 27(2)(m) (en. R.S.C. 1985, c. 10 (4th Supp.), s. 5). In comparison, the U.S. *Copyright Act*, §107, provides:

Notwithstanding the provisions of §106, it is not an infringement for the owner of a copy of a computer program to make or authorize the making of another copy or adaptation of that computer program provided:

(i) that such a new copy or adaptation is created as an essential step in the utilization of the computer program in conjunction with a machine and that it is used in no other manner, or

(ii) that such new copy or adaptation is for archival purposes only and that all archival copies are destroyed in the event that continued possession of the computer program should cease to be rightful.

Note that this section refers to "archival copies" whereas the Canadian counterpart of this section refers to a "single reproduction for backup purposes". Licensees of software should be aware of the significant difference between the Canadian and American rules.

[85] Note: there is no equivalent provision for compatibility with a particular program.

destroyed forthwith when the person ceases to be the owner of the copy of the computer program" [emphasis added].[86]

The person may also make a *single* copy for back-up purposes of the copy that was modified, if the person proves that the reproduction is destroyed forthwith when the person ceases to be the owner of the computer program.[87]

4.21.1 Fair Dealing or Express Permission

Any copying that is not within these fair dealing/use defences *or is not authorized by the licence* granted at the time of acquisition of the copy of the program will result in an infringement of copyright. At present, it is not clear whether in the United States or Canada a licence can take away any fair dealing/use.[88]

4.21.2 What Legitimate Needs for Copying and Modifying Were Not Included

There are many legitimate reasons for copying programs that should be excepted from the general rules against copying: not all of these reasons were covered by the fair dealing software-related amendments to the Canadian Act. A software user normally would like to be able to:

(a)   make more than one back-up copy of the program for internal use to overcome the risk of inadvertent damage or destruction;

(b)   alter the program to tie into the user's own program and use the derivative work for the user's own internal purposes;

(c)   make other copies or modifications to the program (such as may be necessary for normal support), so long as they are solely for the user's internal use.

4.21.3 Only Owners Receive the Benefit of the Right to Copy Computer Programs

It should be noted that under the Canadian and U.S. rules only an *owner* is given the benefit of the fair dealing defences.[89] Thus, anyone who is not an owner (for example, a person who has *borrowed* a copy or who is a true *licensee* of a copy) may not have the benefit of these fair dealing defences that specifically relate to software. The first draft of the Canadian Bill provided that the person had only to be in "lawful and actual possession" of the copy: that would have covered a "licensee". The requirement that the person be an owner may restrict the ability of many legitimately licensed-users to satisfy essential copying needs.

Strategies: Keep in mind that these statutory rights may be extended by any valid licence or any other agreement between the owner of the copyright and the user. The licence may give more rights than the Copyright Act (Canada)

---

[86]   *Copyright Act* (Canada), s. 27(2)(l) (en. R.S.C. 1985, c. 10 (4th Supp.), s. 5).

[87]   *Ibid.*, s. 27(2)(m) (en. R.S.C. 1985, c. 10 (4th Supp.), s. 5).

[88]   For example, see *ProCD, Inc. v. Zeidenberg*, 908 F.Supp. 640 (D. Wis. 1996), summarized in The Computer Law Association Bulletin (1996), Vol. 11, No. 2, p. 28.

[89]   In contrast the European Software Directive gives similar rights to a "lawful acquirer".

would otherwise give, and users should strive to get permission for a number of archival copies reasonably appropriate for their specific purposes. Anyone who has the opportunity to negotiate the terms of the software licence should request that the licence permit the number of copies and the type of modifications required. It is hoped that Canadian consumers of mass-marketed programs will demand that the tear-me-open licences provide additional rights to make back-up copies.[90]

4.21.4 Restricting Back-up Copying

A licensor may want to be cautious about restricting the fair dealing/use right to make a back-up copy, particularly with licences within the European community. Article 5.2 of the European Software Directive provides "the making of a back-up copy by a person having a right to use the computer may not be prevented by contract insofar as it is necessary for that use".

4.22 Reverse Engineering for Interoperability

Because, under the Canadian and U.S. rules, an owner may modify a computer program to make it interoperable with his or her computer, it would seem to be a necessary conclusion that he or she is authorized to reverse engineer the machine code into human readable code if that is necessary to determine how to make the modification. The reverse engineering for computer compatibility may be defensible as fair dealing/use only if there is no other way of making the necessary modification (*i.e.*, the reproduction is "essential" for this purpose).

4.22.1 Reverse Engineering Methods

"Reverse engineering" can be done in several ways. It can involve looking at the software while it is operating to determine its functional and performance specifications. Some technology can be taken apart to see its components. Reverse engineering can involve decompiling or disassembling software to determine how the software functions. Decompiling involves regenerating the form of code used just before it was converted into electronic form. Disassembling involves the translation of this low-level code into a high-level human readable form. With complex programs, however, the revelation of the source code in this fashion may be of little value without the author's annotations explaining what he or she did.

4.22.2 Reverse Engineering As Fair Dealing

Whether reverse engineering is permissible for the development of competing programs has been a subject of several U.S. cases, including *Atari Games Corp. v. Nintendo of America Inc.*,[91] and *Sega Enterprises Ltd. v. Accolade*

---

[90]   See §4.23 of this chapter for tear-me-open licences.
[91]   975 F.2d 832 (Cir. 1992).

Inc.,[92] both of which are the subject-matter of an excellent and succinct article by Philip J. McCabe.[93] In each of the above cases there was intermediate copying of the subject program. In *Sega* it was ruled, as was expected, that this intermediate copying would be an infringement. But, to the surprise of many, it was also ruled that this intermediate copying (obtained through some form of reverse engineering) was a "fair use" and therefore is permissible so long as the intermediate copying

(a)   is only for the purpose of discovering the underlying ideas and the development of the program's functional specifications, and

(b)   these functional specifications are relayed to a "clean room" of developers who independently find methods of expressing (*i.e.*, developing) a new program that meets these functional specifications.

4.22.3 Reverse Engineering is Rarely Legitimately Needed

In a very useful article by Casey P. August and Derek K.W. Smith,[94] the authors suggest that reverse engineering is rarely needed to discover the functional specifications of a computer program. It is their position that:

> [f]unctional ideas expressed in a successful computer program are usually revealed through the information published by its developer or through the normal use of the program in a computer. . . . The source code version produced by reverse compilation is useful primarily for pirates and other so-called "competitors" who do little original software authoring and who do not wish to compete on an equal development cost footing with the originator.[95]

Strategy: Because, under the appropriate circumstances, fair dealings/use might be restricted by contract, consider placing a prohibition against a licensee taking any steps intended to reveal the source code of software, e.g., reverse engineering.

4.22.4 Reverse Engineering for Interoperability in Europe

Reverse engineering to make modifications for interoperability with another computer program is not explicitly covered by the Canadian and U.S. *Copyright Acts*. The European Software Directive encourages some forms of reverse engineering, where reproduction of a program's code and translation of its form are

---

[92]   977 F.2d 1510 (Cir. 1992).

[93]   "Reverse Engineering of Computer Software: A Trap For The Unwary?", in the Computer Law Association Bulletin (1994), Vol. 9, No. 2, p. 4 (hereinafter called "McCabe, 'Reverse Engineering'").

[94]   "Software Expression (SSO), Interfaces, and Reverse Assembly", in Canadian Intellectual Property Review, (1994) Vol. 10, No. 3, p. 679 (hereinafter called "August and Smith 'Software Expression'").

[95]   *Ibid.*, at 690. The August and Smith article attempts to "explain in simple terms some of the relevant concepts of a computer program, their ideas and expression, their sequence, structure and organization (SSO) software 'interfaces', and reverse assembly or reverse compilation (sometimes misnamed as 'reverse engineering')". It is a useful addition to our computer law literature.

indispensable to obtain the information necessary to achieve the interoperability of an independently created computer program with other programs[96]

provided that certain conditions are met and that the information retrieved is not also used for other purposes.

Strategies:

(1) *Licences of software granted to European customers must take into account the fair dealing/use rules of the European Software Directive.*

(2) *Consider making available some means for other developers in Europe to design their software to interoperate with yours to overcome reverse engineering authorized by the European Software Directive.*

4.22.5 Error Correction in Europe

In addition to encouraging interoperability, the European Software Directive permits the correction of errors in a copy of a program that has been lawfully acquired; this includes reproduction, adaptation and other alterations necessary to correct errors.[97] Perhaps the *Atari* and *Sega* cases indicate a movement of the U.S. judiciary to adopt the policy evidenced in the European Software Directive.[98]

Strategy: Since the European Software Directive does not give the right to the "lawful acquirer" to make improvements beyond error correction and measures necessary to achieve interoperability, a licence of software within the European Community should prohibit any use of the information disclosed in the process of correcting errors or achieving interoperability for any other purpose.[99]

TEAR-ME-OPEN LICENCES

4.23 Nature of Tear-me-open Licences

In the case of mass-marketed or "off-the-shelf" software, there are pre-packaged licences or what are referred to as "tear-me-open" licences or "shrink-wrap" licences. In mass-marketed software the licensor does not negotiate the terms of the licence with the licensees; often these licence terms either are apparent on the box, inside the clear shrink-wrap packaging, or are inside the box itself, and, thus, not apparent until the box is opened. Generally, a shrink-wrap licence contains two types of provisions: (1) the grant of a limited right to copy and use the object code, which is protected by copyright, and (2) provisions that endeavour

---

[96] European Software Directive, Art. 6.

[97] Article 5.1 and the Recitals to the Directive.

[98] For a helpful article on this point see Timothy S. Teter "Merger and the Machines: An Analysis of the Pro-compatibility Trend in Computer Software Copyright", in Stan. L. Rev. (1993), Vol. 45, p. 1061.

[99] Even if the current available technology does not now concern a licensor about the possibility of trade secrets being revealed by permitted reverse engineering, the licensor should anticipate such technology becoming available.

to create contractual rights and obligations, such as warranties, disclaimers and limitations of liability, and choice of law and forum.

4.23.1 Effectiveness of Tear-me-open Licences

It is unclear whether shrink-wrap licences have the consent of both buyer and seller. In many cases the software publisher, wishing to impose the terms through the shrink-wrap licence, has no direct contractual relationship (*i.e.*, privity of contract) with the buyer who acquires the copy elsewhere, perhaps at a software store. Contract law usually requires a direct relationship between parties to create obligations that are binding on them. In most common-law jurisdictions

> it is essential to a contract that all necessary terms are present in the offer, and that the acceptance of the offer is on the same terms as the offer itself. Further, reasonable notice of the terms of a contract must be brought to the attention of both parties prior to the conclusion of the agreement. Terms cannot be imposed unilaterally following the conclusion of an agreement. Subsequent terms do not form part of the subject matter in respect of which there was an intention of the acceptor to be bound and for which consideration was given.[100]

A "simple warning on the outside of the box that the box should not be opened unless the terms inside the box are agreed to, and that the opening of the box constitutes agreement to [or acceptance of] those terms"[101] may be ineffective.

Strategies:

(1)   *Place all the terms of a shrink-wrap licence in a visible place on the outside of the packaging if this is acceptable marketing.[102]*

(2)   *If visibility of all terms is physically impossible or is unacceptable for marketing purposes, write the shrink-wrap licence to extend one or more of the fair dealing/use rights (for example, extending the Canadian right to make only one back-up copy) in exchange for limitations on the licensor's obligations (for example, warranties, limitations on liability) or a selection of choice law and forum. The licensee must accept or reject all of the terms of the licence; it cannot choose only those it wants.*

(3)   *At a minimum, allow the user the right to return the product unused if it rejects the terms of the licence (some technical form of copy protection may be necessary).*

4.23.2 Licences on Transfer of Technology Electronically

Licensors involved in transactions that do not involve physical delivery, such as electronic transmission, will need to address a method of directing the licensee's attention to the provisions of the licence at the time of entering into the

---

[100]   Subject 9 Enforceability of Shrink-wrap Licences in Australia, 1993–1994 ABA *Annual Report*, p. 406 (hereinafter "ABA *Annual Report*, 93/94").

[101]   *Ibid.*

[102]   *Ibid.*

transaction. Plain language and interesting licences can be used to encourage the customer to read the licence without detracting from the marketing appeal.

ORIGINAL EXPRESSION

4.24 Copyright Protects Original Expression in Software

Copyright in Canada and the United States protects any "original" work, *i.e.*, a work independently created and not copied from other works.[103] The work does not have to show inventiveness as a patented innovation would. The work expressed may merely be a "unique form of expression of widely understood computer functions".[104]

Delrina Corp. v. Triolet Systems Inc. sets out the basic rules:

> The most basic principle of copyright law is that copyright cannot subsist in an idea but only in the way the author of a work expresses that idea. Perhaps the next most fundamental principle is that to give rise to copyright, the work must be original, that is to say, it must not have been copied by the author from another work, whether that other work was protected by copyright or was in the public domain and free for the taking.[105]

4.24.1 No Copyright Protection for Ideas

In *Delrina*, the judge helpfully enumerates

> . . . some general principles applicable to the law of copyright.

1. An author has no copyright in ideas or information, but only in his expression of them.

2. Copyright subsists in original literary works. There is no copyright in what the author has copied from something already in the public domain or from a work in which another holds the copyright.

3. Even if the expression originated with the author, the expression of the idea is not copyrightable if the expression does no more than embody elements of the idea that are functional in the utilitarian sense: see *Lotus v. Paperback*, 740 F. Supp. 37 (D. Mass. 1990) at pp. 57–8.

4. If an idea can be expressed in only one or in a very limited number of ways, then copyright of that expression will be refused for it would give the originator of the idea a virtual monopoly on the idea. In such a case it is said that the expression merges with the idea and thus is not copyrightable.

5. Copyright does not subsist "in any arrangement, system, scheme, method for doing a particular thing, procedure, process, concept, principle, or discovery,

---

[103] See *University of London Press Ltd. v. University Tutorial Press Ltd.*, [1916] 2 Ch. 601, at 608, 86 L.J. Ch. 107, and *NEC Corp. v. Intel Corp.*, W.L. 67434, at 5 (N.D. Cal. 1989), quoting M. Nimmer, *Nimmer on Copyright*, s. 2.01[A] at 2-8, s. 2.01[B] at 2-15.

[104] August and Smith "Software Expression", at 680.

[105] *Supra* note 15, at 32 (C.P.R.).

but only in an author's original expression of them. Consistent with accepted thinking in copyright law, therefore, a particular expression of a mathematical algorithm or other procedure for solving a problem or accomplishing some end in the form of sets of instructions or statements may be protected by copyright, but the mathematical algorithm or other procedure as such cannot be protected by copyright": *Sookman Computer Law*, pp. 3–96.[106]

Courts are forced to deal with the grey issues. When would one person's method of expression, if protected, preclude others from developing a competitive program if there is only one way of expressing the underlying idea? These issues significantly involve public policy. The garden-variety infringer[107] clearly should be restrained, but copyright should not give patent-like protection.[108]

4.25 Ideas Versus Expression

The courts have tried to develop methods of separating from software the expression that is protectable because it is not the only embodiment of the idea.[109] *Delrina* summarizes the issue as follows:

> [I]t seems clear that before a computer program or some part of it can be held to be copyrightable, some method must be found to weed out or remove from copyright protection those portions which, for the various reasons already mentioned, cannot be protected by copyright. After the portions that are not copyrightable have been filtered out, there may or may not be any kernels or golden nuggets left to which copyright can attach.[110]

4.25.1 Analytical Method of Filtering Out Ideas from Expression

Delrina follows the analytical method offered by the court in *Computer Associates Inc. v. Altai Inc.*,[111] *i.e.*, the abstraction, filtration and comparison method. In the first step of the analysis, *i.e.*, abstraction, the program is broken down into its constituent structural parts. The second step, filtration, requires the court to examine "each of these parts for such things as incorporated ideas, expression that is necessarily incidental to those ideas, and elements that are taken from the public domain".[112] The court is thus "able to sift out all non-protectable mate-

---

[106] *Ibid.*, at 41 (C.P.R.).

[107] McCabe,"Reverse Engineering" p. 10, quoting from *Atari*.

[108] *Ibid.* The Americans may have more protection for their software than Canadians do. Patents are regularly issued in the United States for software, but patents for computer programs in Canada are less frequent. The judges in American cases frequently note that there is patent protection available and that copyright should thus be restricted in its scope of protection. Canadians will be inclined to argue as strongly as the Americans have in the past that copyright protection should be broader because the alternate patent protection is not as readily available in Canada.

[109] *Ibid.*, at 37.

[110] *Supra* note 15, at 37 (C.P.R.).

[111] 982 F.2d 693 (2nd Cir. 1992).

[112] *Delrina, supra* note 15, at 33 (C.P.R), quoting Walker J., p. 4741, in *Computer Associates v. International Inc. v. Altai Inc.*, June 22, 1992 (2nd Cir. U.S.C.A.).

rial".[113] This leaves "a kernel, or possibly kernels, of creative expression";[114] this is the protectable portion of the work. Then, in a suit for infringement, the court will compare the protectable material "with the structure of [the] allegedly infringing program. The result of this comparison will determine whether the protectable elements of the programs at issue are substantially similar so as to warrant a finding of infringement."[115] The appropriate method of analysis is still in the development stage as the courts attempt to apply these principles both in Canada and the United States.

4.26 When Has Copyright Infringement Occurred?

In cases where the idea versus expression dichotomy is not an issue, there are many ways to determine whether there has been a copyright infringement of the subject software:

(a) Access to the subject program may indicate the likelihood of copying, but it is not conclusive. In *Prism Hospital Software Inc. v. Hospital Medical Records Institute*, the defendants had access to the source code and behaved towards the plaintiff with "open arrogance bordering on contempt".[116] In *Delrina*, although the defendant had a copy of the source code, he did not use it. And in *Atari v. Nintendo*, Atari improperly obtained a copy of the source code.[117]

(b) A competitive program developed in an unusually short period of time may indicate copying, but if the creator of the computer program also wrote the subject program that is allegedly infringed, he or she could cut the time down significantly by eliminating the time wasted by design and conceptual errors that was originally encountered.[118]

(c) Programs that are functionally similar indicate copying.[119] The similarities, however, could result from:

    (i) the intention to make [the computer program] capable of performing every function [the subject program] can perform,

    (ii) peculiarities required by another program with which the subject program is intended to interface or support,

    (iii) habits or styles developed by a programmer who developed both programs,

---

[113] *Ibid.*

[114] *Ibid.*

[115] *Computer Associates, supra* note 111, at 735.

[116] (1994), 97 B.C.L.R. (2d) 201, [1994] 10 W.W.R. 305, 18 B.L.R. (2d) 1, 57 C.P.R. (3d) 129 (B.C.), quoted from p. 179 (C.P.R.).

[117] *Supra* note 90. There is a significant problem to developers when "a programmer has kept a copy of a copyrighted program obtained during previous employment. The use of this program, unknown to the present employer, in writing competing software is likely to lead to a finding of copyright infringement". See *Computer Associates, supra* note 111, quoted by McCabe "Reverse Engineering", p. 9.

[118] See *Delrina, supra* note 15, at 12 (C.P.R.).

[119] *Ibid.* at 13 (C.P.R.).

(iv)   common ways of approaching problems,

(v)   the problems encountered in programming not lending them-
       selves to multiple solutions, and

(vi)   the programmer who developed both programs using the
       same tools that he or she remembered using in the first
       program;[120]

(d)   Unusual phrasing, unnecessary instructions or mistakes common to
       both programs suggests copying.[121] It must be established, however,
       that the common item is indeed a defect and not something intrinsi-
       cally necessary;[122]

(e)   Both the programs working on seldom used terminals[123] may be an
       indication of copying, although the full offering may result only
       from a desire to be fully competitive;[124]

(f)   A common hidden command may indicate copying so long as the
       same command does not result from the use of the same program-
       ming convention;[125] and

(g)   An overwhelming similarity of codes may be evidence of copying.[126]

MULTIMEDIA: THE INFORMATION HIGHWAY

4.27 Copyright Law and Multimedia

"Multimedia" brings together copyright law and entertainment law, which previously happily operated separately, each with "their own legal customs and traditional licence terms".[127]

> The multimedia industry currently consists of an inchoate mass of computer
> software and hardware companies, cable television companies, telecommunica-
> tions companies, publishing companies and traditional entertainment compa-
> nies. All those industries have their own culture with their own customs,
> practices and traditions ingrained through years of experience. Each industry
> seeks to impose its own vision of "order" upon the multimedia industry. This
> clash of cultures leaves all these cross-industry alliances uneasy and insecure.
> That culture clash also means that expectations of parties in different industries
> differ markedly in every transaction. Indeed, even approaches to negotiations

---

[120]   *Ibid.*

[121]   *Ibid.*, at 14 (C.P.R) and *Atari*, as quoted by McCabe "Reverse Engineering", p. 10.

[122]   *Ibid.*, at 45 (C.P.R.).

[123]   *Ibid.*, at 16 (C.P.R.).

[124]   *Ibid.*

[125]   *Ibid.*, at 17 (C.P.R.).

[126]   *Ibid.*, and *Prism*, *supra* note 116.

[127]   Mark Radcliffe, "Key Issues for User of Multimedia" in Les Nouvelles, the Journal of the Licens-
       ing Executive Society, Vol. XXX, No. 2, June 1995, p. 93, at 95 (hereinafter "Radcliffe, 'Key
       Issues', Les Nouvelles, June 1995"). See also Michael D. Scott and James L. Talbott, "Multime-
       dia: What is it, Why is it Important and What do I Need to Know About It?" in The Computer
       Law Association Bulletin (1993), Vol. 8, No. 3, p. 14, at 15.

differ among industries, and finding common ground can sometimes be the most important element of a successful negotiation.[128]

4.27.1 No Separate Copyright Category for Multimedia

"Multimedia works are not categorized separately under the *Copyright Act*."[129] The term multimedia is a misnomer;

> it is the types of categories of *works* that are "multiple" . . . , not the types of *media*. The very premise of a so-called "multi-media" work is that it combines several different elements or types of works (*e.g.*, texts, literary works), sound (sound recordings), still images (pictorial works), and moving images (audiovisual works)) into a *single medium* (*e.g.*, a CD-ROM) — not multiple media.[130]

4.28 Bundle of Separate Rights

Copyright gives the holder a number of separate and independent exclusive rights.[131] Let us now briefly review in a multimedia context the exclusive rights that are reserved to the holder of copyright.[132] By definition, multimedia content providers require a number of these exclusive rights.

4.28.1 "[T]o produce or reproduce the work or any substantial part thereof in any material form whatever"[133]

Copying onto any medium, including compact disks or a computer's memory, is covered by this exclusive right, and, thus, can be done only with the permission of the copyright holder or as a fair dealing/use. Frequently, the content provider wants to include in his or her multimedia works a very minuscule portion of another copyrighted work. The content provider may think that taking such a very tiny portion will be permissible, but it must be remembered that it is the *quality* of the material taken, not the *quantity* that determines the substantiality of the copying. A tiny portion may be the "very essence" of the work and, thus, may be protected by copyright.[134] Digital technology allows the user to manipulate material that has been digitized to conceal its origin and, therefore, a content owner might never find out or even suspect, let alone establish, that an image appearing on the screen is something that originally came from his or her work.[135] Drawing the line between what is a "substantial

---

[128] "Multimedia Licensing Issues" written by a committee consisting of William S. Coats and David M. Barkan, presented in "Evolving Strategies in Evolving Industries", 1994 Licencing Executives Society Winter Meeting, February 16, 1994, p. 2 (hereinafter "Coats and Barkan, 'Licensing Issues'").

[129] NII, p. 42.

[130] *Ibid.*, pp. 41–42.

[131] Radcliffe, "Key Issues", Les Nouvelles, June 1995, p. 98 and NII, p. 215.

[132] For a more thorough review, see NII, pp. 63–130.

[133] *Copyright Act* (Canada), s. 3 (1).

[134] Bender and Jarvis, "Multimedia Licensing", p. 12.

[135] Coats and Barkan, "Licensing Issues", p. 8.

part thereof" and what is not is very difficult to do in practice, and may be done at the taker's jeopardy.

4.28.2 *"Distribute"*

The U.S. *Copyright Act* explicitly covers the rights to distribute copyrighted works (and, thus, multimedia works), unlike the Canadian Act that leaves distribution to be controlled by the basic rules against producing or reproducing.

4.28.3 *"Create derivative works"*

One of the great benefits of the delivery of multimedia works in computer use-able form is the ability to manipulate the work (or "morph"). The U.S. *Copyright Act* reserves to the copyright holder the right to create derivative works. The Canadian Act leaves this to be controlled by the basic rules against producing or reproducing. The content provider may manipulate the work before including it in his or her multimedia work. Although he or she may thus produce a derivative work capable of protection under the U.S. *Copyright Act*, he or she will still need consent for the use of the underlying work.

4.28.4 *"Perform . . . the work or any substantial part thereof in public"*[136]

The "public" includes "multiple individual viewers who may watch a work being performed in a variety of locations at several different times".[137] "Therefore, . . . the fact that performances and displays may occur in diverse locations and at different times will not exempt them from the public performance and public display rights."[138] In s. 2 of the Canadian *Copyright Act*, "performance" is defined to mean "any acoustic representation of a work or any visual representation of a dramatic work . . ." and a "dramatic work" includes a "choreographic work or mime", and a "cinematograph".

4.28.5 *"Transmit"*

The Canadian *Copyright Act* gives the copyright holder of a literary, dramatic, musical or artistic work the exclusive right to communicate that work to the public by telecommunication.[139] Transmission rights are presently missing from the rights of a holder of a U.S. copyright, a deficiency that the NII recommends be remedied.[140]

---

[136] *Copyright Act* (Canada), s. 3(1).

[137] NII, p. 71. See also *Canadian Cable Television Assn. v. Canada (Copyright Bd.)* (1993), 46 C.P.R. 359, at 368, [1993] 2 F.C. 138, 60 F.T.R 159n, 151 N.R. 59 (C.A.); leave to appeal to S.C.C. refused (1993), 166 N.R. 238n, 51 C.P.R. (3d) vn (S.C.C.) (referred to in Hughes, *On Copyright*, §46).

[138] *Ibid.*, pp. 71–72.

[139] *Copyright Act* (Canada), s. 3(1)(f) (am. R.S.C. 1985, c. 10 (4th Supp.), s. 2; re-en. 1988, c. 65, s. 62(1); am. 1993, c. 44, s. 55(2)).

[140] See NII, pp. 213 ff.

Strategy: Until the United States adopts transmission rights as exclusive right of the copyright holder, transmission rights should be controlled by contract. The right of transmission is a critical component of the information highway including the Internet.

4.29 Independent Rights

Each of the rights given to a copyright holder is independent, even if relating to the same work. In addition to independent existence, each right is capable of being licensed or assigned for specific and separate applications. The multimedia content provider is faced with the almost overwhelming tasks of:

(a)   identifying the holders of the various copyright interests. A clip from a musical movie may require consent of the holder of copyright for the screen play (perhaps even the novel on which it is based), the score, the lyrics and the singer and, sometimes, even the entertainment unions and the writers' guilds. Copyright notices are not required for copyright works, making the process of identification even more difficult.[141] An owner of copyright should consider placing copyright footprints in the work to overcome the problems of identification and location;

(b)   determining each holder's rights. One holder may have the right to present the work as a live drama, another as a film to be shown only in a theatre, another as a video for home consumption, another as a television miniseries, and yet another as a continuing television program;[142]

(c)   determining when any of the rights are jointly held. An individual who works as an independent contractor, alone or jointly with others, holds copyright to the work created either solely or jointly with others, as the case may be, unless there is an effective assignment of copyright that has not reverted to the assignor.

(d)   valuating the portion of the work to be included in the multimedia work.

> [E]ach licensor fears that its particular contribution will become immensely popular in this new market, which the licensor cannot then fully exploit because it has signed away at least some of its multimedia rights to the CD-ROM licensee.[143] . . .

> Formula and rate structures in use for photographs and movies have not been set with multimedia use in mind, and usually run too high for a multimedia title. Many licensors charge 5% of the final price, often acceptable enough for a traditional work but overwhelming where the multimedia work may use 200 or more sources.[144]

---

[141]   *Ibid.*, p. 52.
[142]   See the litigation surrounding *Lonesome Dove*, referred to in Radcliffe, "Key Issues", Les Nouvelles, June 1995, p. 95, middle column.
[143]   Bender and Jarvis, "Multimedia Licensing", p. 5. See also Coats and Barkan, "Licensing Issues", p. 7.
[144]   *Ibid.*, p. 9.

(e)   negotiating which existing multimedia platforms will be the subject of the licence. The licensor will be anxious about limiting its product to a platform that may be a loser in the market-place. (Do you choose SEGA or Nintendo?) Will it reserve the right to produce the work on other platforms?[145]

(f)   negotiating the application of the licence to future platforms. In the present environment, it will be difficult for the licensor to

> know what the shape of things will be in just a few years, which is within the term of the typical license. In such situations, both licensors and licensees seek to protect their interests. The licensor is worried lest it authorize applications that it does not contemplate, and as a result, grant licenses to its birthright for a pittance. . . . This uncertainty causes problems for both the business people, and their lawyers. How do you protect your rights in the end product when you're not sure what that product will be? And even if you do know what it would be, you may not be able to perceive the universe of future applications for it. . . . Contracting parties should be careful regarding the language they use in the grant and royalty clauses. For example, from the licensee's perspective, where a broad grant is desired, the clause might recite that the license is for performance, distribution, etc., "by any means now known or later conceived". And it may speak of exploitation "in any way, medium, mode, form or language". Where a narrow grant is desired, the clause might recite that no rights are granted other than those expressly granted, and that all rights not expressly granted are reserved to the licensor.[146]

(g)   granting concessions to the copyright holder for the use of the content providers interface. The licensor may want to ensure that all its works can be enjoyed using the same interface and that interface may be controlled by the multimedia content provider.[147]

(h)   avoiding infringement of an author's moral rights in the process of morphing an author's work. Assignment of copyright does not infer that moral rights have been waived.[148]

4.29.1 Clearing Houses for Multimedia Content?

It is hoped that in the near future copyright clearing houses will be operating successfully to reduce some of these difficulties.[149]

---

[145]   Radcliffe, "Key Issues", Les Nouvelles, June 1995, p. 94. See also Bender and Jarvis, "Multimedia Licensing", pp. 14 ff. And see also Coats and Barkan, "Licensing Issues", p. 10, where they discuss the difficulties of deciding on an appropriate platform that will win the day with the consumers.

[146]   Bender and Jarvis "Multimedia Licensing", pp. 15 and 16.

[147]   Radcliffe, "Key Issues", Les Nouvelles, June 1995, p. 94.

[148]   For further discussion of moral rights, see §4.13 ff.

[149]   See Bender and Jarvis, "Multimedia Licensing", pp. 21 ff.

4.30 Demand for Content

The demand for multimedia products is phenomenal and it will escalate as interactive transmission takes over from compact disks as the method of delivery of multimedia products. Content providers may produce their own works, but it is unlikely that they will be able to produce enough "to fill all 200,000 pages on . . . [a] CD with their own original work",[150] let alone to satisfy the demand that will come from electronic transmissions. They will have to acquire third party content and that is "where the problems of multimedia licensing come in".[151]

As Coats and Barkan have stated:

> Unfortunately, using existing content has the disadvantage of having to deal with the people who own it. The producer has to negotiate with people who may not know whether they have the rights to license, because when the work was created (whether it is art, film or television programming) there was no such thing as multimedia rights or digital rights.[152]

4.30.1 Value of Separate Content Clips

What the content provider considers to be a clip of minor importance may be proven subsequently in the market-place to be the sole reason for the success of the provider's multimedia product. How can it be anticipated in advance which portions of the multimedia work will appeal to customers? As well as being a copyright concern, this makes it extremely difficult for the parties to agree on an appropriate value for the individual components of a multimedia work.

4.31 Allocate Risk of Infringement

Because it is so difficult to ascertain the ownership of all the aspects of copyright to a work, the allocation of risk for an infringement should be addressed in each licensing agreement.

Strategies:
- (1) In most licenses, the licensor should be required to warrant that it "does in fact have a valid copyright and [that] the licensee is not simply buying an infringement lawsuit".[153]
- (2) It may be appropriate to set "up some form of shared risk, in which liability costs are apportioned between licensor and licensee," and involve an insurance company.
- (3) "In the early years of [multimedia] licensing, insurance policies are likely to be too expensive, but over time a sufficient risk pool may develop and a sufficient track record of litigation may exist to justify the involvement of the insurance industry."[154]

---

[150] *Ibid.*, p. 3.
[151] *Ibid.*
[152] Coats and Barkan, "Licensing Issues", p. 6.
[153] *Ibid.*, p. 19.
[154] *Ibid.*

EMPLOYEE-CREATED COPYRIGHTED WORKS AND JOINT WORKS OWNERSHIP BY EMPLOYEES AND CONSULTANTS

4.32 Examine Local Work-for-hire Rules

The Canadian and U.S. "work-for-hire" rules are not entirely the same; the scope of "employee" under the U.S. rules may be broader than the Canadian rules. The Canadian rules may be more representative of the international position. Parties contracting for creation of works that will be protected by copyright will be well advised to examine the applicable local laws.

4.32.1 Canadian Work-for-hire Rules

The Canadian rule is contained in the *Copyright Act* (Canada), and components of the rule can be broken down as follows:

    (a)   where the author of a work
    (b)   was employed by some other person
    (c)   under a contract of service or apprenticeship
    (d)   and the work was made in the course of his or her employment
    (e)   the employer shall be the first owner of the copyright
    (f)   in the absence of an agreement to the contrary.[155]

4.32.2 U.S. Rules

In contrast to Canada, in the United States the scope of the relationship between the person paying for the work and the actual developer is broadly defined as more than just an "employee". The U.S. rule states that the author is "the employer or other person for whom the work was prepared".[156]

4.33 Employee Versus Contractor

A person under a "contract *of* service" is an employee under Canadian labour law rules.[157] A useful standard in Canada for determining employment is whether deductions were made at source for income tax purposes. The economic trend of the 1990s is to avoid the cost of employee benefits and to avoid making deductions at source for tax purposes, which can be achieved by hiring individuals as independent contractors ("contracts *for* service"). This practice may have the unexpected result of depriving copyright from the party paying for the development of a work and leaving it with the individual who created the work. It will be difficult for the commissioning party to

---

[155] *Copyright Act* (Canada), s. 13(3).
[156] 17 U.S.C. §201. See §4.33.2 of this text and following for a further discussion of work done in the course of employment.
[157] *C.P. Koch Ltd. v. Continental Steel Ltd.* (1984), 82 C.P.R. (2d) 156, at 163–64 (B.C.S.C.).

argue that, for copyright purposes, the individual was an employee if the employer had not deducted income tax at source and had treated the creator as an independent contractor.

4.33.1 Created in Course of Employment

The issue of whether a work was created in the course of employment can be distilled to "was the work created as an integral part of the working of the enterprise, or did the author create it on his own account?"[158] One factor to consider is the control the employer had over the author, but control is not the determining factor. The more skilled the individual, the less control necessary.[159]

4.33.2 Work Done in Course of Employment — Canada

Barry Sookman, in his text, lists some other factors to consider when determining for Canadian purposes whether a computer program was done in the "course of employment" and, thus, whether the copyright is owned by the employer or employee/contractor:

    (a)   whether the program source code was retained by the programmer,
    (b)   whether the customer ever asked for or demanded it,
    (c)   the nature of the fees charged to the customer,
    (d)   the relationship of the fees to the program's development cost, and
    (e)   whether full documentation relating to the program was provided to the person commissioning the program.[160]

4.33.3 Work Done in Course of Employment — United States

The U.S. Supreme Court in *Community for Creative Non-Violence v. Reid*,[161] identified certain factors (not a conclusive nor a complete list) to consider whether an employment relationship exists. The second circuit court in *Aymes v. Bonelli*[162] emphasized these factors:

    (1)   the hiring party's right to control the manner and means of creation;
    (2)   the skill required;
    (3)   the provision of employee benefits;
    (4)   the tax treatment of the hiring party; and
    (5)   whether the hiring party has the right to assign additional projects to the hired party.[163]

---

[158] *Beloff v. Pressdam Ltd.*, [1973] 1 All E.R. 241, at 250, [1973] R.P.C. 765 (Ch. D.).

[159] *Amusements Wiltron Inc. v. Mainville*, [1991] R.J.Q. 1930 (*sub nom. Amusements Wiltron Inc. v. Mainville*), unofficially translated in 40 C.P.R. (3d) 521 (C.S.).

[160] Barry B. Sookman, *Computer Law: Acquiring and protecting information technology* (Toronto: Carswell, 1989), pp. 3–34 (hereinafter "Sookman, *Computer Law*").

[161] 490 U.S. 730, 109 S. Ct. 2166 (1989).

[162] 980 F.2d 857, at 862 (2nd Cir. 1992).

[163] American Bar Association, Section on Intellectual Property Law, Chicago, Illionois, *Annual Report*, 94/95, p. 291.

Subsequently, the U.S. Supreme Court has said it will apply a uniform test for determining whether an individual is an "employee" regardless of the purpose for making the determination (*e.g.*, copyright, employee benefits, Social Security tax withholding). Accordingly, in the United States additional precedents may be drawn from federal case law outside the copyright area to determine ownership under the "work-for-hire" doctrine.[164] Meadows writes:

> Facts which would support the commissioning party's claim that the consultant was its "employee" based upon payments by the commissioning party to the consultant, would include:
>
> (i)   the payment of a regular periodic (*e.g.*, hourly, daily) "salary" to the consultants;
>
> (ii)   a structured payment schedule (*e.g.*, bi-weekly, monthly);
>
> (iii)   the provision of the employee benefits which are available to the commissioning party's regular employees, to the consultant or in the case of a consulting company, to the consultant's employees;
>
> (iv)   the payment by the commissioning party of applicable payroll and social security taxes (or a legal obligation for the payment thereof) on behalf of the consultant or the consultant's employees; and
>
> (v)   the provision of workers' compensation coverage and contributions to unemployment insurance or workers' compensation funds on behalf of the consultant and the consultant's employees.
>
> Payment by the project or based upon milestones, and without any form of withholding or payment of employment taxes and related charges (or legal obligation therefore), would weigh against the commissioning party's "'payment' argument."[165] [*i.e.*, since it paid, it should own.]

The U.S. courts may be applying the "integral part of the business" test used in the Canadian/English cases.

4.34 Retention of Copyright by Employee

Although the author is an employee, she or he still may own copyright to a work created on her or his own time, without orders from the employer, if the work is entirely unrelated to employment duties.[166] If an employee creates a software program entirely on the employee's own time, but the work created is functionally similar to the employer's program, even if the employee can establish ownership of the copyright under s. 13(3), the employee may be holding that copyright under a constructive trust for the employer as a result of a breach of

---

[164]   James E. Meadows, "Ownership Issues Presented in Independent Consultant Engagements: Applying the 'Work for Hire' Doctrine to Computer Programmers", in The Computer Law Association Bulletin (1992), Vol. 7, No. 2, p. 24, at 26 (hereinafter "Meadows 'Ownership Issues'").

[165]   *Ibid.* p. 28.

[166]   *École de conduite tecnic Aubé Inc. v. 1509 8858 Québec Inc.* (1986), 12 C.I.P.R. 284, at 295 (Que. S.C.).

fiduciary duty to the employer.[167] This illustrates the need to look at all areas of the law[168] rather than narrowly focusing on one area, such as the *Copyright Act*.

4.35 Retention of Copyright by Independent Contractor

If the author of the work is an independent contractor, the author will own copyright and may assign copyright only by written agreement.[169] The commissioning party will not be able to prosecute infringers of "its" software unless it has a written assignment.[170]

4.35.1 Rights Not Covered

The work-for-hire rule does not cover "moral rights" nor the reservation to the author of an article, a contribution to a newspaper, a magazine or a similar periodical, of the right to restrain publication of the work otherwise than as part of a newspaper, a magazine or a similar periodical.[171]

4.35.2 Need for Written Agreement

No written agreement is necessary for employees' work to belong to the employer;[172] ownership of copyright to works created by an employee in the course of business automatically belongs to the employer. For an independent contractor, a written agreement or acknowledgment is necessary.[173]

4.35.3 Equitable Rights in Future Works

For a work that is yet to be developed at the time the assignment agreement is executed, there is a concern that the assignment needs to be perfected from an equitable

---

[167] Sookman, *Computer Law*, p. 3–31 referring to *Missing Link Software v. Magee*, [1989] 1 F.S.R. 36 (Ch. D.). Sookman also refers to a U.S. case on this point, *In re Simplified Systems*, Copyright L.R. (CCH) 26, 255 (Bankr. W.D. Pa 1988). See U.S. case *Avtec Systems v. Peiffer*, No. 92-463-A (ed va) Software Law Bulletin, November, 1994, Vol. 7, No. 9, p. 185, where the employee who was hired to write computer programs developed a program entirely on his own time and on his own initiative. Although the plaintiff had argued constructive trust as well as copyright ownership, the plaintiff was unsuccessful on both accounts. The commentary does not make it clear why the breach of fiduciary duty argument was not successful nor does the commentary make it clear whether the program was functionally similar to a program marketed by the plaintiff. However, an earlier reference in the Software Law Bulletin in April, 1994, Vol. 7, No. 4, pointed out that the employee had started the development of the program before he started his employment and no trade secrets were in violation. This commentary notes that the plaintiff had not demanded the source codes until after it had fired the defendant.

[168] Such as breach of trade secret, breach of contract or unfair trade practices.

[169] *Copyright Act* (Canada), s. 13(4). U.S. *Copyright Act*, U.S.C. §201(b).

[170] *Frank Brunckhorst Co. v. Gainers Inc.* (1993), 47 C.P.R. (3d) 222 (Fed. T.D.).

[171] See the discussion in §4.13 and the following, relating to Moral Rights.

[172] *Copyright Act* (Canada) s. 13(3). U.S. *Copyright Act*, 17 U.S.C. §204(a).

[173] *Copyright Act* (Canada), s. 13(4) and Normand Tamaro, *The Annotated Copyright Act* (Scarborough: Carswell, 1995) (hereinafter "Tamaro, *Annotated Copyright Act*"), p. 238, citing *Canavest House Ltd. v. Lett* (1984), 2 C.P.R. (3d) 386, 4 C.I.P.R. 103 (Ont. H.C.J.).

interest to a legal interest. Section 13(4) of the Canadian *Copyright Act* refers to the owner of a work assigning rights and, thus, the question is raised whether these rights can be effectively assigned before the work, and therefore the right, is created. There is very little case law on this point but the case, *Canadian Performing Rights Society v. Famous Players Canadian Corp. Ltd.*,[174] indicates that an assignment executed prior to the creation of the work creates an equitable interest that will be recognized by the courts. Section 36 of the *Canadian Copyright Act* provides that "any person . . . deriving any right, title or interest by assignment or grant in writing . . . may . . . in his own name . . . enforce such rights as he may hold . . . ". In *Performing Rights Society*, the court recognizes the rights of the equitable assignee to enforce the copyright in its own name, ruling that the words "assignment" and "assignee" should be given the "fuller meaning", to include both legal and equitable assignees.[175]

4.35.4 Loss of Equitable Rights

Even though the equitable assignee's rights may be recognized if the *Performing Rights Society* case properly states the law, the equitable assignee can lose those rights under s. 57(3) of the *Copyright Act,* which provides

> Any grant of an interest in a copyright, either by assignment or licence, shall be adjudged void against any subsequent assignee or licensee for valuable consideration without actual notice, unless the prior assignment or licence is registered in the manner prescribed by this Act before the registering of the instrument under which the subsequent assignee or licensee claims.

In the United States, when dealing with priority disputes between transfers, the transfer first executed is granted priority, only if it is registered one month from execution or at least before the subsequent transfer.[176] Any equitable interest not perfected by registration can thus be defeated by the registration of a *bona fide* assignment. In the United States, however, a non-exclusive licence will not be defeated by a subsequent transfer where the non-exclusive licensee did not know of the transfer and the licence in is writing, signed by the copyright owner.[177]

4.35.5 Constructive Trust

Even if the copyright is owned by the individual, as a result of a fiduciary duty (if one can be established), the individual may be characterized as holding the copyright subject to a constructive trust in favour of the employer. An agreement for the creation of a copyrighted work could require the contractor to hold copyright, one created, in trust for the employer until the assignment is perfected, to make sure that the principles of the *Performing Rights Society* case are implemented.

---

[174] [1929] A.C. 456, 98 L.J.P.C. 70.
[175] *Ibid.*, at 550 (A.C.).
[176] U.S. *Copyright Act*, 17 U.S.C. §205(e).
[177] *Ibid.*, 17 U.S.C. §205(c).

4.36 Exit Interviews

As a practical matter, on completion of a program (or each module of a program), the contractor should be required to formally (*i.e.*, in writing) confirm the assignment of the copyright. Additionally, as part of an "exit" interview with the contractor (*i.e.*, on termination of the contract), all copyright should be assigned for any work in which the contractor participated.

4.37 Corporate Contractor

If the contractor is a company, then each individual whose services are being supplied as subcontractors of the corporate contractor should assign, and agree to assign, copyright.

4.38 Implied Right to Use

Even if the harsh result is that contractor does own the copyright, the person paying for the work may still have an implied right to use and to modify the work,[178] although this is not likely to prohibit the contractor from directly or indirectly competing with the person who paid for the work.

Strategies:

(1) *Although no written agreement is necessary for the employee's works to belong to the employer, a written agreement is necessary for independent contractors.*

(2) *For a work that is yet to be developed at the time the assignment agreement is executed, there is a concern that the assignment needs to be perfected from an equitable interest to a legal interest. Section 13(4) and §201 refer to the "owner" of a work assigning rights, thus, the question is raised whether these rights can be effectively assigned before the work (and therefore the right) is created.*

(3) *As a practical matter, on completion of a program (or each module of a program), the contractor should be required to formally (i.e., in writing) confirm the assignment of the copyright. Additionally, as part of an "exit" interview with the contractor (i.e., on termination of the contract), all copyright should be assigned for any work in which the contractor participated.*

(4) *If the contractor is a company, then each individual whose services are being supplied should assign, and agree to assign, copyright.*

(5) *An agreement for the creation of a copyrighted work could require the contractor to hold copyright, once created, in trust for the employer until the assignment is perfected by a written registered assignment.*

(6) *The contractor should be required to acknowledge:*

1. *the copyright thereto shall belong to the employer when the contractor participates alone or with one or more other individuals in the creation*

---

[178] H. Ward Classen, Marc R. Paul and Gary D. Sprague, "Increasing Corporate Competitiveness By Utilizing Independent Contractors", in The Computer Law Association Bulletin (1996), Vol. 11, No. 1, p. 3, at 6, quoting *Aymes v. Bonnelli*, 47 F.3d 23 (2nd Cir. 1995).

of any computer program, data, documentation or any other written work, whether recorded in human or computer readable form; and

2.   *the contractor shall execute written assignments of copyright to the works on the request of the employer and do all other acts to enforce copyright as the employer may reasonably request, in each case undertaken or prepared at the expense of the employer.*

(7)   *Due Diligence:*

Review the business practices of the transferor of technology to verify that it owns all of the intellectual property rights to that technology. Consider the following:

1.   *Are employees/consultants required to sign secrecy, non-solicitation and assignment of innovation agreements?*

(a)   *Is there consideration for these promises?*

(b)   *Are employees required to disclose innovations in a timely fashion?*

2.   *How is disclosure to be made?*

3.   *Do employees turn over to the employer regular details of research and development performed so these are not lost on termination of employment or death;*

4.   *Is sensitive material placed in safekeeping such as an escrow house, to avoid employee espionage?*

5.   *Are proper procedures set up to protect third party secrets as well as company secrets?*

6.   *Is there a policy to control publications to avoid loss of an opportunity to patent by a premature publication?*

7.   *Are the employees aware of the need to register patents, copyrights or trade-marks?*[179]

JOINT COPYRIGHTED WORKS

4.39 Joint Ownership

If an independent contractor retains copyright pursuant to the Canadian or U.S. *Copyright Acts*[180] there will be a risk of joint ownership if the work can be considered to be a joint work. The U.S. Act defines a joint work as a work "prepared by two or more authors with the intention that their contributions be merged into inseparable or interdependent parts of a unitary whole"[181] The Canadian equivalent is the definition of "work of joint authorship", defined by s. 2 to mean a "work produced by the collaboration of two or more authors in which the contribution of one author is not distinct from the contribution of the other author or authors".

---

[179]   Some of these items are adapted from an article "Clear Policy Can Forestall Data Piracy", in *The Globe & Mail*, January 17, 1995.

[180]   *Copyright Act* (Canada), s. 13 (3); U.S. *Copyright Act*, 17 U.S.C. §101.

[181]   Meadows, "Ownership Issues", p. 29, citing 17 U.S.C. §101.

4.40 Equality Not Necessary

The contribution of the parties need not be equal either in quality or quantity,[182] but there must be "joint labour in carrying out a common design".[183]

4.41 Result of Joint Ownership: Canada Versus the United States

The result of joint ownership is very different in Canada from the result in the United States. The Canadian position is set out in *Forget v. Specialty Tools of Canada*.[184] Although the case relates to patent law, it also applies to copyright law since it is judge-made law rather than law required by statute and the relevant principles of the *Patent Act* and the *Copyright Act* are the same. In Canada, the points of the *Forget* case may be summarized as follows:

(a)   a co-owner may assign the whole of his or her interest without the concurrence of any other co-owner;[185]

(b)   a co-owner may not assign a partial interest without the concurrence of all other co-owners;[186]

(c)   a co-owner may not license the work protected without the concurrence of all other co-owners.[187]

The *Forget* case acknowledges that the Canadian rule differs from the U.S. position. In the United States "joint authors own an individual interest in the whole of the work, and may independently use or license the work, subject to a duty to account for profits to the co-owner".[188]

4.42 Rule Is Not Always Appropriate

Neither the U.S. nor the Canadian rule of joint ownership is generally appropriate; each in its own way can produce a result totally unexpected by the parties before they seek legal advice (which, unfortunately, all too often is sought after the work has been created and the parties are adverse).

4.43 Different Rules for Patents

The standards for patentable inventions of jointly created works are different than the standards for copyrighted works. Melvin Blecher writes the following about the inventive process and its application to joint inventions:

> There are essentially only two elements to inventorship under current legal standards: conception and reduction to practice. Conception is the touchstone of

---

[182]   Tamaro, *Annotated Copyright Act*, p. 117.

[183]   *Ibid.*, p. 115.

[184]   (1993), 48 C.P.R. (3d) 323, 10 B.L.R. (2d) 62 (B.C.S.C.); affd (1995), 62 C.P.R. (3d) 537 (B.C. C.A.).

[185]   *Ibid.*, at 330 (48 C.P.R.).

[186]   *Ibid.*

[187]   *Ibid.*

[188]   Meadows, "Ownership Issues", p. 29, citing *Oddo v. Ries*, 743 F. 2d 630, at 633 (9th Cir. 1984).

inventorship, that is, the completion of the mental part of invention. Conception is the formation in the mind of the inventor(s) of a definite and permanent idea of the complete and operative invention, as it is thereafter to be applied in practice. Conception is complete when only the idea is so clearly defined in the mind of the inventor that only ordinary skill would be necessary to reduce the invention to practice, without extensive research or experimentation. Because it is a mental act, courts require corroborating evidence of a contemporaneous disclosure that would enable one skilled in the art to make the invention; such disclosures could be a dated and signed writing, or a conversation with another party with contemporaneous notes.

An idea is definite and permanent when the inventor has a specific, settled idea, a particular solution to the problem at hand, not just a general goal or a research idea that one would like to pursue. An inventor need not know that his invention will work for conception to be complete. He need only show that he had the idea; the discovery that an invention actually works is part of its reduction to practice.

The second element to inventorship is the reduction of the invention to practice. While the inventor can often exemplify the invention by an actual laboratory experiment and describe it in detail in a patent application, this is not necessary under the law. If the inventor describes prophetically in his patent application how to reduce the invention to practice, the actual filing of the application will be considered to be a legal, *i.e.*, "constructive", reduction to practice. Even in difficult and unpredictable fields such a constructive reduction to practice may satisfy the law.

A joint invention is the product of a collaboration between two or more persons working together to solve the problem addressed. People may be joint inventors even though they do not physically work on the invention together or at the same time, and even though each does not make the same type or amount of contribution.[189]

Strategy: When performing due diligence examine the inventive process and be satisfied that no co-inventors have been omitted from the patent application.

---

[189] Melvin Blecher, "Legal Standards for Inventorship", Foley & Lardner, home page at http://www.biotechlaw.ari.net.

Chapter 5

TRADEMARKS

The differing local trademark and unfair competition laws that conflict with federal laws, and that change from region to region, give rise to uncertainties that are unwelcome to businesses in increasingly global communities.[1]

CONSTITUTIONAL ISSUES

5.1 Introduction

"Trademarks" include words, logos, packaging and other methods of distinguishing one's goods and services from those of others. Both in Canada and the United States, appropriate trademarks are entitled to legal protection whether they are registered or not.

5.2 Origins of Trademark Law

The protection offered in Canada and the United States to trademarks, registered and unregistered, arises out of the common law prohibiting unfair competition.[2]

5.2.1 Dual Jurisdiction

Unlike patents, constitutional jurisdiction over trademarks was not reserved exclusively for the federal government in either Canada or the United States.[3] Thus, there exists (1) a mixture of common-law rules relating to unfair competition generally, (2) provincial or state legislation relating to unfair competition

---

[1] J.H. Reichman, "GATT, TRIPS and NAFTA, the TRIPS component of the GATT's Uruguay Round: Competitive Prospects for Intellectual Property Owners in an Integrated World Market", in M. Goudreau, G. Bisson, N. Lacasse and L. Perret, eds., *Exporting Our Technology: International Protection and Transfers of Industrial Innovations* (Montreal: Wilson & Lafleur, 1995), p. 40.

[2] For a fuller discussion on this topic, see Arthur H. Seidel, Steven J. Meyers and Nancy Rubner-Frandsen, *What the General Practitioner Should Know about Trademarks and Copyrights*, 6th ed. (Philadelphia: American Law Institute-American Bar Association Committee on Continuing Professional Education) (hereinafter "AIL/ABA *Trademarks*"); Also see Roger T. Hughes, *Hughes on Trade Marks*, rev. ed. (Vancouver: Butterworths Canada Ltd.), loose-leaf (hereinafter "Hughes, *On Trade Marks*") and John Drysdale and Michael Silverleaf, *Passing off Law and Practice*, 2nd ed. (London: Butterworths, 1995) (hereinafter "Drysdale and Silverleaf, *Passing Off*").

[3] See Hughes, *On Trade Marks*, §1, p. 311 and AIL/ABA *Trademarks*, p. 1.

with significant effect on trademarks, and (3) the federal legislation on trademarks which, on occasion, attempts to control unfair competition. This gives rise to constitutional conflicts about how much control the different levels of government (federal versus provincial/state) can exert over the areas of trademark and unfair competition.[4] Since the U.S. federal government cannot exert controls over intrastate commerce (*i.e.*, commerce that occurs only within one state), the U.S. trademark legislation passed by the U.S. federal government (including the U.S. *Trademark Act* — known as the *Lanham Act*) covers only interstate commerce, commerce with foreign nations, and commerce with Indian tribes.[5] Likewise the Canadian federal government's attempt to control unfair competition has been subject to constitutional challenges. Section 7(e) of the Canadian *Trade-marks Act* attempts to prohibit a person from doing any act or adopting a "business practice contrary to honest, industrial or commercial usage in Canada"; the constitutionality of this subsection is in doubt since it may be an intrusion by the federal government into exclusively provincial jurisdiction.[6]

Strategy: A review of current law applicable to the specific geographic areas involved will be required whenever trade names and trademarks are involved in a technology transfer agreement.

UNFAIR TRADE PRACTICES

5.3 Examples of Unfair Trade Practices

Some practices that might be suspect as unfair in Canada or the United States, either as a result of common law, provincial or state legislation, or federal legislation are:

(a)   an offending company *passing off* its products as if they were products of another company, either by misrepresenting the source or sponsorship of those products;[7]

(b)   an offending company claiming that another company's products either originated from the offending company or are under "sponsorship" of the offending company ("reverse passing off");[8]

(c)   an offending company engaging in false or misleading advertising about its own products;[9]

---

[4]   This conflict becomes most apparent in the franchising area. See the discussion of franchising later in this chapter at §§5.20–5.23.

[5]   AIL/ABA *Trademarks*, p. 2.

[6]   Hughes, *On Trade Marks*, §74, p. 658.

[7]   AIL/ABA *Trademarks*, p. 12; Hughes, *On Trade Marks*, §§75–80, starting at p. 660. See also Canadian *Trade-marks Act*, R.S.C. 1985, c. T-13, s. 7(c) (hereinafter "*Trade-marks Act* (Canada)").

[8]   See Drysdale and Silverleaf, *Passing Off*, ¶¶4.13 and 4.14, p. 83.

[9]   AIL/ABA *Trademarks*, p. 12. See Drysdale and Silverleaf, *Passing Off*, ¶4.1, p. 86; and see the *Lanham Act*, 15 U.S.C. §43(a).

(d)   disparagement of a competitor, its goods or services,[10] where such disparagement is not permitted by any constitutional or other right protecting freedom of speech;[11]

(e)   an offending company making false statements as to its own intellectual property protection;[12]

(f)   an offending company making false statements as to the intellectual property possessed by another (for example, slander of the other's title);[13]

(g)   an offending company *diluting* the effectiveness of a trademark by using that trademark on an unrelated item with resulting loss of distinctiveness (this may be legally offensive in some jurisdictions only if there is "anti-dilution" legislation in effect in that jurisdiction);[14]

(h)   misappropriating the reputation of a famous individual (for example, hockey player, Wayne Gretzky) for another's commercial benefit;[15] and

---

[10]   AIL/ABA *Trademarks*, p. 12, *Trade-marks Act* (Canada), s. 7(a) and U.S. *Trademark Act*, 15 U.S.C. §1125(a)(1)(B) (1994).

[11]   For further discussion see American Bar Association, Section on Patent, Trademark and Copyright Law, *Annual Report* 94/95, p. 152 (hereinafter "ABA *Annual Report*, 94/95").

[12]   AIL/ABA *Trademarks*, p. 12; Hughes, *On Trade Marks*, §70, pp. 653–62.

[13]   AIL/ABA *Trademarks*, p. 12.

[14]   The *Trade-marks Act* (Canada), s. 22(1) provides "No person shall use a trade-mark registered by another person in a manner that is likely to have the effect of depreciating the value of the goodwill attached thereto." For a further discussion on this topic, see ABA *Annual Report*, 93/94, Report of Subcommittee A, Subject 1, "A Federal Anti-Dilution Statute?" in the Report of Committee No. 205 "Unfair Competition — Trade Identity" (hereinafter "ABA *Annual Report*, 93/94). See also English case *Tainttinger v. Allberv, Ltd.*, [1993] F.S.R. 641 (referred to in the ABA *Annual Report*, 93/94, p. 139). Also §1125(1)(A) and (B) to the U.S. *Federal Trademark Dilution Act of 1995* provides:

(1) Any person who, on or in connection with any goods or services, or any container for goods, uses in commerce any word, term, name, symbol, or device, or any combination thereof, or any false designation of origin, false or misleading description of fact, or false or misleading representation of fact, which,

(A) is likely to cause confusion, or to cause mistake, or to deceive as to the affiliation, connection, or association of such person with another person, or as to the origin, sponsorship, or approval of his or her goods, services, or commercial activities by another person, or

(B) in commercial advertising or promotion, misrepresents the nature, characteristics, qualities, or geographic origin of his or her or another person's goods, services, or commercial activities, shall be liable in a civil action by any person who believes that he or she is or is likely to be damaged by such act.

[15]   See s. 2(a) of the Model Right of Privacy and Publicity Statute, which provides in part:

Right to Use of Identity

(a) No person shall have the right, except as the individual concerned may have consented thereto,

(i) to use an individual's identity publicly in such manner as to state or imply, for purposes of commercial advantage, the individual's endorsement of a product, service, or business, or the individual's affiliation with the source of such product, service, or business;

See ABA *Annual Report* 94/95, p. 212, for a further discussion of this Model Act. For Canada, see Hughes, *On Trademarks*, §81, p. 697 and the *Privacy Acts* of British Columbia, Saskatchewan, Manitoba and Newfoundland and the Quebec Civil Code referred to in Hughes.

(i)   imitating the "get up" or "trade dress" of a competitor's product or service[16] (for example, imitating the shape of the "Coke" bottle). ("Trade dress" traditionally has referred to the appearance of a product or a product's packaging and may include features such as size, shape, colour, texture, graphics and the like, in varying arrangement and combinations.[17])

In each case the plaintiff may have to prove there was confusion to the public and detriment to the "injured" party, particularly if the case is based on the common law. In any event, the law of unfair competition is a flexible, changing legal concept that does, and should, adapt itself to social and business changes.[18]

Strategies:
(1)   A technology transfer agreement involving a trademark should prohibit specific acts that are characteristic of unfair competition, concerning both the products of the parties to the agreement and products of third parties.
(2)   Because claims for unfair competition are becoming more popular, the parties to a technology transfer agreement involving a trademark should consider the appropriateness of insurance that provides indemnification for offences.[19]

5.3.1 Passing Off

Passing off is one type of unfair competition. As the phrase suggests, someone is trying to "pass off" its goods or services for those of another. To establish a passing off claim in a lawsuit, one must establish:

(a)   *goodwill*[20] attached to the plaintiff's goods or services in the relevant geographical area;
(b)   a *misrepresentation*
    (i)   made by a trader in the course of trade, or
    (ii)   to prospective customers somewhere in the appropriate distribution chain;

that leads or is likely to *lead the public in that area to believe* that the goods or services are those of, or are authorized by, the plaintiff and that causes, or is likely to cause, *actual damage* to the plaintiff's business or goodwill.[21]

---

[16]   See Hughes, *On Trade Marks*, §78, pp. 683–84 and the American Bar Association, Section on Patent, Trademark and Copyright Law, *Annual Report*, 91/92, p. 189 (hereinafter "ABA *Annual Report*, 91/92").
[17]   ABA *Annual Report*, 91/92, p. 189.
[18]   AIL/ABA *Trademarks*, p. 13. See also Hughes, *On Trade Marks*, §75, p. 660, and see Drysdale and Silverleaf, *Passing Off*, ¶1.04, p. 3.
[19]   See ABA *Annual Report*, 94/95, p. 219.
[20]   For goodwill to exist, the trademark must be in use. To see how the legislation handles applications for registration prior to usage, see §5.11 of this text.
[21]   Adapted from Drysdale and Silverleaf, *Passing Off*, ¶2.33, p. 19; Hughes, *On Trade Marks*, §76, p. 671; and "Tentative Draft No. 1 of the Restatement of the Law (3rd) of Unfair Competition" discussed in ABA *Annual Report*, 91/92, p. 209, at 214–15.

5.4 Area of Coverage

The public who may be confused by a "passing off" effort may be located in an area smaller than all of Canada or the United States or even a province or state. Goodwill that exists only in one local area therefore will be protected by the common law only within that local area. If the product or service is *known* over a broad area, even though *available* only in a local area, protection may still be available:[22] what is required for protection in an area may only be the "necessary reputation"[23] in that area. One of the advantages of the federal registration of a trademark is protection throughout the entire country rather than only a small area in which there is the necessary reputation.

5.4.1 Residual Reputation

Even if a business has been wound up, there may be residual goodwill that merits protection in a passing off action.[24]

5.5 Continuing Distinctiveness

Because a trademark is used by a business to distinguish its goods and wares from those of other businesses, either by indicating the source or quality,[25] the trademark must be sufficiently distinct to be recognized by the consumer. The trademark must not be merely descriptive of the goods or wares.[26] The owner of a trademark must take the appropriate measures to maintain its distinctiveness; this can be lost if the trademark is allowed to become descriptive of the generic product. Thus, one sees considerable effort being expended to prevent trademarks like "Kleenex", "Teflon" and "Xerox" from becoming generic in the way "escalator", once a trademark, became the generic word for a moving staircase.[27] To avoid distinctiveness being lost by authorized users, controls are necessary. Distinctiveness may also be lost if the trademark is used without challenge by someone, other than the owner, without an appropriate licensing arrangement.

Strategies:

   (1)   Allocate the responsibility of preventing unauthorized use of a licensed trademark, as well as related costs.

---

22   See Drysdale and Silverleaf, *Passing Off*, ¶3.10, p. 31. Consider the difficulty of isolating the "local area" if the product or service is promoted on the Internet. See Sheldon Burshtein, "Surfing the Internet: Canadian Intellectual Property Issues", presented at the 1996 McGill University Meredith Lectures, May, 1996 (hereinafter "Burshtein, 'Surfing'"), ¶ 2.2.2.

23   *Ibid.*, ¶3.12, p. 34.

24   *Ibid.*, ¶3.15, p. 36.

25   See Hughes, *On Trade Marks*, §12, p. 363, and §32, p. 457. See also *Trade-marks Act* (Canada), s. 2 (definition of "distinctive") and ALI/ABA *Trademarks*, ¶103, p. 4.

26   22 U.S.C. §2(e)(i) and *Trade-marks Act* (Canada), s. 12(1)(b).

27   For a Canadian example, see *Unitel Communications Inc. v. Bell Canada* (1995), 61 C.P.R. (3d) 12, at 59–69 (F.C.T.D.).

(2)   Ensure that the licence contains the required controls to maintain distinctiveness.

TYPES OF MARKS

5.6 Different Types of Marks

The types of marks recognized by the Canadian *Trade-marks Act* are traditional trademarks (including distinguishing guises) and certification marks. The U.S. *Trademark Act* recognizes traditional trademarks, service marks, certification marks and collective marks.[28]

5.6.1 Traditional Trademarks

The statutory definitions of a traditional trademark reflect what the law of unfair competition will protect (*i.e.*, the goodwill of a business that is derived from a well-known indication of source of sponsorship or of quality used by that business). The Canadian *Trade-marks Act* in its definition of "trademark" refers to a mark that is *used* by a person to *distinguish* its goods or services from those of others.[29] The U.S. *Trademark Act* separates "service marks" (marks that identify "services") from trademarks (marks restricted to "goods"). Under the General Agreement on Tariff and Trade (GATT), the Trade-Related Aspects of Intellectual Property Rights (TRIPPS) does not distinguish between wares and services in its definition of a trademark:[30] "A trademark shall consist of any sign, or any combination of signs, capable of distinguishing the *goods or services* of one undertaking from those of another, including personal names, letters, numerals, figurative elements, and combinations of colours."[31] Article 16(2) and (3) of TRIPPS requires that "well known trademarks for wares and services shall be protected".[32] The definition in the U.S. *Trademark Act* states what a mark is, requires the feature that the mark identifies and distinguishes the goods or services from the competitors (mark includes a "word, name, symbol, or device, or any combination of those").[33] This definition basically applies in Canada. The U.S. "device" is reflected in s. 2 of the Canadian Act "distinguishing guise" includes a "shaping of wares or their containers" and a "mode of wrapping or packaging wares".

5.6.2 Certification and Collective Marks

A certification mark is used to distinguish wares of a defined standard. It may relate to the character or quality of the goods or services, the working conditions

---

[28]   See also the General Agreement on Tariffs and Trade (GATT) Agreement on Trade-Related Aspects of Intellectual Property Rights (TRIPPS), Art. 15, §1.
[29]   *Trade-marks Act* (Canada), s. 2.
[30]   See the Uruguay Round negotiations of GATT, TRIPPS Art. 15(1).
[31]   ABA *Annual Report*, 94/95, p. 177.
[32]   *Ibid.*
[33]   See ALI/ABA *Trademarks*, p. 4. Also see U.S. *Trademark Act*, 15 U.S.C. §1127.

under which they are produced, the class of persons by whom they have been produced, or the geographic area in which they have been produced.[34] The certification mark is not used by its owner;[35] it is used by the provider of the goods or services, which obligates itself to deliver those goods or services within the defined standards, on being permitted to use the certification mark. Collective marks are not specifically mentioned in the Canadian *Trade-marks Act*.[36] Like certification marks, collective marks identify qualities or groups of goods or service providers.

5.6.3 Marks Versus Names

Trademarks are not the same as trade names. A trade name is the name under which any business is carried on, whether or not it is the name of a corporation, a partnership, or an individual. A company name is not registerable as a trademark except when the company name is also used as a trademark. A trade name, however, may be registrable (indeed may be required to be registered) under federal or provincial/state law in Canada and the United States.[37]

5.7 Prohibited Marks

Certain marks are specifically prohibited by the Canadian and U.S. *Trademark Acts*. These include anything "scandalous, obscene or immoral"[38] or marks "that disparage or falsely suggest a connection with persons, institutions, beliefs, or national symbols, or that would bring them into contempt or disrepute".[39]

STRENGTH OF TRADEMARK

5.8 Elements of Distinctiveness

The essence of a trademark lies in its *distinctiveness*.[40] The purpose of a mark is to identify and distinguish the relevant goods or services. A mark that is merely

---

[34] *Trade-marks Act* (Canada), s. 2 (definition of "certification mark"). See also ALI/ABA *Trademarks*, p. 5.

[35] Unless the same mark is also registered as a traditional trademark by that owner: see Hughes, *On Trade Marks*, §15, p. 367-2.

[36] The ABA, *Annual Report*, 92/93, p. 167, states:
> The Canadian Act has for many decades recognized service marks and certification marks, but has given no specific statutory recognition to collective marks. However, the practice of the Canadian Trade-Marks Office for many years has been to permit U.S. collective marks to be registered in Canada as ordinary trade-marks or as certification marks, even though there has been no statutory or case law basis for doing so. Extending formal statutory recognition to collective marks would make sense of an inane practice.

[37] See Hughes, *On Trade Marks*, §13, p. 365 and ALI/ABA *Trademarks*, p. 8.

[38] Using the words contained in *Trade-marks Act* (Canada), s. 9(1)(j). See also ALI/ABA *Trademarks*, p. 7.

[39] ALI/ABA *Trademarks*, p. 7.

[40] Some trademarks get their distinctiveness from the style of print used. This distinctiveness may be lost in "domain names" used on the Internet.

descriptive of the goods or services therefore has difficulty in attaining the requisite distinctiveness warranted for protection. Trademarks may be ranked by their strength as follows:

(a)   "fanciful" or "a meaningless word specifically coined to serve as a trademark with no descriptive or even suggestive connotation in any language".[41] An example of a fanciful trademark is "KODAK".[42]

(b)   "arbitrary" or "a word in normal usage that is used in an unrelated sense". The "BRICK" is a well-known Canadian furniture retailer using an arbitrary mark. The trademark "BRICK" could not be used as a trademark for a style of bricks, but when arbitrarily used for a furniture retailer, it may give significant strength.[43]

(c)   protectable "descriptive" marks have something extra that serves to provide identity and distinctiveness because of usage, notwithstanding their descriptiveness. Such descriptive marks are often referred to as having "secondary meaning"[44] or having acquired distinctiveness.

5.8.1 Guidelines to Trademarks That Warrant Protection

The *Model State Trademark Bill*, as enacted in the State of Washington, provides as follows in determining the standards required for granting protection:

In determining whether a mark is famous and has distinctive quality, a court shall consider all relevant factors, including, but not limited to the following:

(1)   whether the mark is inherently distinctive[45] or has become distinctive through substantially exclusive and continuous use;[46]

(2)   whether the duration and extent of use of the mark are substantial;

(3)   whether the duration and extent of advertising and publicity of the mark are substantial;

(4)   whether the geographical extent of the trading area in which the mark is used is substantial;

(5)   whether the mark has substantial renown in its and in the other person's trading areas [*i.e.*, the competitor's trading area] and channels of trade; and

(6)   whether substantial use of the same or similar marks is being made by third parties.[47]

---

[41] ALI/ABA *Trademarks*, pp. 5–6.

[42] *Ibid.*, p. 5.

[43] *Ibid.*, p. 6.

[44] See Hughes, *On Trade Marks*, §30, pp. 453-6 and ff. and ALI/ABA *Trademarks*, p. 6. Article 15(1) of TRIPPS provides: "where a trademark is not inherently capable of distinguishing the relevant goods or services a Member may make registrability depend on distinctiveness through use". *Per* ABA *Annual Report*, 94/95, p. 177. Note that there will be a difference between suggestive marks which are somewhat descriptive, but registerable, and marks which are clearly descriptive and, therefore, not registerable.

[45] Such as a "fanciful" or "arbitrary" trademark.

[46] Although otherwise somewhat descriptive.

[47] The ABA *Annual Report*, 90/91, p. 125. The *Trade-marks Act* (Canada), s. 6(5), produces substantially the same result.

5.8.2 Federal Trademark Dilution Act of 1995

On January 16, 1996, the United States enacted an amendment to the *Trademark Act,* which effectively grants remedies to the owner of a famous mark to prevent activities that will lead to dilution (*i.e.*, "conduct which weakens the distinctiveness or the goodwill associated with a mark").

> Dilution can occur through blurring or tarnishment. Blurring is the unauthorized use of a mark on dissimilar products or for dissimilar services that may cause the mark to cease functioning as a unique identifier of the mark owner's goods. Tarnishment occurs where a mark becomes consciously or unconsciously linked with poor quality, unsavory, or unwholesome goods or services.

> For various reasons, state statutes are ineffective. First, not all states have dilution statutes, currently only about half the states have such statutes. Second, there is no uniform definition of dilution. Thus, some courts will only enjoin non-competitive, non-confusing uses, while others protect uses on both similar as well as dissimilar products. Third, courts are reluctant to issue nationwide injunctions. Consequently, the recently enacted Federal Trademark Dilution Act of 1995 is expected to provide uniform and nationwide protection for famous marks.[48]

The amendment provides remedies for dilution of famous marks.

(1) The owner of a famous mark shall be entitled, subject to the principles of equity and upon such terms as the court deems reasonable, to an injunction against another person's commercial use in commerce of a mark or trade name, if such use begins after the mark has become famous and causes dilution of the distinctive quality of the mark, and to obtain such other relief as is provided in this subsection. In determining whether a mark is distinctive and famous, a court may consider factors such as, but not limited to

   (A) the degree of inherent or acquired distinctiveness of the mark;

   (B) the duration and extent of use of the mark in connection with the goods or services with which the mark is used;

   (C) the duration and extent of advertising and publicity of the mark;

   (D) the geographical extent of the trading area in which the mark is used;

   (E) the channels of trade for the goods or services with which the mark is used;

   (F) the degree of recognition of the mark in the trading areas and channels of trade used by the mark's owner and the person against whom the injunction is sought;

   (G) the nature and extent of use of the same or similar marks by third parties; and

   (H) whether the mark was registered under the Act of March 3, 1881, or the Act of February 20, 1905, or on the principal register.[49]

---

[48] Jonathan Agmon, Stacey Helpern and David Parker, *The Federal Trademark Dilution Act of 1995*, http://www.ll.georgetown.edu/lc/internic/trademarks/dilut1.html.

[49] U.S. *Trademark Act*, 15 U.S.C. §1125(c).

REGISTRATION

5.9 Requirement to Register

Although sometimes beneficial, registration is not necessary under the Canadian or U.S. *Trademark Acts*; however, registration may be necessary under other legislation and, particularly, provincial/state legislation. Trademarks with the appropriate qualities are registrable at the separate trademarks offices for Canada and the United States. Unless specifically stated when registered, the registration offers protection for usage in the entire country (but, in the United States, not for commerce that occurs only within one state).

5.9.1 Benefits of Registering Federally

Article 16(1) of TRIPPS sets out a reasonable summary of the effect of registration in Canada and the United States:

> The owner of a registered trademark shall have the exclusive right to prevent the use in the course of trade of the identical or similar trademark for goods or services that are identical or similar to those goods or services in respect of which the owner's trademark is registered where such use would result in a likelihood of confusion. Such confusion shall be presumed where there is use of the identical mark with the identical wares or services.[50]

Other benefits of registering federally include the rights to

(a)   use the trademark throughout the country[51] and to preclude others from using a confusing mark anywhere in the country;[52]

(b)   place the trademark on a data base that is readily accessible nationally (for example, the NUANS database in Canada or the T-SEARCH database in the United States);[53]

(c)   a presumption that a registered trademark is valid, placing the onus on the challenger to establish invalidity;[54]

(d)   sue in the U.S. federal courts, as well as in a state court, for an infringement of a U.S. registered trademark;

(e)   sue in the Federal Court of Canada, as well as in a provincial court, such as Alberta's Court of Queen's Bench, for an infringement of a Canadian registered trademark;

---

[50]   See ABA *Annual Report,* 94/95, p. 177. See also *Trade-marks Act* (Canada), s. 19 (rep. & sub. S.C. 1993, c. 15, s. 60).

[51]   For Canada, see Hughes, *On Trade Marks,* §17, p. 371; for U.S., see *Trademark Act,* 15 U.S.C. §1051. But consider the problem raised by two businesses owning the same trademark, one in use, for example, in Canada, and one in Germany. Burshtein, "Surfing", at 2.3.8.6, queries: "Does the European company's advertising of its mark as a domain name worldwide on the Internet infringe the Canadian company's trade-mark in Canada?" See also Drysdale and Silverleaf, *Passing Off,* ¶3.10, p. 31.

[52]   For Canada, see *Trade-marks Act* (Canada), s. 19 (rep. & sub. S.C. 1993, c. 15, s. 60). For the United States, see *Trademarks Act,* 15 U.S.C. §§1051 and 1063.

[53]   See ALI/ABA *Trademarks,* p. 31.

[54]   For Canada, see Hughes, *On Trade Marks,* §17, p. 371.

(f)   register in other countries under international treaties;[55]
(g)   prevent importation of goods bearing infringing marks;[56]
(h)   a broader scope of protection than is offered under common law or provincial/state legislation;[57] and
(i)   the availability of a court order compelling seizure of material bearing infringing trademarks.[58]

TERM

5.10 Term of Federally Registered Trademarks

In Canada, the term of a trademark is 15 years, indefinitely renewable for 15-year periods.[59] In the United States, the term is 10 years: however, after 6 years the registrant must notify the registrar that the trademark is still in use.[60] Thereafter, additional terms of 10 years are available.[61] Article 18 of TRIPPS provides that the initial term for protection of a trademark in the subscribing countries must be at least 7 years, renewable indefinitely for terms of not less than 7 years.[62]

5.10.1 Loss for Non-use

Reflecting the basics of the law of unfair competition — that protection is offered for marks that are in use and, by that usage, generate goodwill — a Canadian trademark may be expunged from the Trademark Register for non-use.[63] Article 19(1) of TRIPPS allows for cancellation of a trademark "after an uninterrupted period of at least three years of non-use".

REGISTRATION PRIOR TO USE

5.11 Registration Federally Prior to Use

The basic principles of the rules against unfair competition require usage of the trademark and, thus, generation of goodwill to warrant protection (*i.e.*, existing goodwill must be injured to give rise to the claim). In practice under a registry system, however, businesses will often want to "reserve"

---

[55]   The "Paris Union" was established by convention in 1883 and includes Canada, the United States and most industrialized countries.
[56]   See *Trade-marks Act* (Canada), s. 53(1) and (4) (rep. & sub. S.C. 1993, c. 44, s. 234); U.S. *Trademarks Act*, 15 U.S.C. §1124.
[57]   Items (a) through (h) are adapted from ALI/ABA, *Trademarks*, p. 17.
[58]   *Trade-marks Act* (Canada), s. 53(1) (rep. & sub. S.C. 1993, c. 44, s. 234); U.S. *Trademarks Act*, 15 U.S.C. §1116(d).
[59]   See *Trade-marks Act* (Canada), s. 46(1).
[60]   U.S. *Trademarks Act*, 15 U.S.C. §1058.
[61]   *Ibid.*, §1059.
[62]   See Quote in ABA *Annual Report*, 94/95, p. 177.
[63]   *Trade-marks Act* (Canada), ss. 44 and 45 (s. 45 am. S.C. 1993, c. 44, s. 232(1); 1994, c. 47, s. 200(1) and (2) (to come into force on proclamation)).

trademarks[64] they intend to use. This will give them the requisite lead time to develop the marketing for the identified product or service. The *Trademarks Act* of Canada currently allows an application to be filed on the basis that the applicant intends to use the proposed trademark, but final registration of the trademark will not occur until the applicant files a Declaration of Use confirming that the trademark is being used in commerce. Article 15(3) of TRIPPS provides that usage, although a condition to *registration*, cannot be a condition to *filing*, and refusal of the application cannot be made "on the ground that use has not been commenced within 3 years from filing". The Canadian government passed s. 45(1) that contemplates evidence of use three years after filing. The United States implemented TRIPPS, effective January 1, 1996.[65]

MARKING

5.12 Marking Not Required

Using a mark to designate a trademark is not required under the Canadian *Trademarks Act*. Using ® or the letters **TM** as a superscript ™ or within a circle, however, will convey to the public the message that trademark rights are being claimed.[66] In addition, this is a valuable way to give notice to the public that the trademark is not a generic term. In the United States, the registrant has the option to display the words "Registered in U.S. Patent and Trademark Office" or "Reg. U.S. Pat. & Tm. Off." or "®". If these words are not displayed, the registrant has to show that the other person using the trademark had actual knowledge that the mark was registered or the registrant will not be entitled to any of the statutory profit and damage remedies offered by the U.S. *Trademarks Act*.[67]

REGISTRATION IN A PROVINCE/STATE

5.13 Inconsistent Rules

One of the greatest barriers to global, and sometimes even national, commerce is the lack of conformity from jurisdiction to jurisdiction for registration requirements (including necessity for registration and extent of disclosure required to the government and the prospective licensee).[68] In the United States, a *Model Trademarks Act* was developed to provide uniformity, but it has not been adopted in all states and has not been applied consistently in the states that have adopted it.

---

[64] See Burshtein, "Surfing", ¶ 2.2.4.3.

[65] ABA *Annual Report*, 94/95, p. 179.

[66] See Hughes, *On Trade Marks*, §39, p. 509.

[67] 15 U.S.C. §1111.

[68] See also American Bar Association, Section on Patent, Trademark and Copyright Law, *Annual Report*, 90/91, p. 126 (hereinafter "ABA *Annual Report*, 90/91").

Strategy:
   (1)   Be aware of relevant provincial/state registration/disclosure requirements.
   (2)   Make necessary revisions to standard form licence agreements to reflect regional differences.

5.14 Benefit of Registration in a Province/State

These benefits include:

   (a)   permission to register a trade name which might not otherwise satisfy the standards of the *Trademark Acts*;
   (b)   satisfaction of registration requirements that impose penalties for non-registration;[69] and
   (c)   protection for use of a trademark only within one state (and, thus, not covered by the U.S. *Trademark Act*).

REGISTERING INTERNATIONALLY

5.15 International Treaties

TRIPPS, one of the results of the recent GATT negotiations, was included in the Final Document signed in April 1994 by Canada, the United States and over 120 other countries[70] and provides certain minimum requirements for registration. Canada and the United States are in the process of enacting the legislation necessary to bring their *Trademark Acts* into line with the requirements of TRIPPS. Preceding TRIPPS, Canada, the United States and Mexico established minimum standards for trademark protection when they entered into the North American Free Trade Agreement (NAFTA).[71]

LICENSEES

5.16 Registration of Licensees

As a result of NAFTA and TRIPPS, the Canadian *Trade-marks Act* no longer requires a licensee of a trademark to be recorded as a "registered user". Now s. 50 requires "direct or indirect control" over the "character of quality of the wares or services".[72] This brought the Canadian Act more into line with the U.S. *Trademark Act*.

5.17 Requisite Controls Over Licensees

In both Canada and the United States, the distinctiveness of trademarks can be lost due to insufficient management and policing of trademarks which gives rise

---

[69]   See ALI/ABA *Trademarks*, p. 16 and the Alberta *Partnership Act*, R.S.A. 1980, c. P-2, s. 87.
[70]   ABA *Annual Report*, 94/95, p. 176.
[71]   See Art. 1708 of NAFTA.
[72]   Repealed & sub. S.C. 1993, c. 15, s. 69.

to extensive uncontrolled use and may lead to the loss of distinctive trade-marks.[73] The following sets out some good advice to licensors of trademarks:

> Trade-mark owners in Canada, including franchisors, should ensure that all trade-mark licenses are in writing, and that the written agreements contained adequate control provisions over the licensee's or franchisee's goods or services. In a franchise system, the trade-mark license and control provisions will typically be found in and as part of the franchise agreement. The agreement should clearly identify every use that the franchisee is entitled to make of the marks and should give the franchisor a contractual right to exercise control over the character or quality of the franchisee's wares or services. The agreement should also specify the manner in which control may be exercised (for example, by periodic inspection). Franchisors also should include, or consider adding to the agreement, a right to terminate the agreement in the event that the franchisee fails to comply with the franchisor's quality standards.
>
> It is not sufficient for a trade-mark owner to have an appropriate trade-mark license agreement in place if the owner does not exercise control in fact. However, . . . [the *Trade-marks Act* (Canada)] specifically allows a trade-mark owner to exercise control over a licensee's wares or services, either directly or indirectly. Direct control may be exercised by supplying proper use guidelines, approving samples of the product at various stages of its manufacture, visiting the licensee's premises, acting on consumer complaints and, in some cases, supplying the product. Indirect control, on the other hand, may be exercised by appointing an independent agent or representative to exercise direct control over the licensee. This method will frequently be used in master franchise transactions where the trade-mark owner (the franchisor) will appoint a representative (the master franchisee) to exercise quality control supervision over the use of the trade-marks by sublicensees (the franchisees).[74]

Strategy: A licensor of a trademark must impose controls over the use of the trademark to avoid loss of distinctiveness.

5.18 Protecting Licensee Against Infringers

Section 50(3) of the *Trade-marks Act* (Canada) has a provision that requires a licensor of a trademark to protect the licensee against harm caused by a third party infringer, unless the licence agreement has a contrary provision.[75]

Strategy: A technology transfer agreement that includes the licence of a Canadian trademark should address who has the obligation, if any, to take action against third-party infringers. Remember, the default provision is that the licensor has the obligation to protect the licensee.

---

[73] See *Unitel Communications Inc. v. Bell Canada* (1995), 61 C.P.R. (3d) 12 (F.C.T.D.) and ABA *Annual Report*, 94/95, p. 246. See U.S. *Trademark Act*, 15 U.S.C. §1064.

[74] ABA *Annual Report*, 93/94, p. 237.

[75] Repealed & sub. S.C. 1993, c. 15, s. 69.

CO-OWNERSHIP OF TRADEMARKS

5.19 Co-ownership of Trademarks

If two or more companies have the right to use the same trademark as result of some form of co-ownership, s. 48(2) of the *Trade-marks Act* (Canada) implies that distinctiveness can be lost if the co-owners exercise their rights in a manner that confuses the public.

Strategy: Co-owners of a trademark should agree to take appropriate steps to preserve the distinctiveness of that trademark.

FRANCHISES

5.20 Franchise Legislation

There is no commonly accepted definition of a "franchise". An element common to most franchises, however, is a licence of a trademark.[76] The definition of "franchise" may vary with the particular legislation.[77]

> The types of businesses that have been found to constitute franchises for purposes of various franchise laws have included a broad array of distribution and licensing relationships in numerous industries. Whether a relationship is referred to as a distributorship, dealership, partnership, license, or by some other name, it may be subject to a variety of laws that regulate franchising if it is found to possess the legal attributes of a franchise.[78]

5.21 Disclosure Legislation

Some franchise legislation requires registration of the franchisor with a governmental authority and compulsory disclosure of facts to the franchisee and, in some cases, to the government. This legislation is intended to:[79]

(a) prohibit misrepresentation and other potentially fraudulent activities in the sale of franchises;[80]

(b) force "disclosure of information to prospective purchasers [*i.e.*, franchisees] to aid them in making an informed decision";[81] and

---

[76] ABA *Annual Report,* 94/95, p. 246.
[77] Currently, Alberta is the only Canadian jurisdiction to enact a *Franchises Act*, S.A. 1995, c. F-17. The definition of franchise in s.1(1), of the new Alberta Act defines franchise as "a right to engage in a business . . . (ii) that is substantially associated with a trademark, service mark, trade name, logotype or advertising of the franchisor or its associate or designating the franchisor or its associate . . .".
[78] ABA *Annual Report,* 91/92, p. 182.
[79] The Alberta *Franchises Act* states a similar purpose in s. 2.
[80] ABA *Annual Report,* 90/91, p. 150.
[81] *Ibid.*

(c)   require "registration and approval by the [governmental] administrators prior to offering or selling franchises".[82]

Disclosure required by the Uniform Franchises Offering Circular includes descriptions of:

> all trademarks and related commercial symbols to be licensed, including information as to federal or state registration; any litigation, past or pending, in any court or administrative tribunal, state or federal; any agreements significantly limiting the rights to use the trademark; whether the franchise agreements will obligate the franchisor to protect the trademarks and the franchisee against claims of infringement or unfair competition; and whether the franchisor knows of any infringing uses which could materially affect the franchisee's use of the trademarks.[83]

5.21.1 Franchise Disclosure

The franchise disclosure rules of many states are the same as those imposed by the U.S. Federal Trade Commission (FTC). To be a franchise[84] within the scope of the FTC Rules generally these elements must exist:

(i)   an agreement between the franchisor and the franchisee that permits the franchisee to use the franchisor's trade name, trademark or service mark;

(ii)   significant assistance to the franchisee or significant control over the franchisee's method of business operation, or the franchisor's provision of a marketing plan to the franchisee; and

(iii) a required payment of consideration deemed to be a "franchise fee" to the franchisor or its affiliate by the franchisee.[85]

5.21.2 Control

The FTC has indicated that any one of the following forms of control or assistance is sufficient to cause a franchise to fit within the scope of its franchise disclosure legislation:[86]

(i)   restrictions on business location or sales area;

(ii)   furnishing management, marketing or personnel advice;

(iii)   restrictions on customers;

(iv)   location or sales area restrictions;

(v)   formal sales, repair or business training programs;

(vi)   furnishing a detailed operations manual;

(vii)   promotional campaigns requiring franchisee participation or financial contribution;

(viii) mandatory personnel policies and practices;

(ix)   control over production techniques;

---

[82]   *Ibid.*

[83]   *Ibid.*, quoting "Business Franchise Guide (CCH)", para. 5813.

[84]   Also see Alberta *Franchises Act*, s. 1(1)(d).

[85]   ABA *Annual Report*, 90/91, p. 151.

[86]   Alberta has a similar provision in the definition, in s. 1(1), of "marketing or business plan" which outlines many of the material aspects of conducting business specified by the franchisor.

(x)   establishing accounting systems or requiring accounting practices;

(xi)   location and site approval;

(xii)   location design or appearance requirements;

(xiii)   control over hours of operation.[87]

5.21.3 Payment to Fall Within the Definition of a Franchise

For FTC purposes there must be a payment.[88] "The 'required payment' is interpreted broadly in order to capture all sources of revenue that the licensee must pay to the licensor for the right to market goods or services under the licensor's mark, whether those payments are required by contract or practical necessity."[89]

5.22 Business Opportunity Legislation

In addition to franchise legislation, some provinces/states have business opportunity legislation that is intended to protect against ventures that "historically have been marketed to unsophisticated purchasers at a low level of investment and have been subject to frequent fraudulent practices and abuses".[90] The scope of the business opportunity legislation could pick up some franchises unexpectedly.[91] The provision of certain types of representations by the franchisor could trigger the application of some business opportunity legislation, for examples, (1) "the seller will refund the buyer's initial payment or buy back the materials that the buyer purchased from the seller if the buyer is dissatisfied with the business opportunity", and (2) "the seller will provide some sort of marketing plan to the buyer".[92]

Strategies:

(1)   *Become familiar with any applicable "business opportunity" legislation.*

(2)   *Examine the applicable business opportunity legislation for any appropriate exemptions.*[93]

(3)   *If possible, avoid representations and other licence provisions that trigger the application of business opportunity legislation; consider disclaiming offensive representations.*[94]

(4)   *Restrict franchises to entities that are not covered by the legislation (i.e., purchasers having the required business experience, financial strength, sales performance history).*[95]

---

[87]   ABA *Annual Report*, 93/94, p. 223, quoting FTC Interpretive Guides to Franchising and Business Opportunity Ventures Trade Regulation Rule, 44 Fed. Reg. 49, 966, 49, 967 (1979).

[88]   In Alberta, a payment is only one of the elements included in the definition of "franchise", however a "continuing financial obligation" is also part of the definition in the alternative to the payment of a franchise fee (s. 1(1)).

[89]   ABA *Annual Report*, 93/94, p. 223.

[90]   ABA *Annual Report*, 90/91, p. 151.

[91]   *Ibid.*

[92]   ABA *Annual Report*, 94/95, p. 250.

[93]   *Ibid.*, p. 251.

[94]   *Ibid.*, p. 252; see also ABA *Annual Report*, 91/92, pp. 185–86.

[95]   ABA *Annual Report*, 94/95, p. 252.

(5)   Consider marketing the products/services directly rather than through franchisees in states where compliance will be difficult.[96]

5.22.1 Effects of Business Opportunity Legislation

In addition to registration and disclosure, if a "franchise" is within the scope of business opportunity legislation, it may be:

(a)   required to repurchase inventory on termination,
(b)   restricted to termination only for cause,
(c)   required to permit renewal unless there is a cause for termination.[97]

5.23 Controls under Franchise Acts

As previously mentioned, the Canadian and U.S. *Trademark Acts* require a licensor of a trademark to maintain control over the use of the trademark, failing which the trademark may be lost because it loses its "distinctiveness". While the strength of a trademark may be described as the "cornerstone" of a franchise,[98] a key to the success of a franchise may be "uniformity of product and control of . . . [the] quality and distribution [of the product that] causes the public to turn to the franchise stores for the product".[99] The *Trademarks Acts* of Canada and the United States therefore impose the need for controls over the franchisee. The extent of control necessary may bring the franchise relationship into one governed by a provincial/state *Franchise Act*[100] and may, indeed, contravene the provisions of a provincial/state Act. In contrast with this federal requirement, some provincial/state franchise legislation attempts to restrict the extent of the controls a purchaser can impose on its franchisees.[101] Because these vary so much from state to state, this topic will not be discussed in this text.

Strategy: There is a "tight rope" between imposition of controls required by the Trademark Acts and imposition of controls that will bring the relationship within the scope of registration/disclosure franchise legislation or business opportunity legislation, or that will offend legislation that precludes excess controls.[102] Walk it carefully.

---

[96]   *Ibid.*, p. 253.
[97]   ABA *Annual Report*, 91/92, p. 182.
[98]   ABA *Annual Report*, 94/95, p. 246, quoting *Susser v. Carval Corp.*, 206 F.Supp. 636, at 640 (S.D.N.Y. 1962); affd 332 F.2d 505.
[99]   ABA *Annual Report*, 94/95.
[100]   See ABA *Annual Report*, 90/91, p. 207.
[101]   See ABA *Annual Report*, 94/95, pp. 245 ff.
[102]   See ABA *Annual Report*, 93/94, p. 228.

Chapter 6

TRADE SECRETS

Trade secrecy is such a powerful form of protection that innovators are offered a long-term monopoly via a patent in exchange for disclosure of the best mode of implementing that technology.

APPLICABLE LEGISLATION

6.1 North American Free Trade Agreement (NAFTA) and Trade Secrets

On becoming a party to NAFTA, Canada, the United States and Mexico agreed to provide protection to trade secrets.[1]

1. Each Party shall provide the legal means for any person to prevent trade secrets from being disclosed to, acquired by, or used by others without the consent of the person lawfully in control of the information in a manner contrary to honest commercial practices, in so far as:
   (a) the information is secret in the sense that it is not, as a body or in the precise configuration and assembly of its components, generally known among or readily accessible to persons that normally deal with the kind of information in question;
   (b) the information has actual or potential commercial value because it is secret; and
   (c) the person lawfully in control of the information has taken reasonable steps under the circumstances to keep it secret.
2. A Party may require that to qualify for protection a trade secret must be evidenced in documents, electronic or magnetic means, optical discs, microfilms, films or other similar instruments.
3. No Party may limit the duration of protection for trade secrets, so long as the conditions in paragraph 1 exist.
4. No Party may discourage or impede the voluntary licensing of trade secrets by imposing excessive or discriminatory conditions on such licenses or conditions that dilute the value of the trade secrets.[2]

---

[1] North American Free Trade Agreement, Art. 17.11.1 (hereinafter "NAFTA"). For corresponding provisions under the Trade Related Intellectual Property Protection Agreement (hereinafter "TRIPPS"), see Art. 39, discussion relating to "undisclosed information".

[2] Items 5, 6(a)–(d), and 7 of Art. 1711 describe protections against disclosure when applying for approval of the marketing of pharmaceutical or agricultural chemical products that utilize new chemical entities.

6.1.1 Canadian Rules

Trade secrecy in Canada is a matter within the jurisdiction of the provinces. None of the nine common-law provinces has passed any legislation covering the protection offered to trade secrets, let alone defining what a trade secret is.[3] Likewise, the Province of Quebec, governed by civil law, has not enacted any codes specifically related to trade secrets.[4]

6.1.2 U.S. Rules

Many of the U.S. states have adopted variations of the *Uniform Trade Secrets Act*, though not all enactments are, in fact, uniform.[5] Courts in the United States refer to the 1939 *Restatement of Torts*, §757,[6] even though the section was not continued into the *Restatement (Second)*[7] or into the more recently adopted Restatement (Third) of Unfair Competition.[8]

PROTECTION OFFERED

6.2 Works Covered

There seems to be no limit to the scope of protection offered by trade secrecy.[9] Indeed the definition of the *Restatement (Third) of Unfair Competition* refers to "*any* information that can be used in the operation of a business or other enterprise" (emphasis added). The distinction between "trade secrets" and "confidential information" seems to be minimal, but may depend on the nature of the secret.[10] If in a particular U.S. state a "trade secret" is defined by the local version of the *Uniform Trade Secrets Act*, "confidential information" may be a better phrase to use because it may be free of limitations to the phrase "trade secret" imposed by that Act. Similarly, there does not seem to be a finite legal distinction between a trade secret, confidential information and "know how". Thus, these words should not be used separately in an agreement with the assumption that each has a distinct and separate meaning.

Strategy: Avoid using the phrase "trade secrets"; instead, use "confidential information" with a specifically prepared definition.

---

[3]   See John T. Ramsay in *Intellectual Property: Worldwide Trade Secrets Law*, Terrence F. MacLaren, ed., rev. ed. (New York: Clark Boardman Callaghan, 1995), p. A2-5 (hereinafter "Ramsay, *Intellectual Property*").

[4]   *Ibid.*, p. A2-33.

[5]   Gale R. Peterson, "Trade Secrets In an Information Age" in (1995), Houston Law Review, Vol. 32, No. 2, p. 385, at 389 (hereinafter "Peterson 'Trade Secrets'").

[6]   *Ibid.*, p. 389.

[7]   *Ibid.*

[8]   *Ibid.*, p. 391

[9]   See Ramsay, *Intellectual Property*, p. A2-35 and Institute of Law Research and Reform, *Trade Secrets*, Report No. 46, p. 157.

[10] Ramsay, *Intellectual Property*, p. A2-35.

NECESSARY QUALITIES FOR PROTECTION
6.3 Secrecy

To be protected, the information must be secret. As mentioned in §6.1 of this text, Art. 17.11.1 of NAFTA specifies that the protected information "is secret in the sense that it is not, as a body or in the precise configuration and assembly of its components, generally known among or readily accessible to persons that normally deal with the kind of information in question". This seems to be a reasonable summary of the Canadian case law[11] and of the U.S. law[12] — absolute secrecy is not necessary.[13] The factors to be closely examined in determining whether there is sufficient secrecy to warrant protection include:

(a) the extent to which the information is known outside the business;
(b) the extent to which it is known by employees and others involved in the business;
(c) the extent of measures taken to guard the secrecy of information;
(d) the value of the information to the holder of the secret and to his competitors;
(e) the amount of effort or money expended in developing the information;
(f) the ease or difficulty with which the information can be properly acquired or duplicated by others;
(g) whether the holder of the secret and the taker treat the information as secret; and
(h) the custom in the industry concerning this specific type of information.[14]

Strategy: Agree to keep confidential only what has been defined to be a secret.

6.4 Economic Value

To warrant protection, the information must have present or future commercial value.[15]

Strategy: Agree to keep secret only information that has value.

---

[11] *Ibid.*, p. A2-8.
[12] See generally Peterson "Trade Secrets". See also TRIPPS, Art. 29, ¶2, where it states:
2. Natural and legal persons shall have the possibility of preventing information lawfully within their control from being disclosed to, acquired by, or used by others without their consent in a manner contrary to honest commercial practices so long as such information:
is secret in the sense that it is not, as a body or in the precise configuration and assembly of its components, generally known among or readily accessible to persons within the circles that normally deal with the kind of information in question;
has commercial value because it is secret; and
has been subject to reasonable steps under the circumstances, by the person lawfully in control of the information, to keep it secret.
[13] Adapted from Ramsay, *Intellectual Property*, p. A2-8 and Peterson, "Trade Secrets", p. 429.
[14] Items (a) to (h) listed in David Vavor, "What is a Trade Secret," in Roger T. Hughes, ed., *Trade Secrets* (Toronto: Law Society of Upper Canada, 1990), p. A-18 (papers presented at a conference held at Osgoode Hall, November 24, 1989). A substantially similar list appears in Peterson, "Trade Secrets", p. 421, quoting from the *Bando* case, 9 F.3d 823, at 848 (10th Cir. 1993) and see Terrence F. MacLaren in *Intellectual Property: Worldwide Trade Secrets Law*, Terrence F. MacLaren, ed., rev. ed. (New York: Clark Boardman Callaghan, 1995), p. A1.02.
[15] See NAFTA, Art. 17.11(1.b); Ramsay, *Intellectual Property*, p. A2-3 and Peterson, "Trade Secrets", p. 417.

6.5 Novelty

The degree of novelty required for patents is not necessary for a trade secret because trade secrecy does not prevent independent development.[16] Only a minimum level of novelty is required;[17] information will not be protected if it is of a trivial nature.[18]

6.6 Imposition of Duties of Confidence

Confidentiality obligations may arise from express contract, implied contract or from a duty that arises by operation of law, whether based on property, tort or trust law. Parties may contract expressly concerning the obligations of secrecy. A contract may imply those obligations particularly in employment contracts.[19] The courts have had much more difficulty in finding non-contractual ways of protecting secrets and often seem to stretch the law of property and trust (*i.e.*, fiduciary duty); some are predicting a separate tort for a breach of duty of confidence.[20]

Strategy: Be careful in your use of words; legal words, such as "trust" and "fiduciary," give rise to special remedies that may not be available under contract law.

6.6.1 Explicit Imposition of the Duties of Secrecy is Unnecessary

At common law, a duty of confidence can arise without the parties agreeing in writing to maintain confidentiality or even discussing the need for secrecy. If a duty is so obviously an implied part of the communication, a court will impose that duty.[21]

Strategy: Rather than having secrecy obligations imposed by the common law, the negotiations for a technology transfer shall early on establish what secrecy duties will be assumed and what duties will be disclaimed.

SECRECY AGREEMENTS

6.7 Imposing Obligations of Confidentiality by Contract

When drafting a confidentiality agreement, the drafter should not assume that there is a clear legal definition of "trade secret" or a precise distinction between the words "confidential information," "trade secret" or "know-how". The definition should be drafted each time for the specific circumstances.

---

[16] Ramsay, *Intellectual Property*, p. A2-13 and Peterson, "Trade Secrets", p. 416.
[17] Peterson, "Trade Secrets", p. 417.
[18] Ramsay, *Intellectual Property*, p. A2-13.
[19] Peterson, "Trade Secrets", p. 404, referring to Jager on *Trade Secrets*.
[20] See *International Corona Resources Ltd. v. LAC Minerals Ltd.*, [1989] 2 S.C.R. 574, 69 O.R. (2d) 287, 36 O.A.C. 57, 61 D.L.R. (4th) 14, 101 N.R. 239, 44 B.L.R. 1, 26 C.P.R. (3d) 97, 35 E.T.R. 1, 6 R.P.R. (2d) 1.
[21] *Ibid.*

6.7.1 Compare to Restrictions on Competition

An imposition of obligations of confidentiality may be similar to restrictions on competition and, thus, if unduly restrictive, are challengeable for being in contravention of public policy against restrictions on competition. The secrecy obligations should therefore be sufficiently precise and appropriately written for the particular circumstances.

6.8 Information that is the Subject of the Contractual Secrecy Obligations

The disclosing party will want the definition of "confidential information" to be drafted in the broadest terms available, particularly if it cannot be readily anticipated what will be disclosed in an on-going relationship. Conversely, the recipient of the information will want to restrict the definition as much as possible to narrow down its restriction on use and to limit the quantity of information that must be stored in a secured manner.

Strategy: Draft the scope of the definition of "confidentiality" to produce a fair balance between the needs of the disclosing party and the duties of the recipient.

6.8.1 Who Describes the Secret?

The drafter, taking the easy way out, may leave it to others to draft a definition of trade secrecy and write "'Confidential Information' means the information described on Schedule 'A'". The drafter's confidence that a person with the appropriate technical skills will insert the proper words may be misplaced. That person may forget to attach Schedule "A" altogether and leave the agreement uncertain at best and entirely unenforceable at worst. The drafter may find that the scheduled definition contains puffery that could be considered to be specific statements of quality that a court might decide constitute an express warranty that overrides the effect of a general statement disclaiming all express warranties. The drafter might be upset to find that Schedule "A" is so well prepared and in such detail that the schedule itself reveals the trade secrets. Rarely is the agreement imposing confidentiality kept secret, and the instrument designed to preserve secrecy may very well be the instrument that reveals the secrets.[22]

Strategy: Too much can be as bad as too little.

6.8.2 Mark as Confidential

Some agreements state that the disclosing party must mark as "Confidential" all information that is to be the subject of confidentiality and restricted use. This

---

[22] John H. Woodley, "Taking Care of Trade Secrets: Controlling and Exploiting Trade Secrets in Law and Practice" in Roger T. Hughes, ed., *Trade Secrets* (Toronto: Law Society of Upper Canada, 1990), p. C-1, at C-4 (papers presented at a conference held at Osgoode Hall, November 24, 1989).

may be appropriate when all the information will be disclosed in writing at one time; it is not as practical if the information will be disclosed orally or over a period of time.

6.8.3 Oral Disclosures

In contemplation of oral disclosure, some agreements provide that the obligation of confidentiality must be imposed by written notice delivered within a certain period of time; otherwise there will be no obligation of confidentiality on an oral disclosure. This helps to control the scope of information that is to be kept secret, but will be overlooked more often than not, especially during lively technical discussions. If the technical staff have been properly warned about oral disclosures, this requirement to put the disclosed information into writing may interfere with a normal robust exchange of information. With the normal pressures of negotiating and implementing a technology transfer, individuals may forget to do the requisite written confirmation (assuming they were even aware that they were necessary).

Strategy: Be reasonable about oral disclosures: remember what is reasonable to the negotiators is not necessarily reasonable to the implementers.

6.9 Exceptions to Information that is to be Kept Secret

The recipient will want to except out certain information from the subject-matter of the duties of confidentiality and restrictions on use, including the following standard exceptions:

   (a)   information that is within the public domain at the time of the disclosure;
   (b)   information subsequently entering the public domain without fault on the part of the recipient;
   (c)   information that the recipient already knows.

Perhaps the recipient could be required to immediately disclaim confidentiality on receipt of information it already knows, though this may not be practical in a larger organization where individual employees will not know what other information is in the possession of the recipient.

6.9.1 Onus of Proof

The drafter could specify who has the onus to prove whether specific information is within one of the exceptions. Will the disclosing party have to establish that the information is not generally known in its trade or business? Will the recipient have to prove that it possessed the information at the time of disclosure? Will the recipient have to claim the benefit of the exception within a specified period after disclosure?

Strategy: Specify who has the onus to establish existence of an exception.

6.9.2 Public Domain

The phrase "public domain", though frequently used in Canada, may not be familiar to many licensing executives. It may have different meanings in different countries. Rather than being faced with having to determine the number of people that comprise the "public" and whether that "public" can be restricted to a narrow area of business, the drafter of the confidentiality clause could use a phrase more generally used in trade secrecy legislation, such as "not generally known in the disclosing party's trade" or "not generally known by the disclosing party's competitors".

Strategy: Avoid phrases such as "public domain" that may have conflicting legal meanings and little or no commercial meaning.

6.10 Mixture of Public and Private

Mixed public and secret information may be protectable if the combination has been brought into "being by the application of the skill and ingenuity of the human brain",[23] but only the portion of the material that is secret will be protected.[24] Some collections of data may contain both information that is obtained from the public domain and information that is private, or they may present public domain information in a novel manner. To overcome a contrary inference from a disclaimer of confidentiality for information within the public domain, the confidentiality clause could specifically protect a blend of public and private information if the private information enhances the public information.[25]

COMMUNICATING TRADE SECRETS

6.11 Methods of Communication

The many different ways of communicating disclosure of trade secrets must be considered. Some will be disclosed in written material (including manuals), some at training sessions, some will be transferred in digital format, either physically, in the form of floppy disks or compact discs, or transmitted electronically by telecommunication, including the Internet.

6.11.1 Full and Useful Disclosure

The recipient will expect a full and useful disclosure. Conversely, the disclosing party will want to restrict the quantity of information that must be collected and physically transferred.

---

[23] Ramsay, *Intellectual Property*, p. A2-12 ; and see Peterson, "Trade Secrets", p. 418.
[24] Ramsay, *Intellectual Property*, p. A2-8.
[25] *Lac Minerals, supra* note 20, at 78 (D.L.R.).

6.11.2 Training Communicates Trade Secrets

One of the most significant methods of transferring the know-how portion of technology is the training provided by the disclosing party. By this process, data is converted into useable information. The recipient will want to obtain "an appreciation of the benefits of doing things a certain way, an understanding of research objectives to achieve a certain result, knowledge of which avenues of research may be productive and insight into what mistakes to avoid".[26]

6.11.3 Selection of the Site for Training

The selection of the site for training is particularly relevant if the parties' places of business are remote from each other (for example, one party is in Atlanta and the other in Calgary, Moscow or Almaty). An Internet "chat" line could be used to benefit multiple users if the information so disclosed is not confidential.

6.12 Factors to Consider When Offering Training

1. Will the teacher travel to the students, or vice versa?
2. Who pays the cost of travel and accommodation?
3. How many students will be trained at one time (both a minimum and a maximum)?
4. Whose equipment will be made available to the students?
5. What is the requisite training or expertise of the teachers/students?
6. What accreditation will be given after successful completion of the training and will the students then train other students?
7. How long will the training sessions be (both minimum and maximum)? Consider hours per day as well as days per week, and consider religious and statutory holidays that are not shared by both the teachers and the students;
8. How often will training sessions be given (both minimum and maximum)?
9. What language will be used?
10. Will interpreters with the requisite scientific and language skills be provided?
11. Which party will pay any medical expenses incurred by the students or teachers while in a foreign country?
12. What provisions will be made for the safe departure of the teacher and students in the event of civil unrest or political revolution, or illness?
13. What are the minimum safety conditions required at the transferee's plant site? and
14. Will the teacher have full and free access to the licensee's plant, phone and fax?

---

[26] Rule No. 3 in Alan H. Melincoe, "Locked out licensees", counsel at the San Jose law firm of Hoge, Fenton, Jones & Appel, "Intellectual Property" at http://www.portal.com/~recorder/melon.html.

MEASURES TO BE ADOPTED TO MAINTAIN SECRECY

6.13 Requisite Standards

The propensity for highly skilled "hackers" to gain illegal access to computers thought to be secured will be a concern for all parties. The recent publicity that hackers have produced draws attention to an already serious problem. The most likely intruders into a computer system are competitors, followed by employees and ex-employees. Other likely intruders are customers, public interest groups, suppliers, foreign governments and junior high school students.[27] As a result, the requisite standards adopted to maintain secrecy must be specified. Some agreements provide that the "recipient shall take measures to *ensure* that secrecy is maintained". Because a strict definition of the word "ensure" is to "guarantee" or "insure,"[28] use of "ensure" may, inadvertently perhaps, impose a higher standard of care than the standard of care adopted by the disclosing party for the same information. "Ensure" does not mean to "strive" or to give a good try, though it is often used in that context. When commonplace usage and the dictionary definition seem to be contradictory, a more precise word should be used.

6.13.1 "Use Own Precautions"

Many agreements provide that a recipient "shall take the same precautions to hold information in confidence as it takes for its own trade secrets". This may be an acceptable standard for a company that is known to have adopted very stringent standards, but it could cause disappointment to the disclosing party if its secrets are disclosed along with those of a recipient that has allowed its standards to become dangerously lax.

6.13.2 "All Reasonable Measures"

Often, agreements provide that the "recipient shall take all reasonable measures available to it". What is "reasonable," however, will depend on the individual circumstances.[29] It may require a "balance of cost and benefits that will vary from case to case".[30] It is unlikely that an owner of a trade secret will be required, in order to qualify for the legal benefits offered to trade secrets, to "take extravagant, productivity-impairing measures to maintain their secrecy".[31]

---

[27] Economic Security, press clippings published by Canadian Security Intelligence Service, p. 5, complied February 1995, quoting National Security Institute's Advisory, January 1995.

[28] See *The Oxford English Dictionary*, J.B. Sykes, ed. (England: Oxford University Press, 1982).

[29] See Peterson, "Trade Secrets", p. 442.

[30] *Ibid.*, p. 446, citing *Rockwell*, 925 F.2d, at 178.

[31] *Ibid.*, p. 447, again citing *Rockwell*.

6.14 Proprietary Rights Protection Policy

When prudent companies receive or develop confidential information, they should adopt a proprietary rights policy. This policy should be written in clear language and distributed to all employees and contractors.[32] One essential item for this policy will be confidentiality agreements with employees and statements setting out company policies for the treatment of confidential information. These agreements and policies will consider

    (a)   the consideration granted to the employee that is sufficient to justify the promises obtained;[33]

    (b)   the duty of an employee/contractor to disclose innovations made by that individual while employed or retained by the company. Is the duty of disclosure restricted to innovations made in the course of employment or to any innovations made in that time period?

    (c)   the ownership of innovations made in the course of employment;

    (d)   the ownership of innovations that were made outside the course of employment but using company time and equipment;

    (e)   the ownership of innovations that were made entirely on the employee's own time and off the premises of the company but that are still within the type of business conducted by the company;

    (f)   the duty of the company to keep confidential the innovations disclosed by the employee that are not owned by the company (most agreements with employees fail to make the confidentiality bilateral);

    (g)   the duty of the employee to assign or to waive any intellectual property rights vested in the employee by operation of law, keeping in mind, particularly, copyright to works that have not yet been created;[34]

    (h)   the company's policy towards unsolicited disclosures and any standard policy of refusing such disclosures or accepting them only with a disclaimer of confidentiality;

    (i)   security measures taken to prevent loss of trade secrets merely as a result of key employees taking jobs elsewhere and not creating and leaving documentation necessary to re-create the research and development done to date of termination; consider the appropriateness of continually depositing research records with a neutral third party;

    (j)   provisions that will prevent the employee from competing with the company or soliciting its customers and employees;[35]

    (k)   all the other issues related to confidentiality agreements generally.

---

[32]   Canadian Security Intelligence Service, "Clear Policy Can Forestall Data Piracy", January 17, 1995.

[33]   For example, see *Watson v. Moore Corp. Ltd.* (1996), 134 D.L.R. (4th) 252 (B.C. C.A.)

[34]   See §§4.34 and 4.35 of this text.

[35]   See Chapter 10, Restraint of Trade.

It is essential to implement a thorough proprietary rights protection policy. This will ensure that no door is left unsecured.[36]

6.14.1 Other Measures to be Adopted to Maintain Secrecy

The confidentiality provisions could specify what measures must be adopted to maintain secrecy, particularly in the case of highly sensitive material or where it is not clear that the recipient has adopted strict standards for maintaining secrecy. Some of these measures are:

(a) having enforceable non-disclosure and confidentiality agreements with those individuals who are permitted access to confidential information;[37]
(b) taking sensible precautions against industrial espionage;
(c) labelling plans and documents "confidential";
(d) employing confidentiality legends, warnings and agreements;
(e) limiting visitors and employing similar types of security;
(f) locking up, or otherwise securing, sensitive information;
(g) taking technical precautions (for example, dividing the system into steps to be handled by separate individuals or departments);
(h) using copy protection and embedded codes to trace copies and carrying out regular employee exit interviews.[38]
(i) specifying physical security of areas where access may be gained to the confidential information;
(j) specifying security measures for electronic storage and transmission of data including, or derived from, any confidential information;
(k) specifying controls on access to any computer facility and tape or disk library where any confidential information may be stored; and
(l) specifying document and computer network control systems that limit access to the confidential information to employees and agents who have a need to know, which control system provides for a secured method of protection of sensitive data.

Strategy: Specify the required secrecy controls.

RESTRICTIONS ON USE/DISCLOSURE

6.15 Permitted Use

In the case of copyright and patents, the right to *use* is controlled by the statutory restrictions. In the case of trade secrets, however, restrictions on use must be imposed by contract. The confidentiality clause might specify: (a) the confidential

---

[36] Canadian Security Intelligence Service, "Clear Policy Can Forestall Data Piracy," January 17, 1995.
[37] Peterson, "Trade Secrets", pp. 441–42.
[38] Items (b)–(h) are extracted from Peterson, *"Trade Secrets,"* pp. 448–49.

information shall be used only for the recipient's internal use or, perhaps, only for a specific project; (b) the right to reproduce material, since reproduction not only is controlled by trade secrecy but also is prohibited by copyright law; and (c) the rights of affiliates to use the disclosed material, as well as the rights of the recipient, and the responsibility of the recipient for the conduct of its affiliates.

6.16 Permitted Disclosure

Even though information may not have become generally available to the relevant trade or business, the recipient may require the right to use or to disclose information without breaching its duties and, perhaps, without triggering a royalty.

    (a)   if the information has been released to a third party without obligations of confidence, even though it is not generally available;

    (b)   as a result of a government order or a court order, though the disclosing party could demand that it be given advance notice to permit it to oppose the disclosure;[39]

    (c)   to a professional advisor;

    (d)   to employees or consultants who have a need to know, whether subject to express confidentiality agreement in a form provided by the agreement or in the recipient's standard form; and

    (e)   to bankers and other lenders,to permit them to assess the merits of financing the project involving the exploitation of the confidential information.

Strategy: Specify both the permitted uses and the permitted disclosures.

6.17 Duration

The parties could agree on the duration of the obligations of restricted use and non-disclosure. There is no industry standard that can be applied in all cases since the nature of the information will vary. A reasonable anticipation of the economic life of the information may be an appropriate standard. From the recipient's point of view, the duration of its duties must not be taken lightly due to the cost of maintaining secrecy.

Strategy: Negotiate a term for the duties of confidence that reasonably matches the information's economic life.

6.17.1 Termination

On termination of the duties of confidentiality, the agreement could require that the recipient return all copies of the information that it has in material form and render unusable all materials stored on a computer. Some agreements require an officer or an appropriate employee with authority to certify that the recipient has no further copies in its possession. The recipient may be reluctant to return or to

---

[39]   The parties should consider the effect of any freedom of information legislation.

destroy all copies of the confidential information if it is concerned that the disclosing party will subsequently claim misappropriation or misuse of the secrets. Having lost possession of all copies, the recipient may not be able to properly defend itself. On termination, such a recipient may require at least one copy of all of the material to be deposited securely with access limited for the purposes of such a defence. All continued rights of use should specifically be prohibited, subject to appropriate exceptions for individual circumstances.

Strategies:
   (1)   Specify what action is to be taken on termination of the agreement.
   (2)   Allow confidentiality obligations to survive termination of a technology transfer agreement, where appropriate.

Part III

THE TRANSFER

Chapter 7

TRANSFER OF RIGHTS

7.1 Introduction

Each party will strive to clearly define what technology is being transferred as well as the extent of the transferred interest. They will precisely establish the express terms and delete the application of inappropriate compiled terms. The right to favourable terms and exclusivity will be subject to specified conditions.

7.2 Subject-Matter

The subject-matter of the transfer can be a process or product protected by patent or trade secret, a name or logo protected by trademark, or a work (literary, artistic, musical, dramatic, etc.) protected by copyright. If the process or product is protected by patent, the grant clause could specifically refer to the subject patent. The ABA Draft Model Software Agreement[1] uses a broad-brush approach. A "Licensable Activity", *i.e.*, one permitted by the license, is "an activity encompassed by one or more Intellectual Property Rights, *i.e.*, an activity which, absent a license, would give rise to liability for infringement (or inducement of infringement or contributory infringement) of the Intellectual Property Right(s)".[2] This definition may not fully cover trade secrets unless "infringement" is expanded to cover "misappropriation" or "misuse". The ABA Draft Model Software Agreement uses the words "grants to LICENSEE . . . a license under any and all Intellectual Property Rights owned or otherwise assertible by a Transferor to engage in the following Licensable Activities".[3]

7.2.1 Characterization of Technology Transfer

To make sure a licence agreement is characterized as a licence (with a retention of some rights) rather than as a sale or an assignment (with a disposition of all

---

[1] American Bar Association, Section on Patent, Trademark and Copyright Law, Committee on Computer Programs, *Model Software License Provisions*, Committee Chair: D.C. Toedt III of Arnold, White & Durke, Houston, Texas (hereinafter "ABA Draft Model Software Agreement").

[2] *Ibid.*, Section 1001.57.

[3] *Ibid.*, Section 102.2. The author would prefer to use the words "Permitted Activities". This precedent uses BLOCK CAPITALS only for Licensor and Licensee and not for other defined phrases. Perhaps this can be used as a reminder to replace each word with a word or acronym appropriate for the purpose. The use of the words "Licensor" and "Licensee," besides being unfriendly, almost guarantees that somewhere in the document one word ("Licensor") will be inadvertently switched with the other ("Licensee"), perhaps with wholly unintended and, perhaps, irreparable consequences.

rights), the grant clause should state that the licence is subject to every term of the agreement being fulfilled.[4] Mayers and Brunsvold[5] characterize technology transfer agreement into assignments (a complete transfer of an interest even if that interest may be a partial interest), licences (mere permissions to do something) and exclusive licences (more than a 'mere licence' and less than an assignment). The characterization of the technology transfer may produce significantly different results for tax purposes, and these differences will vary from country to country and may differ depending on the various types of intellectual property.[6] As well, there could be a significant difference in the application of bankruptcy law. Although, for business purposes, an exclusive licence for the full term of the patent with a running royalty based on net sales may seem identical to an assignment where the consideration is a percentage of net sales, "it is possible that in the creditors' rights context, the two transactions might be treated differently".[7]

7.2.2 Use of Word "Rights"

If the drafter of a licence agreement refers to a grant of "rights," it might be appropriate to specifically state that only a licence is being granted since the phrase "grant of rights" could be considered to be an assignment of intellectual property *rights* rather than the grant of a "permission" to do something.

7.2.3 Get All the Rights Needed

The transferee will want to ensure that it has received a transfer granting all of the rights the transferor has relating to the subject-matter of the transfer and that the transferor does not possess separate rights that may overlap with the rights specifically granted to the licensee.[8]

7.2.4 Do Not Exceed Rights

The grant of licence should not exceed the rights possessed by the transferor. A holder of a U.S. patent that is not issued in any other country cannot grant the right to use that patented technology in any other country. Conversely, a U.S.

---

[4]   Ronald B. Coolley, "Drafting a Granting Clause", in Les Nouvelles, the Journal of the Licensing Executive Society, Vol. XXVII, No. 4, December 1992, p. 212 (hereinafter "Coolley, 'Drafting', Les Nouvelles, December 1992"). See also Robert Goldscheider, *Companion to Licensing Negotiations, Licensing Law Handbook* (New York: Clark Boardman Callaghan, 1993-94), where he uses the phrase "subject to the terms and conditions of this Agreement", at p. 153 (hereinafter "Goldscheider, *Licensing Negotiations*"). The ABA Draft Model Agreement uses similar words in its Section 102.2.

[5]   Harry R. Mayers and Brian G. Brunsvold, *Drafting Patent License Agreements*, 3rd ed. (Washington: BNA Books, 1994), p. 32 (hereinafter "Mayers and Brunsvold, *License Agreements*").

[6]   See Chapter 12 of this text.

[7]   R.M. Milgrim, *Milgrim On Licensing*, rev. ed. (New York: Matthew Bender, 1995), §15.00, p. 15-3 (hereinafter "Milgrim, *On Licensing*").

[8]   This is important patented technology (see Chapter 3 of this text) for patents as well as for copyrighted works, particularly multimedia content (see Chapter 4 of this text).

transferor may run into antitrust violations if it tries to restrict the licensee from using the patented technology outside of the United States.[9] This territorial restriction in a grant of licence may be more acceptable if the subject-matter of the licence is a trade secret rather than a patent, the benefit of trade secret protection not being limited to any particular jurisdiction.

IMPLIED LICENCES

7.3 Implied Licences

The negotiators to a technology transfer agreement should consider not only the rights expressly granted or transferred but also those that may be implied. Brunsvold and O'Reilly point out that equitable principles "prohibit a party to a contract from taking legal actions that would interfere with the expected consideration and rights of the other party to the contract".[10] Some of the implied grants are appropriate and some should be excluded. They list some grants that a court could choose to imply on equitable grounds (*e.g.*, plain indications that a grant of licence should be inferred).[11]

(a) A license to "make and sell" may imply a right to use "for if not, why would anyone purchase from the licensee".

(b) "[A] license to make and use does *not* imply a licence to sell."[12]

(c) "[A] license to sell does not logically imply the right to make if it can be presumed that the licensed product can be obtained by purchase."[13]

(d) "[A] license to use and sell implies the right to make unless the license expressly excludes the right to make."[14]

(e) Once a product that embodies technology covered by a patent is sold, patent rights cannot be used to control the manner of its use or the right to resell that product.[15]

(f) U.S. cases have established that the purchaser of a patented product has the right, in the absence of an express restriction imposed at or prior to sale, to also resell and repair the patented product free of patent infringement suits by the seller.[16] Any restriction imposed must not violate U.S. antitrust rules.[17]

---

[9] Coolley "Drafting", Les Nouvelles, December 1992, p. 213.

[10] Brian G. Brunsvold and Dennis P. O'Reilly, "Implied Licenses", October 1993, Annual Meeting of the Licensing Executives Society (U.S.A. and Canada) (unpublished), p. 4 (hereinafter "Brunsvold and O'Reilly, 'Implied Licenses'").

[11] *Ibid.*

[12] *Ibid.*

[13] *Ibid.*

[14] *Ibid.*

[15] *Ibid.*, p. 14, referring to the doctrine of exhaustion enunciated by the U.S. Supreme Court in *Adams v. Burke*, 84 U.S. (17 Wall) 453 (1873).

[16] *Ibid.*, p. 14.

[17] *Ibid.*

Although the grant of licence implies the agreement of the transferor not to assert its intellectual property rights against the licensee,[18] the implied agreement may cover only the precise subject-matter of the express grant.[19] Brunsvold and O'Reilly suggest that, if there is bad faith on the part of the transferor, a court may imply a licence to exploit the undisclosed but necessary patentable technology.[20] "However, bad faith by the patent owner is not necessary to create an implied license. . . . Inadvertence or sloppy practise will also suffice if the party asserting the implied license could reasonably infer from the patent owner's actions that the patent owner consented to the use of the patented invention."[21] Brunsvold and O'Reilly suggest that if it is intended to restrict a licence grant to a specific patent, even though there are related patents, these related patents and patent applications should be disclosed by number and title, and a licence or other transfer of these rights should be disclaimed.[22] The licensee may want an express agreement that the transferor will not assert its rights under any of its intellectual property rights against the licensee so long as the licensee is engaged only in the functions intended to be covered by the licence.[23] In the multimedia area, the licensee may need more than the traditional intellectual property rights. It may need a waiver of moral rights if the work was created outside of the United States.[24]

Strategies:

(1)   *In a patent licence, specify whether the grant is intended to cover every activity covered by the patent. Precise wording is necessary to avoid "unnecessary and undesirable questions as to what limitations, if any, were intended".[25]*

(2)   *Expressly negate any implied licence that is not intended, or provide an express licence for the intended scope with an exclusion of all other uses.[26]*

---

[18]   See Mayers and Brunsvold, *License Agreements*, p. 30, and §7.3 of this text.

[19]   *Ibid.*, p. 31, where Mayers and Brunsvold propose a non-assertion clause, but caution against making the language too broad. They suggest (at p. 31) that the drafter distinguish between "licensed patents" and "non-asserted patents" throughout the agreement.

[20]   See Brunsvold and O'Reilly "Implied Licenses", at pp. 1–2.

[21]   *Ibid.*, p. 2, referring to *DeForest Radio Telephone & Telegraph v. United States*, 273 U.S. 236, at 241 (1927).

[22]   *Ibid.*, p. 10.

[23]   Coolley, "Drafting," Les Nouvelles, December 1992, p. 213.

[24]   See §4.16 of this text and Kenneth M. Kaufman, "Legal and Business Issues for On-Line Publishers and Content Providers," in *The Internet and Business: A Lawyer's Guide to the Emerging Legal Issues*, Joseph F. Ruh, Jr., ed. (The Computer Law Association, Current Issues Publications series, 1996), p. 107, at 108.

[25]   See Mayers and Brunsvold, *License Agreements*, p. 61. See also Goldscheider, *Licensing Negotiations*, Model Clauses 1-39 and 1-40, pp. 145 and 146, where he provides examples of activities described by a reference to a patent as well as activities that are functionally described.

[26]   Brunsvold and O'Reilly, "Implied Licenses", p. 6.

PERMITTED/RESTRICTED USES

7.4 Uses Covered by the Grant

In addition to the subject-matter, the licence agreement should specify what uses are permitted in the case of patents, trademark and copyright and what uses are restricted in the case of trade secrets. The permitted rights for patents are variations of "make, use and sell".[27] The transferor could give Alice the right to make, but not to sell and use, and could require her to comply with quality control standards. Bob could get the right to sell only, *i.e.*, he would be allowed to act as a distributor of some kind, with a requirement for him to comply with the transferor's marketing program.[28] Charlie could get the right to use the patented technology, perhaps only at a specified plant site, and may be required to use the technology only in a specified manner, complying with all safety and environmental rules. There is a long list of permitted uses of a copyrighted work including the following: the right to produce or reproduce it; to perform it; to publish it; to translate it and to produce, reproduce or perform the translation;[29] to make a record or other way of mechanically performing a work; to import a copy of the work; and, in the case of a computer program, to rent it.[30] Each of these rights possessed by the copyright holder are independent of each other, and each may be licensed as to different, specific and separate applications.[31] The copyright holder of a painting can thus grant to Alice the right to publish the painting in a book; to Bob, the right to sell separate reproductions; and, to Charlie, the right to digitize it and place it in a clip art catalogue. The holder of a trade secret has the right to maintain secrecy. Once the secret information is released to another, the holder of the secret must impose restrictions on use; usage is not prohibited by statute, as is the case with patent or copyright. Instead of permitted uses, as are contained in a patent or copyright licence, a licence of a trade secret thus *restricts* uses as well as imposes obligations on the licensee to maintain secrecy. Often, a trade secret licence will permit one or more specific uses and restrict all other uses.

7.4.1 Non-physical Delivery

For any work that is stored in digital or electronic form, the right to transmit the word by telecommunication should be considered, as well as other methods of non-physical delivery that may be developed in the future. Developers of computer games are hard pressed to decide what computer platforms and

---

[27] See §3.2 of this text.
[28] Since this may be a franchise, the rules relating to franchises, disclosures by the transferor and restrictions on permitted controls may be relevant — see Chapter 5 of this text starting at §5.20.
[29] See §4.20.2 of this text.
[30] See §4.20.8 of this text.
[31] See §4.28 of this text.

what methods of delivery are appropriate uses for each licence (physical delivery at retail stores versus non-physical delivery over the Internet).[32]

7.4.2 "Have Made"

If a patent licence grants a right to make, the licence should clarify whether the licensee may permit a subcontractor to make the product for it, even though that may be implied by law. Likewise, rather than relying on terms implied by the local law, the agreement could specify whether a licensee that only has the right to "use" also has the right to "sell" the protected product to another user, or, if that is excluded, the right to dispose of it for scrap. As Mayers and Brunsvold point out, since there is a "presumption that the grantor intended to make his grant enjoyable," a licence to *make* may be "found to imply the right to use or sell (or, in some circumstances, both) on the theory that without such an implication, the grant would be of no value to the licensee".[33] To better communicate with the implementers of the technology transfer, the negotiators could spell out the implied grants.

7.4.3 Grant of All Rights — What's Left?

If the grant in a patent licence is to "make, use and sell," it is possible that no rights have been reserved from the licensee since these words are co-extensive with the protection offered by the U.S. and Canadian *Patent Acts*. Mayers and Brunsvold thus question whether anything is added by including additional words such as "to . . . have made, . . . lease, or otherwise dispose of . . . ," though these words are often added for comfort.[34] It might be appropriate to say that the rights "make, use and sell" include, without limitation, specific rights such as "have made," "lease," or "dispose of."[35] So long as the words "without limiting the generality of the foregoing" or some other phrase of similar effect is used, the business principles are often better developed by using the more explanatory language. The agreement could also clarify whether "have made" means to be made only by someone under the control of the licensee who is subject to confidentiality and restrictions on the use of any trade secrets involved.[36]

7.5 Field of Use

The granted rights may be restricted to specific uses or purposes, often referred to as "fields of use". For example, an expert learning software system could be licensed to Alice, for use with devices that assist spine-injured individuals to walk, and to Bob, for use in the financial derivatives market.[37] If, however, the

---

[32] *Atari Games Corp. v. Nintendo of America Inc*, 995 F.2d 832 (Fed. Cir. 1992).
[33] Mayers and Brunsvold, *License Agreements*, p. 58.
[34] *Ibid.*, p. 57.
[35] *Ibid.*
[36] *Ibid.*, pp. 56–57.
[37] These varied, divergent uses are not at all the result of my imagination running rampant, but were suggested to me as appropriate uses for the product produced by one of my software clients.

separation of fields of use are too finely divided and could "divide a naturally competitive market", in the United States there could be antitrust issues; thus, the field of use clause must be "handled with care".[38]

7.5.1 Difficulty in Separating Fields of Use

In a business sense, it is often very difficult to separate the various uses to provide exclusivity to different entities for the separate fields of use. This difficulty increases if the extent of the usefulness of the technology is not yet proven. The business deal often reflects the parties' differing predictions of the merit of the foreseeable applications. The negotiators of the technology transfer agreement will be challenged to produce language that is precise and that resolves the complications resulting from the "ever-increasing commercial and industrial complexity and overlap".[39] A licensee could be restricted to use the licensed technology, whether it be protected by patent, copyright or trade secrecy, only

(a)   in specified combinations — if the licensee has some product or process that will be combined by utilizing the transferor's technology, the licence could restrict the licensee to use the transferor's technology only with that product or process;

(b)   with specified styles or sizes of product; or

(c)   with product to be sold or used by specified customers, or marketed through specified trade channels.

7.6 Quantity Limitations

In performance clauses, there is often a requirement that the licensee will manufacture or sell a minimum number of units.[40] In the "grant" clause there may be requirements that the licensee sell in minimum blocks of a stated number of products. Conversely, it could be specified that the licensee cannot sell more than a specified number of units in a year, or in total. In recognition of different distribution channels that need to be maintained, some distributors could be licensed to sell in blocks of at least 100,000 units per sale; others could sell in smaller blocks. Instead of using a fixed number of units, the licence could restrict the licensee from selling more than 10 per cent of the product's total sales, perhaps to prevent it from obtaining a dominant position as a buyer.

7.7 Price Limitations

Some transferors would like to restrict the licensee from selling below a specified price. Such a restriction will contravene antirestraint of trade rules against

---

[38] Coolley, "*Drafting,*" Les Nouvelles, December 1992, p. 213. See also Milgrim, *On Licensing,* §15.12, pp. 15–28, and Chapter 10 of this text.

[39] Milgrim, "*On Licensing,*" §15.13, p. 15–29.

[40] For further discussion see §§12.3 ff. of this text.

price maintenance and should be avoided.[41] An alternative might be to let the licensee charge the price it chooses, but to provide for a minimum level of royalty. Increasingly, royalties are being based on suggested retail price to allow the licensee the maximum flexibility and to provide the transferor with an assured level of royalties without having to resort to price fixing. The licensee then can engage in price wars but, without the consent of the transferor, the transferor's revenue will not drop below a pre-agreed level.[42]

TERRITORY

7.8 Territory

The licence may permit the licensee to engage in the licensed activities only in a particular territory. In the United States and Canada, there seem to be few legal restrictions on the size of the territory (for examples, the portion of the City of Calgary lying north of the Bow River, all of the Province of Alberta, or all of Canada). The licence may give exclusive rights to some territories and non-exclusive rights to others, and it may give the right to manufacture and sell in one territory, but only the right to use in another. These territorial restrictions, frequently seen in trademark licences or franchises, are useful in distribution agreements and manufacturing licences. These restrictions must be carefully reviewed for any licence to a licensee within the European Community where the market is intended to be seamless.

7.8.1 Doctrine of Exhaustion

Once an item has been manufactured and sold, it may be impossible to restrict the purchaser from reselling the item, causing a relocation of the item from a permitted territory into a restricted territory. There is a rule of law referred to as the "doctrine of exhaustion" of rights that must be reviewed to determine the ability to control such movement of goods.[43]

7.8.2 Site Licences: Relocation and Replacement

If a licence of technology is specific to a certain site or plant, the possible relocation or replacement of the plant must be addressed. The intent of the restriction is to limit the number of sites at which the licensee can engage in a licensed activity, and the restriction should not prevent an appropriate relocation or replacement.

---

[41]   See Chapter 12 of this text.

[42]   In any event, local advice on restraint of trade rules is essential.

[43]   For additional discussion, see Ronald B. Coolley, "Recent Developments in Emerging Issues in Licensing" in The Licensing Journal, Vol. 14, No. 86, p. 7, and Michael Burnside, "Intellectual Property as a Non-Tariff Barrier", presented to the Canadian Bar Association, September 26, 1990, at its annual meeting in London, England.

MOST FAVOURABLE TERMS

7.9 Most Favourable Terms and Conditions

A licensee who is in a strong bargaining position will want to have a deal that is at least as good as those its competitors have.

> There is no general rule of law which requires the patent owner to extend identical licensing terms to all licensees, or to refrain from granting to a subsequent licensee terms which are more generous in some respect than those contractually assured to a prior licensee. It is therefore quite natural for the prospective acceptor of a license to request that the agreement contain provisions assuring him [of most favoured licensee terms].[44]

Even if the transferor has sympathy with the licensee's position, it should not concede a most favoured licensee position without caution. A most favoured licensee clause can lead to inflexibility and, perhaps, even disclosure of strategic alliances or other relationships that would otherwise be kept secret.

7.9.1 Cherry-picking Selected Terms

The transferor will wish to avoid allowing the licensee to "cherry-pick" the terms it likes best. For example a more favourable royalty rate due to a greater access to the licensee's improvements. Some transactions may be so unique, due to the nature of the players, that no concession should be made to other licensees who do not have the same market presence. For example inclusion in the IBM product line may warrant terms that others should not have. To avoid being faced with these variables, a strong licensee may require that "future licensees shall be subject to the same royalty rate, royalty base, time and reporting of payments and other pertinent terms" as were granted to it.[45]

Strategy: The most favoured licensee clause could require the licensee to elect to take all terms in the licence that appear more favourable, rather than cherry-picking selected terms.[46]

7.10 Benefits of Most Favoured Licensee Clause to Transferor

Using a most favoured licensee clause may occasionally have benefits for a transferor. It may use the most favoured licensee term as a "shield against the downward royalty pressures that subsequent negotiations may present," and may avoid charges of price fixing.[47]

Strategy:
The most favoured licence clause will address the following:
(a)   how and when the transferor will notify the licensee of the details of the other licence;

---

44   Mayers and Brunsvold, *License Agreements*, p. 103.
45   Milgrim, *On Licensing*, §26.13.
46   See Goldscheider, *Licensing Negotiations*, Model Clause 3-2, p. 156.
47   Milgrim, *On Licensing*, §§26.01 and 26.02.

(b)   *a territory or field of use in which the favourable terms apply;*

(c)   *the duration of the more favourable terms;*

(d)   *the method of valuing non-cash consideration (for examples, cross-licences or equity);*

(e)   *whether the adjustment will be retroactive;*

(f)   *how to deal with prior licences; and*

(g)   *how the licensee will elect to accept the most favoured licensee clause, if the adjustment is not made automatically.*

OTHER LICENCES

7.11 Right to Receive Other Licences

A licensee, which has received rights for a restricted territory or field of use, may wish to be considered as a candidate when the transferor is ready to licence other territories or fields of use. The right to be considered may range from a first right to negotiate, to a soft first refusal (where the transferor has not yet located the potential licensee and established the terms), to a hard first refusal (the name of the licensee and pertinent terms are both established), or to an option to acquire rights to additional territories on pre-determined terms.

7.12 Use of Other Party's Name in Promotions

A licence may restrict the right of either party to use the other party's name in promotions; some licences prevent the licensee from even announcing that it has a licence.[48]

EFFECT OF INVALIDITY

7.13 Effect of Invalidity of the Licenced Intellectual Property Right

The licensee may want to be protected against paying royalties if one of the intellectual property rights that it considers material subsequently is established to be invalid or of no beneficial effect. Consider the effect on the agreement of such a determination in the following instances (does the invalidity terminate the agreement, reduce the royalties or result in some other negotiated consequence):

(a)   if a licence was based on a patent application and the patent does not issue;

(b)   if an issued patent is held to be invalid;

(c)   if an issued patent expires due to passage of time or as a result of unpaid maintenance fees;

(d)   if a material claim in a patent is held to be invalid, but other claims remain valid;

---

[48]   See, for example, Goldscheider, *Licensing Negotiations,* Model Clause M24-3, p. 273.

(e)   if a material trade secret becomes generally available to competitors; and

(f)   if a work ceases to be protected by copyright.

The result may vary from country to country, assuming that the licence agreement does not address the issue. In Canada, the licensee might continue to bound by the licence agreement in all of those events, the law is not well developed. In the United States, the licensee may be relieved of its obligations by law if the licence relates to a patent or a patent application, but not if it relates to a trade secret or copyright.[49]

7.13.1 Estoppel

In Canada, the licensee is estopped from disputing the validity of its transferor's intellectual property right; entering into the licence is considered to concede that point.[50] In the United States, there is no such estoppel; in contrast the antirestraint of trade rules encourage the licensee to dispute such validity.[51] A Canadian licence might disclaim an admission of validity when appropriate.

7.14 Payment Even Though Invalid

In Canada, the licensee may be required to pay royalties even if the patent is invalid, unless the licence agreement provides otherwise. In the United States, if a licence is solely for the impugned patent, future royalties are excused no matter what the contract provides. If the patent is only one of a package of patents, the requirement for continued royalties may be lawful.[52] Milgrim offers the following suggestion:

> If, therefore, a prospective licensee is asked to take a license under a group of patents, but only one or a few of the patents are particularly significant to that licensee, the parties might negotiate a revised royalty schedule in the event of invalidity or expiration of the significant patent(s). Otherwise, the licensee may be forced to decide, after a determination of invalidity of such patent(s) whether to remain licenced under the other patents in the package, seek to negotiate a new rate, terminate the licence agreement unilaterally or cease paying royalty on the ground that the licensee's activities do not infringe any of the remaining licenced patents.[53]

The U.S. rule may be different if copyright or trade secret protection is lost. In either of those cases, intellectual property rights do not prevent independent development and therefore cannot have the same monopolistic result.[54]

---

[49]   Milgrim, *On Licensing*, §18.50.
[50]   *Rymland v. Regal Bedding Co.* (1966), 59 D.L.R. (2d) 316, 58 W.W.R. 182, 51 C.P.R. 137, 34 Fox Pat. C. 145 (Man. C.A.).
[51]   Milgrim, *On Licensing*, §18.50.
[52]   *Ibid.*
[53]   *Ibid.*, p. 18-91.
[54]   *Ibid.*, §§18.50 and 18.51 and see *Aronson v. Quick Point Pencil Co.*, 440 U.S. 257, 99 S. Ct. 1096, 59 L.Ed. 2d 296, 201 U.S.P.Q. No. 1 (1979).

7.14.1 Withholding Royalties During Licensee's Challenge of Transferor's Intellectual Property Rights

Since the U.S. technology transfer agreement cannot restrict the licensee from challenging the transferor's intellectual property rights, there could be an unfair result. At the same time that the licensee derives benefit from the transferor's intellectual property rights (the exclusion of all others) and from the licensed activities, the licensee can be trying to deny the transferor of its reward, challenging the validity of the transferor's intellectual property rights and withholding royalties during that challenge.[55] This withholding of royalties could be considered to contravene antirestraint of trade rules if the licensee dominates the industry. Permitting the licensee to challenge the patent may be required in the United States; requiring the licensee to elect between paying royalties or repudiating the licence may be permissible. Milgrim suggests requiring the licensee to represent that it believes the patent to be valid[56] and allocating costs of any challenge (from whatever resource) between the parties in a pre-agreed fashion.[57]

Strategies:
In any event and depending on the countries involved, the following issues should be considered:

   (a)   *prohibiting/permitting the licensee to challenge the transferor's intellectual property rights (these related rights may vary from country to country and the right to challenge may depend upon the type of intellectual property);*

   (b)   *stating whether the royalty remains payable after the intellectual property rights cease to be effective;*

   (c)   *stating whether the royalty is suspended during the challenge (consider restraint of trade implications);*

   (d)   *stating whether the royalty, though remaining payable, must be paid into escrow; and*

   (e)   *stating whether the granted rights are lost if permits are withheld and the licensee looses its challenge of the transferor's intellectual property rights.*

EXCLUSIVITY

7.15 Exclusive Licence

If the licence is exclusive, it will exclude the transferor as well as all third parties.[58] If the transferor wishes to reserve some rights to itself, these rights must be expressly reserved and, thus, make the licence exclusive subject to these

---

[55]   *Ibid.*, §27.04.
[56]   *Ibid.*
[57]   *Ibid.*
[58]   See D.G. Henderson, "Patent Licensing: Problems from the Impression of the English Language" in (1970), 4 Ottawa L. Rev. 62, p. 66 (hereinafter "Henderson 'Patent Licensing'") and Mayers and Brunsvold, *License Agreements*, p. 39.

specified reservations. A transferor may be using the licensed technology in its own business or may have outstanding licences, "limiting [its] ability to grant total exclusivity".[59]

7.15.1 Sole Licence

A "sole" licence does not exclude the transferor; it agrees only that the transferor will not grant any other licences to third parties.[60]

7.15.2 "Sole and Exclusive"

The use of these words together is a contradiction of terms.[61] This specialized legal meaning, however, is not clearly apparent and, perhaps, it would be more appropriate to specify in the technology transfer agreement:

(a)   what rights granted exclude all others, including the transferor;

(b)   what rights are reserved by the transferor for its use alone;

(c)   what rights are reserved by the transferor for its use and for the use of others currently licensed, but to the exclusion of all others except the licensee; and

(d)   what rights are reserved by the transferor for its use and for the use of others now or hereafter licensed.

Strategy: Assist the negotiators: set out the business issues, alternatives and consequences in the early draft agreements, perhaps using annotations.

7.16 Limited Exclusivity

Exclusivity can be restricted to:

(a)   specified fields of use;

(b)   specified distribution methods;

(c)   specified territories;

(d)   specified time periods;

(e)   specified levels of sales, production, purchases or other appropriate milestones.

7.17 Conditional Exclusivity

It could be a condition of maintaining continued exclusivity that the licensee:

(a)   attain certain levels of sales, purchases, production or other appropriate milestones;

(b)   produce specified royalties;

(c)   pay specified amounts if required royalty levels are not attained;

---

[59]   Milgrim, *On Licensing*, §15.09.

[60]   See Henderson, "Patent Licensing," p. 66 and Milgrim, *On Licensing*, §15.33.

[61]   Henderson, "Patent Licensing" p. 66.

(d)   engage in certain research, development, production or sales activities appropriate to the circumstances.

PERFORMANCE REQUIREMENTS

7.18 Best Efforts

The phrase "best efforts" is often used in technology transfer agreements, and not always as a result of drafting laziness. It may be used because:

(a)   the parties have developed a level of trust between them and do not want to disrupt the relationship by pressing for more precision;

(b)   the parties are unable to predict market acceptance of the product; and

(c)   the negotiators think the phrase has a well recognized meaning.

Unfortunately, when the trust relationship collapses or the transferor feels that its technology is not being adequately exploited, the parties will find that though the term "best efforts" has been the subject of frequent litigation, particularly in the United States, its meaning is uncertain and ambiguous. In Canada, there is case law that would indicate that the phrase means "leave no stone unturned". The words "do not mean second-best endeavours . . . . They do not mean that the limits of reason must be overstepped with regard to the cost of the service; but short of these qualifications the words mean that the [licensee] must, broadly speaking, leave no stone unturned . . . ."[62]

In the United States as well, there does not seem to be a clear meaning of the phrase "best efforts". Its use gives little or no guidance — indeed there is no "direct reference . . . to the scope or direction in which the efforts should be made".[63]

Strategy: The best advice is do not to use the phrase "best efforts".[64]

7.19 Minimum Levels

The parties might be better served if they addressed what "minimum performance" will be acceptable. This performance may be in terms of:

---

[62]   *C.A.E. Industries Ltd. v. R.*, [1983] 2 F.C. 616, at 638, 639 (T.D.); additional reasons (1983), 79 C.P.R. (2d) 88 (Fed. T.D.); leave to appeal refused (1985), 20 D.L.R. (4th) 347n, [1986] 2 W.W.R. xxin (S.C.C.), referring to *Sheffield Dist. Ry. Co. v. Great Central Ry. Co.* (1911), 27 T.L.R. 451. There seems to be no distinction between "best efforts" and "best endeavours" for this purpose. This case law seems to be totally out of line with commercial expectations in technology transfer agreements.

[63]   Mayers and Brunsvold, *License Agreements*, p. 42, quoting *Western Geophysical*, 285 F. Supp. 815, 157 U.S.P.Q. 129 (D. Conn. 1968).

[64]   See Charles W. Shiftley, and Bradley J. Hulbert, "'Best Efforts' May Not Be The Best Advice" in Les Nouvelles, the Journal of the Licensing Executive Society, Vol. XXVII, No. 1, March 9, 1992, p. 37, at 39. This article has an interesting analysis of "best efforts" clauses providing a summary of legal decisions, practical examples of difficulties caused by the phrase and suggested improvements.

(a)   media advertising to be undertaken;

(b)   displays at trade shows;

(c)   direct mail promotions;

(d)   minimum number of licences to be obtained in a year; and

(e)   minimum revenue to be earned in a year.

The request for "minimum performance" requirements cuts through the "puffery" of the licensee; suddenly, the transferor sees the licensee realistically assessing the product and the market-place.

7.20 Effect of Not Satisfying Performance Requirements

If the licensee does not satisfy the conditions for maintaining exclusivity, some of the consequences may be

(a)   loss of exclusivity — the licence could convert from an exclusive licence to an non-exclusive licence.[65] This allows the transferor either to exploit the technology itself or to license others for that purpose. It may, however, not always be possible to find other licensees who are prepared to compete with the formerly exclusive licensee, and the benefit of the conversion from exclusivity to non-exclusivity may be illusory;

(b)   maintenance of exclusivity by payment of a specified amount;

(c)   termination of agreement;

(d)   loss of rights only after a "cure" period has expired, giving the licensee a second chance to attain the specified milestones; and

(e)   forbearance of loss of rights if the failure to attain the milestones is due to factors beyond the licensee's control. A good and prompt dispute resolution mechanism will be necessary for the transferor to avoid any dispute over whether the failure was caused by the transferor or by the licensee or by external causes.[66]

---

[65]   Mayers and Brunsvold, *License Agreements*, p. 41.

[66]   See Milgrim, *On Licensing*, §15.14.

Chapter 8

CUSTOMIZATION AND ACCEPTANCE TESTS: WHO, WHY, WHEN, WHERE AND HOW

8.1 Introduction

Frequently, the transferor's existing technology must be adapted or further developed for the licensee's particular needs. This adaptation may give rise to an issue over ownership of improvements[1] and over joint ownership.[2] In any event, acceptance criteria for the adaptation must be addressed; this is the subject-matter of this Chapter.

8.2 Specifications/Acceptance Tests Yet to be Developed

Often, when a technology transfer agreement is being prepared, the parties have not yet developed mutually acceptable functional or performance specifications. When technology is being adapted or improved, the licensee will want to subject the resulting product or process to acceptance tests. If the specifications have not been developed at the time of formation of the agreement, it is unlikely that the acceptance tests have then been established. A mechanism is necessary for establishing acceptance tests as the project proceeds. The negotiators must contemplate how the parties will interact generally in the further development of the technology. The agreement might set out, perhaps in chronological order, flexible provisions covering the appropriate tests for remedial action if the acceptance tests are not passed. Although legally trained individuals like certainty in their agreements establishing such a working relationship, "an on-going dynamic process" may be more desirable than the "locked-in" relationship that is produced in most agreements.[3]

8.2.1 Conceptual Description of Specifications

The development agreement could provide a conceptual description of what the parties intend to achieve in the development project, perhaps discussing the general business or scientific problems intended to be solved. Although only

---

[1] See Chapter 9.
[2] See §§4.39 ff. of this text.
[3] American Bar Association, Section on Patent, Trademark and Copyright Law, Committee on Computer Programs, *Model Software License Provisions*, Committee Chair: D.C. Toedt III of Arnold, White & Durke, Houston, Texas (hereinafter "ABA Draft Model Software Agreement").

concepts can be described at this point of the research and development, the expectations of the parties should be stated as precisely as possible to avoid uncertainty and unrealistic expectations. If the licensee is inexperienced, it may be wise for the transferor to insist that a consultant be retained to clarify the licensee's expectations. In any event, each party "should have experienced technical advisers to help establish the specifications".[4]

8.2.2 Types of Specifications

Lawrence Chesler's useful article on system specification and acceptance testing guidance may be summarized as follows:[5]

(a)   there are two types of specifications that may be defined for a system: functional specifications and performance specifications;[6]

(b)   functional specifications define the capabilities of the system at a functional level, *i.e.*, what features and functions the system will have;

(c)   performance specifications define *how efficiently* the system will perform its functions;

(d)   although accurately defined, functional capabilities of a system can be complex, it is usually the performance specifications that are most difficult to define with sufficient clarity to avoid contractual disputes; and

(e)   to the extent practicable, define all acceptance tests criteria, and especially performance specifications, by reference to well-drafted bench-mark tests in which all relevant variables are carefully and systematically controlled.

8.2.3 Development Team

Appropriately trained and experienced personnel should be appointed to a team that will co-ordinate the development of the customized technology;[7] the team could be the same group that established the specifications. This development team could be given the exclusive right to approve the initial specifications and any deviations from them.

---

[4]   Pegi A. Groundwater, "General Considerations in Drafting Software Licenses", a paper presented at the Licensing Executives Society Annual Meeting, October 26, 1992 (unpublished), p. 3-64. See also William P. Andrews, Jr., "Limiting Risks in International Transactions: Current Legal Issues in the United States Domestic Transactions for Computer Goods and the Unsigned Services", a paper presented to the World Computer Law Congress, 1991, p. 12 (hereinafter "Andrews 'Limiting Risks'").

[5]   Lawrence Chesler, "Specifications, Acceptance Testing, Acceptance Procedures and Risk Allocations in Agreements for Complex Systems: The Vendor's Perspective" in The Computer Law Asociation Bulletin, 1991, Vol. 6, No. 1, p. 8 (hereinafter "Chesler 'Specifications'").

[6]   *Ibid.*, p. 9.

[7]   ABA Draft Model Software Agreement, Section 211.1.

8.3 Needs – Study Plan

The first task of the development team might be to design the method for per-forming a detailed study of the parties' goals or a "Needs – Study Plan".[8] The agreement could address what would happen if the development team cannot reach agreement on a Needs – Study Plan within the desired time period, as well as the method and timing of any payment to each of the parties for its contribu-tion to the Needs – Study Plan.

8.3.1 Development Plan

Once the parties have achieved agreement on a Needs – Study Plan, they can move on to prepare a detailed Development Plan and a related Progress Sched-ule. The Development Plan could consist of critical path charts setting out the generally anticipated project tasks and task phases with reasonable estimates of the time anticipated and charges for each project task. "The contract must pro-vide a clear, well-defined mechanism for finalizing the specifications and accep-tance test procedures well in advance of system installation, in order to avoid disputes when the time comes for acceptance testing."[9] As Chesler writes:

> The best mechanism for accomplishing this goal is to build into the contract a series of milestones, to set forth in the contract the interim tasks that must be com-pleted in order to insure that such milestones are met, and to assign responsibility for those tasks to the appropriate party. There should be a clear understanding that the vendor's ability to meet milestones by the dates projected is contingent upon timely performance by the user of all tasks for which the user is responsible.[10]

8.3.2 Contributions of Each Party

The responsibility of each party must be specified, including (a) payment, (b) provision of previously developed intellectual property, personnel and equip-ment, (c) the right to use previously developed intellectual property contributed to the project by one party, and (d) consideration of the ownership of any deriva-tive work.

8.3.3 Binding Effect of Development Plan and Progress Schedule

The agreement must consider what, if any, binding effect the Development Plan and Progress Schedule will have — whether it will be established for guidance only, or will a unilateral deviation result in damages or, perhaps, termination. The parties might agree to periodically review the Develop-ment Plan and Progress Schedule with the intention of revising both the specifications and the timetables to take into account the result achieved to date. The agreement must address the effect of parties being unable to agree

---

[8]   *Ibid.*, Section 213.1.
[9]   Chesler, "Specifications", p. 10.
[10] *Ibid.*

on the initial Development Plan and Progress Schedule or on deviations that are "essential" in the eyes of one party.

8.4 Performance of Acceptance Tests

The Development Plan and Progress Schedule should also include methods of testing the resulting technology; some payments may depend on acceptance tests being passed. The agreement could consider:

(a)   the time period within which the acceptance tests must be conducted, and the effect of a test not being performed within that period;

(b)   the location of the test;

(c)   the rights and obligations of the developer to attend at the test and to conduct or participate in the test;

(d)   the right of the non-testing party to receive full details of the test results;

(e)   control over quality of material to be processed in the test, and which party has the right or obligation to provide that material (if the user is performing the test, the developer may want to pre-test the material to make sure it is appropriate to be used in the test);

(f)   detailed standards that will establish acceptance or rejection, perhaps as to quality, quantity and speed of input/output;[11]

(g)   partial acceptance if the test is "almost passed";

(h)   the consequence of a failure, including an extension to allow the developer to attempt to remedy the problems (with or without a penalty), and the ability of either party to abandon if the remedial action is not done in a timely fashion or cannot be done economically;

(i)   allowances for failures or delays not attributable to the parties;

(j)   the right to re-test after modifications have been made, and how many times tests must be performed; and

(k)   the effect on any warranty if the tests are passed — are the tests in lieu of a warranty?

8.4.1 Delays and Deficiencies

As Chesler writes:

> In some instances it may be reasonable for the vendor's performance dates to slip by one day for each day the user is late in performing its obligations; in other instances, it may be reasonable for the vendor's performance dates to slip by a longer period of time than a one for one slippage, where, for example the vendor is forced to divert resources to other projects while waiting for the user to complete its obligations. The contract should also specify that if the user's approval

---

[11]   *Ibid.*, p. 9. Andrews "Limiting Risks" writes that the "single best avenue for avoidance of litigation in computer contracts is to establish in excruciating detail the expectations for the performance of the system" (p. 12). The author of this text has experienced too much excruciating detail in contracts, and, as a plain language drafter, would prefer "precisely accurate detail".

of specifications and acceptance tests procedures is delayed beyond a specified milestone date, all subsequent vendor milestone dates for implementation and deliver will be delayed . . . If the vendor submits specifications or acceptance test procedures to a user for review and approval, the user should be required to approve or disapprove such materials in writing in a reasonably short period of time (*e.g.*, fifteen business days). Because of the possibility that a user may never approve specifications or acceptance criteria, or the process may drag on for extended period, the contract should specify that the user's failure to provide written notice of disapproval within the specified period of time constitutes approval; . . . The contract also should provide a mechanism for terminating the contract if such specifications or test procedures are not approved by a certain date.[12]

8.4.2 Rejections

One potential consequence of technology failing to pass acceptance tests is the right to reject the technology and, perhaps, to cancel any remaining obligations under the technology transfer agreement.[13] In allowing for rejection, the following might be considered:

(a) the extent of failure of the acceptance tests that permit rejection or other reasons giving rise to such a drastic remedy;

(b) the time within which rejection must be made;

(c) the consequences of not rejecting within that time period;

(d) the method of giving notice of rejection;

(e) any period in which the transferor has the opportunity to cure the defect giving rise to the rejection;

(f) which party has the responsibility to remove the rejected technology from the licensee's premises (this is particularly important if the technology is embodied in a plant or major system) and the incidental costs of restoring the condition of the licensee's premises;

(g) whether rejection is the sole remedy available to the licensee; and

(h) whether the contractual right to reject is instead of any implied right of rejection granted by Sale of Goods legislation.[14]

8.4.3 Abandonment

Each party may want the opportunity to abandon the project if it feels that the project is not viable or that it is not getting what it anticipated out of the project. Either party may come to the conclusion that a project is not economically viable and, thus, may wish to abandon the entire project or only the tasks that are causing the uneconomic result (assuming that viable tasks can be separated from non-viable tasks). The agreement could allow for abandonment on a specified, but reasonable notice and provide for a pre-agreed payment for the abandonment.

---

[12] *Ibid.*, p. 11.
[13] See also §13.5 of this text.
[14] For example, ss. 36 and 37 of Alberta's *Sale of Goods Act*, R.S.A. 1980, c. S-2, or the *Uniform Commercial Code*, Art. 2, s. 2-602.

The agreement could also go on to resolve the rights of ownership and the continued use of the abandoned technology.

8.5 Documentation to be Delivered

If documentation will be required, its details and format must be established by the parties. In many cases, particularly with software, the completeness of documentation may determine the actual usefulness of the technology. The details of the documentation could vary depending on the stage of development.

8.6 Records and Reports

In order to establish independent development, the parties might require that their researchers maintain records of all third-party sources of research, scientific principles and data used in the development. These records might be necessary to defend against a claim of misappropriation of copyrighted material (including source code for software) or trade secrets. They could include the names of all individuals who worked on the project and a cross-reference to their files which contain the appropriate secrecy and assignment of novations agreement.[15]

---

[15] See, for example, the ABA Draft Model Software Agreement, Section 215.3.

Chapter 9

IMPROVEMENTS

9.1 Introduction

As the relationship continues, either party may make improvements to the technology that was initially transferred. The negotiators must determine how these improvements will be shared and which party will own them.

9.2 Business Reasons for the Transferor to Share Improvements

The transferor may want to share improvements with its licensees

   (a)   to keep its product competitive and, thus, maintain the income flow from running royalties;

   (b)   to maintain a position for the technology as the one that sets the standard for the industry;

   (c)   to increase its royalty income by exploiting the improvement throughout its distribution chain;

   (d)   to extend the economic life of the product/process and, thus, extend the life of the income stream;

   (e)   to decrease the licensee's exposure to product liability by keeping the product/process in a state-of-the-art condition; and

   (f)   to be able to provide support; if the licensee has changed the technology without disclosure to the transferor, the transferor's attempts to provide support may be frustrated. If all users are not implementing the same technology, support will become increasingly complex. Most software suppliers will cease to support obsolete products after a period of time, and will want their licensees to have only the improved versions. Many updates to software are made to overcome problems that caused a high demand for support; implementation of these updates will reduce the cost of providing support. If standardization is the goal, lack of implementation of all the improvements will detract from standardization.

9.3 Business Reasons for Licensee to Want Access to Improvements

The licensee may want to gain access to improvements for the following reasons:

   (a)   to maintain or improve sales;

   (b)   to improve its productivity if it is a user of the licensed technology;

   (c)   to maintain its revenue stream from sublicensees;

The licensee may also want to share improvements made by other licensees, as well as those made by its transferor.

9.4 Additional Compensation for Providing Improvements

The transferor may not want to automatically extend the licence to include improvements without obtaining further compensation

(a)   if the improvement can be marketed independently;

(b)   if the improvement will not be fully commercialized by the licensee but, rather, could be "locked-up" by a disinterested exclusive licensee.

The licensee may not want to share its improvements with its transferor without compensation

(a)   if the improvement can be used independently of the licensed technology;

(b)   if it is toward the end of a licence term; and

(c)   if the obligation to disclose can be considered too broad or onerous.

9.5 Patent Versus Copyright Improvements

Improvements for patented technology are fundamentally different in a legal sense from improvements to copyrighted works.[1] A patent holder does not have the exclusive right to improve its technology, whereas the copyright holder has the exclusive right to make "translations," "adaptations" to its work and, in the United States, "derivative works".[2] In Canada, the exclusive right (if any) to make "adaptations" and "derivative works" must be inferred from the exclusive right to copy since it is not expressly covered by the Canadian *Copyright Act*.[3] That it may be inferred is suggested by the express provision in the Canadian *Copyright Act* that provides a fair dealing defence for modifications of computer programs for use on a different computer.[4]

9.6 Types of Improvement to Patented Technology

Some agreements may leave the scope of the word "improvement" to be determined by the courts, but the business decision makers should be alerted to the fact that the word "improvement" by itself may not have a precise legal meaning even with patents. Some improvements could be subject to sharing and improvements could be retained to the exclusion of the other party. The distinction must be carefully made, considering the appropriate circumstances, and one definition may not be sufficient throughout the agreement. A list of

---

[1]   R.M. Milgrim, *Milgrim On Licensing*, rev. ed. (New York: Matthew Bender, 1995), §17.00 (hereinafter "Milgrim, *On Licensing*").

[2]   U.S. *Copyright Act*, 17 U.S.C. §106.

[3]   R.S.C. 1985, c. C-42.

[4]   *Ibid.*, s. 27(2) (am. R.S.C. 1985, c. 1 (3rd Supp.), s. 13; R.S.C. 1985, c. 10 (4th Supp.), s. 5; 1993, c. 44, s. 64(1) and (2)). See also §4.4 of this text.

types of improvements[5] to patented technology may assist in negotiating what improvements are to be shared. Some types are

    (a)   improvements that cannot be used without infringing the transferor's patent:
            (i)   those capable of being patented in the applicable country; or
            (ii)   those more like "know-how" and not patentable;

    (b)   improvements that will be considered to result from disclosure by the transferor of trade secrets related to the patented technology, unless the licensee can establish it made the improvement independently or as a result of prior knowledge;

    (c)   improvements that relate to function,
            (i)   those that reduce the cost of the manufacture of the product by at least a specified per cent;
            (ii)   those that increase the sales of the product by at least a specified per cent;
          (iii)   those that reduce the cost of the application by at least a specified per cent;
          (iv)   those that increase the output of the application of the process by at least a specified per cent;[6]

    (d)   improvements that relate to similarity, for example, any product/process that has substantially similar features to the transferor's products/process; and

    (e)   improvements that relate to competitiveness, for example, an improvement is any product/process that could competitively displace demand for the transferor's product/process[7] and would infringe the licensor's patents.[8]

An improvement that would be an appropriate subject of a grant-back falls within the scope of one or more of the valid claims of the licensed patent.[9] The definition of "improvement" could operate by the elimination of what it does not include as well as by what it does include.[10] In any event, "because of uncertainty as to what individual courts might, in their wisdom, do with this term if undefined, it is highly desirable that the parties eliminate potential

---

[5]   Including modifications, enhancements and additions.

[6]   John Crispen and Terry Marsh, "Preparing for the Future — Implement a Grant-Back", presentation at the 1994 Annual Meeting of Licensing Executives Society (Canada), quoting from World Intellectual Property Organization "Licensing Guide For Developing Countries", p. 9. See also Harry R. Mayers and Brian G. Brunsvold, *Drafting Patent License Agreements*, 3rd ed. (Washington: BNA Books, 1994), p. 63 (hereinafter "Mayers and Brunsvold, *License Agreements*").

[7]   For a comparable list see Milgrim, *On Licensing*, §1702.

[8]   See Mayers and Brunsvold, *License Agreements*, p. 64.

[9]   See Robert Goldscheider, *Companion to Licensing Negotiations, Licensing Law Handbook* (New York: Clark Boardman Callaghan, 1993-94), Model Clause MC 10.8 (hereinafter "Goldscheider, *Licensing Negotiations*"); also see Mayers and Brunsvold, *License Agreements*, p. 64.

[10]   See Mayers and Brunsvold, *License Agreements*, p. 65.

argument by providing a definition of their choosing".[11] The definition chosen may be different for improvements that are included by the transferor in its grant than for improvements that are the subject of a grant-back by the licensee.

9.6.1 Infringement is Not a Good Standard for Copyright

The case law has established that copying of the literal code of a computer program is prohibited, but it does not establish what non-literal copying is prohibited.[12] An original method of expressing an idea is protected under copyright rules unless it has merged with the idea being expressed (the idea not being protected by copyright). Recently, Canadian and American courts have been struggling to "weed out or remove from copyright protection those portions [of a computer program] which, . . . cannot be protected . . . ".[13] Cases relying on *Computer Associates v. Altai, Inc.*[14] use the abstraction/filtration method and reject the structure, sequence and organization analysis propounded by *Whelan v. Jaslow.*[15] Whether either analytical method is practically sound, let alone legally correct, remains unsettled and the scope of protection offered by copyright to computer programs presently is far from clear.[16] Relying on copyright infringement as a standard for a software improvement thus provides little certainty to the business decision makers.

9.6.2 Functionality May be a Better Standard for Copyright Improvements

The following are examples of different kinds of improvements that could be made to licensed software.

> *Type A.* An improvement[17] to the source code (the human readable portion of a computer program) that is made to remedy or "work around" an error that prevents the program from working as intended.

> *Type B.* An improvement to the source code that is made to provide features that were described in the functional specifications, but were not achieved in the current version.

> *Type C.* An improvement[18] to the source code that provides features that were not contemplated by the current version.

---

[11] *Ibid.*, p. 64.
[12] See Chapter 4 of this text.
[13] *Delrina Corp. v. Triolet Systems Inc.* (1993), 47 C.P.R. (3d) 1, at 37, 9 B.L.R. (2d) 140 (Ont. Ct.(Gen. Div.)).
[14] 982 F.693, at 705 (2nd Cir. 1992).
[15] 797 F.2d 1222.
[16] Philip J. McCabe, "Reverse Engineering of Computer Software: A Trap for the Unwary?" in The Computer Law Association Bulletin (1994), Vol. 9, No. 2, p. 4, at 10–11.
[17] Often referred to as a "modification". There seems to be no difference between "improvement" and "modification" or "enhancement".
[18] Often referred to as an "enhancement".

Type D. An improvement that provides new features but does not modify the source code of the transferor's program, though it interfaces with it and can call upon the transferor's program to perform functions; this type of improvement is sometimes called a "stand-alone module".

The transferor needs disclosure of Type A and B improvements made by the licensee. Even with Type C improvements, errors in normal operation may relate to a change of the source code that inadvertently disrupted other operations, making support difficult or impossible. The transferor needs disclosure of, and the rights to use, Type A and B improvements in order to maintain standards. The transferor may need the right to use Type A, B and C improvements to keep its product vibrant and in the current state of the art. The transferor would like to have Type D to expand the life of its technology and related income stream.

9.7 Grant-backs

The rights granted back by the party making the improvement (the "improver") in favour of the party that produced the basic technology that was modified (the "basic innovator") can be either a transfer of all rights, a transfer of ownership with a reservation of rights of continued use, or a license back to the basic innovator.

(a) *Transfer of Rights.* Generally, a transfer back of all rights will be resisted by all improvers. Indeed, anything more than a non-exclusive grant-back may be a violation of rules against restraint of trade in the United States.[19] There is a barrier, sometimes only an emotional barrier, to giving up ownership to an improvement. Historically, such a transfer has been demanded when there has been an imbalance of bargaining power, for example, a large multinational corporation dealing with a national in a developing country. In many such countries, a grant-back that involves a transfer of ownership is prohibited.[20]

(b) *Transfer of Ownership With a Reservation For Continued Use.* There may be good reason for a transfer of ownership. If one party is charged with prosecuting third-party infringers or with obtaining patents for all improvements, it may find it more expedient to own the improvements. Where the transfer of the improver's improvement is made to the basic innovator the rights reserved to the improver should address whether the improver has the right to sublicense the rights of use to its affiliates or to any other third party and, if so authorized, whether there is a duty to report such licences and account for royalties. The term of continued use of the improvement

---

[19] Anti-Trust Guidelines for the Licensing of Intellectual Property. These guidelines are reproduced in "Expanded European Communities Interfacing with North American, Technology, Marketing and Commercial Implications," Symposium 4, Licensing Executives Society (U.S.A. and Canada) September 11–13, 1994 (hereinafter "LES Symposium 4"). (Guidelines hereinafter referred to as "U.S. Anti-Trust I.P. Guidelines"). Also, see Chapter 10 of this text.

[20] See Chapter 10 of this text.

by the improver who transferred its rights to the basic innovator should not necessarily cease with expiration of the term of the basic improvement, or the improver may find itself unable to use its own innovation on expiry of the basic licence.

(c)   *Grant of a Non-exclusive Licence-back.* A grant of a non-exclusive licence-back of an improvement is more generally acceptable to improvers, particularly when there is a real or a perceived imbalance of bargaining power, and may be the only way to share improvements when a grant-back assignment is prohibited or potentially illegal, whether on account of rules against restraint of trade or otherwise.[21] The licence must state the respective rights of the basic innovator and the improver to produce, improve and sell the improvement and the duties to account between themselves for its use, essentially covering most of the points contained in any licence of technology of a similar nature.

9.7.1 Disclosure of Improvements

Because the disclosure of the improvements will be similar to any disclosure of confidential information, the basic principles that apply to trade secrets will apply to these improvements.[22] The time when a disclosure of an improvement must be made should be specifically set out in the agreement. It could be at one of the following stages of development:

(a)   reduction to practice for a patentable improvement;[23]
(b)   commercially marketable stage;
(c)   third party site beta testing stage;
(d)   alpha testing stage; or
(e)   first conception stage.

The choice of the timing will be important, especially toward the end of the relationship when each party will want to retain everything from the other. The parties may wish to choose a cut-off date that is earlier than the termination date.[24] Milgrim suggests that a licensee could negotiate for disclosure to occur as the improvement develops module by module to avoid losing all disclosure if completion of the improvement will not occur until after the cut-off date.[25] Additionally, the agreement will have to specify how often disclosure will be made, for example, at least quarterly. The agreement could provide what details of the improvement must be disclosed. These details could be:

---

[21]   A non-exclusive grant-back does not necessarily pass the U.S. rules against restraint of trade but it has a better chance of passing them than an exclusive grant-back does. See the U.S. Anti-Trust I.P. Guidelines, Section 5.6.
[22]   See Chapter 6 of this text.
[23]   See Milgrim, *On Licensing*, §17.13, p. 17-21.
[24]   *Ibid.*, p. 17-20.
[25]   *Ibid.*, p. 17-22.

(i)   enough information to permit the user to commercially use the technology;

(ii)   only the material disclosed in a relevant patent; or

(iii) only that an innovation has been made and a brief description of its functional specifications.

Part IV

RESTRICTIONS ON ABILITY
TO CONTRACT

Chapter 10

Restraint of Trade

Monopolies in times past were ever without the law [i.e., illegal], but never without friends.[1]

10.1 Introduction

There are three main types of restraints of trade that apply in technology transfers: monopolies or cartels, employee non-competition agreements and non-competition covenants granted concurrently with a sale of a business. Restraint of trade resulting in monopolies is essentially covered by legislation: in Canada, the *Competition Act*,[2] and in the United States, the *Clayton Act*[3] and the *Sherman Act*.[4] The other types of non-competition agreements may be the subject of the common law and specific local legislation.

MONOPOLIES OR CARTELS

10.2 Effect on Licensing

The U.S. antitrust rules that prohibit what are considered to be anticompetitive practices have broad application to technology transfers. Every business term of a technology transfer agreement should be reviewed to ensure there is no realistic potential for a violation of those rules. In Canada, the rules are not nearly as extensive nor as troublesome as they are in the United States. Canadians should not relax, however, since even a technology transfer agreement only among Canadians does not preclude the United States applying its rules extraterritorially.[5]

---

[1] Coke, 3 *Institutes of the Laws of England*, 4th ed. (1670), p. 182, quoted by Michael J. Trebilcock, *The Common Law of Restraint of Trade, A Legal and Economic Analysis* (Toronto: Carswell, 1986), p. 13 (hereinafter "Trebilcock, *The Common Law*").

[2] R.S.C. 1985, c. C-34.

[3] 15 U.S.C.

[4] 15 U.S.C.

[5] See R.J. Roberts, "Technology Transfer Agreements and North American Competition" in Intellectual Property Journal, December 1995, Vol. 9, No. 3, 247, at 249 and 254; also printed in M. Goudreau, G. Bisson, N. Lacasse and L. Perret., eds., *Exporting Our Technology: International Protection and Transfers of Industrial Innovations* (Montreal: Wilson & Lafleur, 1995), p. 154 (hereinafter "Roberts 'Technology Transfer Agreements'") (all cites to Intellectual Property Journal). Also see "Expanded European Communities Interfacing with North American, Technology, Marketing and Commercial Implications," Symposium 4, Licensing Executives Society (U.S.A. and Canada) September 11–13, 1994 (hereinafter "LES Symposium 4"), p. 78.

Strategy: In every technology transfer agreement, the negotiators must determine the possibility of an unlawful restraint of trade.

10.3 Effect of Violation of Antitrust Rules in Canada

A material difference between the American and Canadian systems is the effect of a violation of antitrust rules. In Canada, action under the *Competition Act* can be brought only before the Competition Tribunal and then only by a representative of the government.[6] "The injured party must complain to the Director and if the Director decides not to proceed the complainant has little, if any, recourse . . . . Even if the Director proceeds and the Tribunal concludes that a violation occurred, the question whether to issue an order remains in the discretion of the tribunal."[7] A violation of an antitrust rule in Canada produces a private action only under very limited circumstances, including "violations of the conspiracy, bid-rigging, banking, price discrimination, predatory pricing or price maintenance provisions of the criminal section of the *Competition Act*".[8] No private action is available for offences based on "abuse of dominant position (monopolisation), merger, joint venture, tied selling, exclusive dealing and market restriction".[9] Even when a private action is available, the "Canadian private action limits recovery to single damages".[10] The Canadian private action "has not played a significant role in developing competition law as it relates to intellectual property".[11]

10.4 Effect of Violation of Antitrust Rules in the United States

The results of violating the antitrust rules are far more drastic in the United States than they are in Canada. The *Clayton Act* authorizes and encourages private actions. It "has enlisted as 'private attorneys-general' those who have been injured by virtue of violations of the antitrust laws. As an incentive, the *Clayton Act* provided private parties with a potential recovery of, inter alia, treble damages,"[12] as well as "the cost of the suit, including a reasonable attorney's fee".[13] All this is in addition to significant fines for a violation.

10.4.1 Enforcement Policy

During the Reagan/Bush regimes, enforcement of the U.S. antitrust rules relaxed. The rules did not go away; only the enforcement dropped.[14]

---

[6]   Roberts, "Technology Transfer Agrements", p. 254.
[7]   *Ibid.*
[8]   *Ibid.*
[9]   *Ibid.*
[10] *Ibid.*, p. 253.
[11] *Ibid.*
[12] *Ibid.*, citing the *Clayton Act*, 15 U.S.C. §4.
[13] *Ibid.*, quoting 15 U.S.C. §4, ¶12-27.
[14] *Ibid.*, p. 258. The Roberts article is now somewhat out of date as a result of increased enforcement by the Clinton administration and the 1995 U.S. Antitrust I.P. Guidelines.

10.4.2 U.S. Guidelines

The U.S. administration released "Antitrust Guidelines for the Licensing of Intellectual Property" on April 6, 1995, replacing, in part, the 1988 rules. The 1995 rules provide guidelines to the current antitrust enforcement policy in Section 1.0.[15] Whether the courts will follow the U.S. Antitrust I.P. Guidelines remains to be seen.[16]

Strategy: In any event, these Antitrust I.P. Guidelines should be kept in mind by the negotiators of any technology transfer agreement where any term may be considered to harm "competition among entities that would have been actual or likely competitors in the absence of such an arrangement"[17] or where there is any display of an apparent exercise of market power, i.e., "the ability profitably to maintain prices, or output, below competitive levels for a significant period of time".[18]

10.4.3 Intellectual Property by Itself Does Not Necessarily Confer Market Power

The U.S. Antitrust I.P. Guidelines provide that the "Agencies will not presume that a patent, copyright, or trade secret, necessarily confers market power upon its owner."[19] Normally intellectual property "derives its value by being combined with other factors of production",[20] *i.e.*, normally it must be used to have any market power — "standing by itself [it] is not worth very much".[21]

Strategy: Particularly here, remember that this statement is a guideline, not a statement of the law binding on the courts.

10.4.4 No Requirement to License

The U.S. Antitrust I.P. Guidelines suggest that the owner of intellectual property is not obligated to license its use to others[22] nor to create competitors in its own technology,[23] but collecting intellectual property or forming alliances that collect intellectual property with the intention of "blocking" all competitors may be reviewable.[24]

---

[15]   These guidelines are reproduced in LES Symposium 4. These guidelines are hereinafter referred to as "U.S. Antitrust I.P. Guidelines".

[16]   LES Symposium 4, p. 41.

[17]   U.S. Anti-Trust I.P. Guidelines, discussion of Example 1 following Section 2.3.

[18]   *Ibid.*, Section 2.2.

[19]   *Ibid.*

[20]   LES Symposium 4, p. 38.

[21]   *Ibid.*, p. 38. This does not seem to take into consideration the effect of merely possessing patents that encircle the competitor's patent.

[22]   U.S. Anti-Trust I.P. Guidelines, Section 2.2.

[23]   *Ibid.*, Section 3.1. See also Roberts "Technology Transfer Agreements," p. 260, where he discusses *Continental Paper Bag Co. v. Eastern Paper Bag Co.*, 210 U.S. 405, at 424 (1908), where the "Supreme Court of the United States rejected the notion that a patentee was in the position of a quasi-trustee for the public, that he is under a sort of moral obligation to see that the public acquires the right to the free use of that invention as soon as conveniently possible".

[24]   *Ibid.*, Sections 2.2 and 3.1.

10.4.5 Per Se Violations

Some activities are considered so restrictive of competition that they are treated as violations without the requirement to prove actual restraint of trade; these are often referred to as *"per se* violations". "Among the restraints that have been per se unlawful are naked-price-fixing, output restraints, and market division among horizontal competitors, as well as certain group boycotts and resale price maintenance."[25]

Strategy: Keep a checklist of the per se violations and apply it to every technology transfer agreement in the early stages of negotiation.[26]

10.4.6 Rule of Reason

"In the vast majority of cases, restraints in intellectual property licensing arrangements are evaluated under the rule of reason. The Agencies' general approach in analyzing a licensing restraint under the rule of reason is to inquire whether the restraint is likely to have anti-competitive effects and, if so, whether the restraint is reasonably necessary to achieve pro-competitive benefits that outweigh those anti-competitive effects."[27] An arrangement deserves "rule of reason" treatment rather than *per se* treatment if the

> restraint in question can be expected to contribute to an efficiency-enhancing integration of economic activity. In general, licensing arrangements promote such integration because they facilitate the combination of the licensor's intellectual property with complementary factors of production owned by the licensee. A restraint in such a licensing arrangement may further such integration by, for example, aligning the incentives of the licensor and the licensees to promote the development and marketing of the licensed technology, or by substantially reducing transaction costs. If there is no efficiency-enhancing integration of economic activity and if the type of restraint is one that has been accorded *per se* treatment, the Agencies will challenge the restraint under the *per se* rule. Otherwise, the Agencies will apply a rule of reason analysis.[28]

Strategy: Gather and maintain evidence to support a rule of reason defence.

---

[25]   *Ibid.*, Section 3.4.

[26]   Kathleen R. Terry in "Antitrust and Technology Licensing" in Journal of the Association of University Technology Managers, 1995, Vol. VII, p. 83, at 85, lists the "Nine No-No's" considered by the Agency (but never ratified by a court) to be *per se* antitrust violations: (1) requiring a patent licensee to purchase an unpatented material from the licensor; (2) grant-back of title to the licensor of the licensee's improvements to the patented technology; (3) attempting to impose restrictions after sale of the patented product; (4) tie-in and tie-out: tying of products or services outside the scope of the patent claims, or restricting the licensee's freedom to deal with other suppliers; (5) an agreement outside the licence not to grant other licences (that is, concealing the exclusive nature of the agreement); (6) mandatory package licences; (7) any broadening of the royalty base; (8) restriction on sale of products made with the patented process; and (9) price fixing.

[27]   U.S. Antitrust I.P. Guidelines, Section 3.4.

[28]   *Ibid.*

10.4.7 Hot Spots

Although not *per se* violations, transactions that should give immediate concern for violation of the restraint of trade rules include:

(a) Technology transfers between horizontal competitors;[29]

(b) Resale price maintenance;[30]

(c) A "tying" arrangement — *i.e.*, "an agreement by a party to sell one product . . . on the condition that the buyer also purchases a different or 'tied' product or at least agrees that he will not purchase that [tied] product from any other supplier".[31] Instead of products, the offence could relate to the tying of the acquisition of one intellectual property right (for example, a patent) to the acquisition of other intellectual property rights (for example, a trade secret);

(d) Packaged Licensing — *i.e.*, the licensing of multiple items of intellectual property in a single license or in a group of related licenses;[32]

(e) Exclusive Dealing — *e.g.*, preventing "the licensee from licensing, selling, distributing or using competing technologies";[33]

(f) Cross Licensing and pooling arrangements[34] — *i.e.*, "agreements of two or more owners of different items of intellectual property to license one another or third parties";[35]

(g) Grant-back — *i.e.*, an arrangement under which a licensee agrees to extend to the licensor of intellectual property the right to use the licensee's improvements to the licensed technology:[36] These grant backs can be non-exclusive or exclusive; the former is "less likely [than the latter] to have anti-competitive effects";[37]

(h) Acquisitions rather than licenses — These will be reviewed applying the "1992 Horizontal Merger Guidelines" rather than the U.S. Antitrust I.P. Guidelines; and

(i) Enforcement or attempted enforcement of invalid intellectual property rights.[38]

Strategy: Add the Hot Spot Checklist to the Per Se Checklist.

---

[29] *Ibid.*, Section 5.1.

[30] *Ibid.*, Section 5.2.

[31] *Ibid.*, Section 5.3.

[32] *Ibid.*

[33] *Ibid.*, Section 5.4.

[34] *Ibid.*, Section 5.5.

[35] *Ibid.*

[36] *Ibid.*, Section 5.6.

[37] *Ibid.*

[38] *Ibid.*, Section 6.

10.4.8 How to Conduct Business without Fear of Antitrust Violation

As mentioned above, each technology transfer agreement must be reviewed by competent counsel to determine if there is a possible violation, using many of the principles set out in the U.S. Antitrust I.P. Guidelines. Unfortunately, it may be costly to obtain even a very restricted opinion. The legal advisors have to anticipate how the markets may develop, using the limited market information available for such analysis. In contrast, the Agencies or the self appointed "private attorneys-general" have the benefit of hindsight. Additionally, the Agencies have material available to them that is not available to the general public.

10.5 Analysis

The analysis to determine the balance between the economic benefits of the arrangement and its anticompetitiveness can be both extensive and expensive. The market must be narrowed, to the extent data is available, "to the smallest group of technologies and goods [and services] over which a hypothetical monopolist of those technologies and goods would exercise market power, for example, by imposing a small but significant and non-transitory price increase".[39] The "markets" consist of "goods markets,"[40] "technology markets"[41] and "innovative markets".[42] In the analysis, the Agencies "will not engage in a search for a theoretically least restrictive alternative [to the offending activity] that is not realistic in the practical prospective business solutions faced by the parties".[43]

Strategy: The parties should be able to establish that there are no existing practical and significantly less restrictive alternatives to their selected arrangement; their claims to efficiency are not enough.[44]

10.5.1 Safety Zone

To "provide some degree of certainty" and to reduce the costs associated with antirestraint of trade opinions and defences, "the Agencies will not challenge a restraint in an intellectual property licensing arrangement if (1) the restraint is not facially anti-competitive and (2) the licensor and its licensees, collectively account for no more than 20% of each relevant market significantly affected by the restraint".[45] A challenge to an arrangement in a technology market or innovation market is unlikely (but not precluded) if:

---

[39]   *Ibid.*, Section 3.2.2.
[40]   *Ibid.*, Section 3.2.1.
[41]   *Ibid.*, Section 3.2.2.
[42]   *Ibid.*, Section 3.2.3.
[43]   *Ibid.*, Section 4.2.
[44]   *Ibid.*
[45]   *Ibid.*, Section 4.3.

(a)   the restraint is not "facially anti-competitive" — in violation of a *per se* rule or other similar rule "that would always or almost always tend to reduce output or increased prices";[46] or

(b)   in addition to the parties for the technology, there are four or more parties in that technology market or innovation market.[47]

If these safety zones are exceeded, there is not an automatic violation; arrangements outside the safety zone are encouraged and are assessed under the U.S. Antitrust I.P. Guidelines.[48]

Strategy: Take comfort in the safety zone, but remember that it is a moving standard; the qualification is determined at the time of entering into the transaction as well as at the time of "the subsequent implementation of the restraint".[49]

EMPLOYMENT CONTRACTS

10.6 Need

Because an employee, (including, in this context, independent contractors who are similar to employees) gains access to sensitive trade secrets, an employer will wish to impose restrictions on the employee's use of these trade secrets. The employer may wish to restrict the employee from using the information for any purpose other than the specified project and from developing a competing product or service. Without adequate protection the interest of the public, as well as the interest of the employer, could be harmed: "businesses would cease to invest sufficiently in these activities and overall levels of economic development would suffer".[50] The employee, on the other hand, does not want his or her professional expertise to be restricted; the employee will wish to preserve employment mobility. Just as the U.S. courts have done in the antitrust cases, the courts can be expected to impose a standard of reasonableness on employee-related restrictive covenants.

10.7 The Test of Reasonableness

The Canadian rules will be examined to develop the basic principles involved, their application in any locality, including a Canadian jurisdiction, must be examined in light of local law as it applies to the particular fact situation. This chapter is not intended to develop legal principles that may be relied on; it is intended to develop only the basic principles. Any restrictive covenant must be reasonable, not only in regard to the interest of the parties, but also in regard to the interest of

---

[46]   *Ibid.*
[47]   *Ibid.*
[48]   *Ibid.*
[49]   *Ibid.*
[50]   Trebilcock, *The Common Law*, p. 52.

the public.[51] The basic Canadian premise is that "all restraints of trade themselves, if there is nothing more, are contrary to public policy, and therefore void".[52] Restraints are justifiable "if the restriction is reasonable — reasonable, that is, in reference to the interests of parties concerned and reasonable in reference to the interests of the public, so framed and so guarded as to afford adequate protection to the party in whose favour it is imposed, while at the same time it is in no way injurious to the public".[53] The public interest is "always upon the side of liberty, including the liberty to exercise one's powers or to earn a livelihood".[54]

10.7.1 Only "Adequate" Protection will be Provided

Adequate levels of protection can be identified by means of five distinct elements:

> (1) only proprietary interest will be protected; (2) such interest will be protected no more extensively than is reasonably necessary; (3) the onus of proving both that a legitimate interest exists and that it is not too wide normally falls upon the promisee; (4) failure to meet this onus in either respect will often result in the unenforceability of the entire restrictive covenant (that is, it will generally not be severed); and (5) where a covenant is held to be enforceable, the primary relief for breach is injunctive.[55]

10.7.2 Proprietary Interest

Interests that are deserving of protection include protection of trade secrets, which should not be improperly divulged or used, and relations with customers which should not be subject to improper solicitation by employees or ex-employees.[56]

Strategy: Define clearly what activity is being restricted and establish why the proposed restriction on that activity is reasonable.

10.7.3 Reasonable Scope

Trebilcock writes:

> In practice, a restrictive covenant "will be too wide," and hence unenforceable, if it is found to: (a) endure for a longer time period; (b) apply to a wider range of types of employee activities; or (c) apply across a greater geographical area, than is considered by the courts to be reasonably necessary for the adequate protection of the employer's legitimate interest.[57]

---

[51] *Nordenfelt v. Maxim Nordenfelt Guns & Ammunition Co.*, [1894] A.C. 535, at 565, [1891-4] All E.R. Rep. 1 (H.L.).

[52] *Ibid.*, at 565 (A.C.).

[53] *Ibid.*

[54] *Mason v. Provident Clothing & Supply Co. Ltd.*, [1913] A.C. 724, at 739–40, [1911-13] All E.R. Rep. 400 (H.L.).

[55] Trebilcock, *The Common Law*, p. 67.

[56] See *Herbert Morris Ltd. v. Saxelby*, [1916] 1 A.C. 688, [1916-17] All E.R. Rep. 305 (H.L.) and Trebilcock, *The Common Law*, pp. 67 ff.

[57] Trebilcock, *The Common Law*, p. 70.

Reasonableness is decided "at the date at which the agreement was entered into,"[58] taking into account the parties then-existing expectations of what might possibly happen in the future.[59]

Strategy: Design the restrictive covenant, for the specific facts, to apply only for a reasonable time period and within a reasonable geographical area.

10.7.4 Onus

The party wishing to enforce a restrictive covenant has the responsibility or onus to establish that it is reasonable *in the interest of the parties*. The party wishing to resist enforcement of a restrictive covenant has the onus to establish that it is not reasonable *in the public interest*.[60]

10.8 Application of Test of Reasonableness to Employees

The test of reasonableness applies to restrictive covenants imposed on employees (such as secrecy obligations, non-solicitation or non-competition covenants). There must be a reasonable balance between the interests of the parties, and the result must not injure the public interest. The employer has the obligation to establish that the restriction is reasonable for the parties; the employee has to establish that the restriction is not within the public interest. One factor to be considered is the bargaining power of the parties. The court will protect an employee who is not in a strong bargaining position with the employer against any restriction that may prevent the employee from using his or her professional expertise. But if the proprietary interest of the employer is exceptional, a broad restrictive covenant may be appropriate.

> Whether a restriction is reasonably required for the protection of the covenantee can only be decided by considering the nature of the covenantee's business and the nature and character of the employment. Admittedly, an employer could not have a proprietary interest in people who were not actual or potential customers. Nevertheless, in exceptional cases, of which I think this is one, the nature of the employment may justify a covenant prohibiting an employee not only from soliciting customers, but also from establishing his own business or working for others so as to be likely to appropriate the employer's trade connection through his acquaintance with the employer's customers. This may indeed be the only effective covenant to protect the proprietary interest of the employer. A simple non-solicitation clause would not suffice.[61]

10.8.1 Dimensions to Reasonableness

There are three "dimensions" to reasonableness of the scope of employee-restrictive covenants that are designed to prevent unauthorized use of trade

---

[58]   *Gledhow Autoparts Ltd. v. Delaney,* [1965] 3 All E.R. 288, [1965] 1 W.L.R. 1366, at 295 (C.A.).
[59]   *Tank Lining Corp. v. Dunlop Industrial Ltd.* (1982), 140 D.L.R. (3d) 659, at 665 (Ont. C.A.).
[60]   *Ibid.*
[61]   *Elsley v. J.G. Collins Insurance Agencies Ltd.* (1978), 83 D.L.R. (3d) 1, at 7, [1978] 2 S.C.R. 916, 20 N.R. 1, 3 B.L.R. 183, 36 C.P.R. (2d) 65.

secrets, solicitation of customers, or non-competition agreements: "(i) the range of people that the employee will be prevented from serving; (ii) the range of services that he will be prevented from providing; and (iii) the duration of the restraint".[62]

SELLER OF A BUSINESS

10.9 Seller of a Business

A non-competition covenant is a standard part of the sale of a business, including an assignment of all intellectual property rights for specified technology. The courts are more likely to find an equality of bargaining power in a case involving a sale of a business than would be found in a case involving an employee.[63] The same dimensions of reasonableness apply to restrictive covenants granted on the sale of businesses as apply to employees.

SEVERANCE

10.10 Severance

Frequently, at the time of drafting a restrictive covenant, it is difficult to determine what scope, duration and area, is reasonable. The drafter of the restrictive covenant will be concerned that if the clause is too broad it will be held to be unenforceable and no restrictive covenant will be in place. The drafter would like the courts to decide what is appropriate and then reduce the scope of the restrictive covenant accordingly. Unfortunately, the Canadian courts will not do that. "The courts have always resisted rewriting a contract that the parties have made."[64] This may be the opposite result to the position taken by some American courts who "have asserted a jurisdiction to rewrite contracts to provide reasonable restraints where the covenant agreed between the parties has been held to be unreasonable".[65] The Canadian courts will restrict themselves to severing unenforceable covenants from enforceable ones. "[T]he severance can be effected when the part severed can be removed by running a blue pencil through it."[66] This "blue pencil" rule does not authorize a Canadian court to add words or to rewrite the clause.[67] The part that is left after a severance must "be a sensible and reasonable obligation in itself and such that the parties would have unquestionably had agreed

---

[62] Trebilcock, *The Common Law*, p. 99.
[63] *Elsley, supra* note 61, at 5–6 (D.L.R.).
[64] *Canadian American Financial Corp. (Canada) Ltd. v. King* (1989), 60 D.L.R. (4th) 293, at 305, 36 B.C.L.R. (2d) 257, 25 C.P.R. (3d) 315 (C.A.).
[65] *Ibid.*, at 303 (D.L.R.).
[66] *Attwood v. Lamont*, [1920] 3 K.B. 571, at 578, [1920] All E.R. Rep. 55 (C.A.), quoted favourably in *Canadian American, supra* note 64, at 299–300.
[67] *Canadian American, supra* note 64, at 306 (D.L.R.).

to it without varying any other terms of the contract or otherwise changing the bargain ".[68]

10.10.1 Telescope Clauses: Uncertainty Versus Severability

Some drafters, counting on severability of void clauses, provide a series of decreasing areas of restriction. The British Columbia Court of Appeal has refused to sever the components of a telescope clause that said that the "employee will not compete in (a) Canada, (b) British Columbia, and (c) Vancouver, for (i) 10 years, (ii) five years, and (iii) one year". It held that the clause was void for uncertainty and it refused to make it valid by severance.[69]

10.10.2 Draft as Separate Covenants

Some writers will now draft a Canadian restrictive covenant selecting the widest geographical area that can be bargained, and stating that the covenant will be construed as a series of separate covenants, one for each province (or smallest area that is reasonable). The agreement could specifically provide why the protection is necessary. The same principle could be adopted for each of the restricted activities. The intent of the drafter is to provide certainty on the agreed restrictions but to allow them to be independently severed, leaving the balance of the agreement a complete and reasonable bargain without change.

---

[68] *Ibid.*
[69] *Ibid.*

Part V

CONSIDERATION

Chapter 11

PAYMENT

a billion here, a billion there, and pretty soon you're talking about real money[1]

11.1 Introduction

Payments for the technology transfer may be made in a number of ways; what is best may depend on the individual nature of the parties to the transfer as well as on the technology.[2]

11.2 One-time Fixed Payment

One of the simplest licences to administer involves a fixed payment made in one instalment at a specified date, perhaps on execution of the licence or on attainment of a specified milestone. In addition to offering administrative simplicity, a fixed payment or instalment licence will be attractive to

    (a)   competitors who do not want to reveal their sales/financial records to each other;

    (b)   a transferor which does not have the staff to collect and audit running royalties;

    (c)   a transferor who needs the working capital immediately to continue development of either the technology that is the subject-matter of the transfer or the development of other technology that it wishes to commercialize.[3]

Lump sum technology transfer fees are appropriate when the continuing benefit of the technology that a licensee can be expected to receive can be calculated with reasonable accuracy and then discounted to take into account the time and risk factors.

---

[1]   Everett McKinley Dirksen, quoted in John Bartlett, *Familiar Quotations: A Collection of Passages, Phrases, and Proverbs Traced to Their Sources in Ancient and Modern Literature*, ed. Justin Kaplan (Boston: Little, Brown, 1992), p. 694, No. 4.

[2]   The prevailing tax system may influence the choice of payments. See Chapter 12 of this text.

[3]   For a discussion on Customization, see Chapter 8 of this text and for Improvements see Chapter 9 of this text.

11.2.1 Fixed Periodic Payments

Instead of the fixed technology transfer fee being payable in one instalment, the payment could be made over a period of time in fixed amounts.

Strategies: In the case of fixed periodic payments, consider:
  (a)   *acceleration of the remaining payments if an instalment is missed;*
  (b)   *interest on delayed payments or overdue payments (but watch for laws relating to usury or laws that prohibit a higher rate after default than was charged before default); and*
  (c)   *the possibility that the delayed payments will still be payable even if the subject intellectual property rights are declared invalid (in contrast to a running royalty that might cease to be payable as a result of antitrust rules).*

11.2.2 Fixed Payments Credited Against Future Royalties

In some cases, the fixed payment is an advance against royalties that will subsequently be earned.

Strategies:
  (1)   *How much of the running royalty payment will be credited against the advance? The licensee may need some of the funds for income taxes and working capital.*
  (2)   *Is the advance non-refundable if the earned royalties do not cover the advance?*
  (3)   *What is the effect of bankruptcy on the advance?*

11.3 Running Royalties

When it is difficult to determine the potential commercial success of the technology, when the parties cannot agree on the discount rates, or when the licensee cannot afford an appropriate lump-sum payment, running royalties may be appropriate. Running royalties may be combined with a fixed payment, which is either independent of the running royalties or is an advance against them.

11.3.1 Different Royalty Rates for Different Intellectual Property Rights

In the case of a technology transfer consisting of a number of intellectual property rights, such as a number of patents or a combination of patents and trade secrets, it may be appropriate to separate the consideration for each component, or, at least, agree on the amount of reduction if one or more of the rights is invalid or ineffective (for examples, a patent application not resulting in an issued patent, an issued patent being declared invalid, or a trade secret entering the public domain). United States antitrust rules may provide that a blended royalty in a "hybrid" licence (a licence of both a patent and trade secrets) will be entirely ineffective if a licence of the patent fails to provide the intended benefit, even though the secrets continue to be

licensed.[4] United States antitrust rules do not seem to obviate the requirement to pay a royalty for a trade secret, even if the trade secret becomes part
of the public domain.[5] Under Canadian rules, the licensee may be required to
continue to pay even though the patent is invalid, unless the contract specifies otherwise.

*Strategy: In any event, it is good business practice to contemplate the ineffec-
tiveness of a licensed intellectual property right.*

11.3.2 Variable Consideration

The running royalty could be based on the following:

(a) A flat sum per unit — this basis is attractive to the transferor
because payment is made at an early stage in the manufacturing and
distribution cycle. It is a useful standard when the technology that is
transferred is included as one of many components of a product marketed by the licensee, or when the licensee does not wish to reveal
its sales revenue.

(b) A fixed percentage of revenue — this method allows the royalty to
reflect the commercial success of the technology that is transferred
and is often the fairest allocation of the risks and benefits of commercialization. What is considered to be "revenue" will require careful consideration. It will be net of sales taxes, but will it be net of the
costs of packaging, transportation, return allowances, sales commis-
sions or other appropriate deductions? Will the revenue that is the
subject of the royalty calculation include indirect benefits, such as
charges for installation, maintenance and training (significant
amounts in the cases of licensing of software)?

(c) Increasing or decreasing rates — in order to encourage a prompt
incline in the growth of sales, the royalty rate may decrease as certain milestones are reached. Conversely, the entry into the market-
place may involve significant one-time costs and, thus, will initially
require low royalty rates that can be increased as the licensee's fixed
costs are being amortized over a higher level of sales.

(d) Flat sum — the licence could provide that the annual royalty will
have minimums or maximums. If the transferor is concerned about
its technology not being adequately exploited, it may require a
minimum royalty payable for each specified time period. If there
is concern that the transferor's revenue could be excessive in comparison to its contribution to the successful commercialization of

---

[4] See, for example, *Brulotte v. Thys Co.*, 379 U.S. 29 (1964); rehearing denied, 379 U.S. 985 (S.C.
1965), and *Lear, Inc. v. Adkins*, 395 U.S. 653 (1969).

[5] See *Warner-Lambert Pharmaceutical Co. v. John J. Reynolds*, 178 F.Supp 655, 123 U.S.P.Q. 431
(S.D. N.Y. 1959); affd 280 F.2d 197 (2nd Cir. 1960) and also *Aronson v. Quick Point Pencil*, 440
U.S. 257, 99 S. Ct. 1096, 59 L.Ed. 2d 296, 201 U.S.P.Q. No. 1 (1979) (U.S. Supreme Court).

the resulting product, a maximum amount could be specified to protect the licensee.

(e)   Lower royalties — if a lump sum is paid when the success of the commercialization is not easily predictable, the parties could agree that the royalty rate will decrease if a fixed sum is paid. In this case, the royalty rate might be higher than fair market value to compensate the transferor for the reduction in rate.

11.3.3 Base for Calculation of Royalty

The base for calculating royalties could be

(a)   the number of units manufactured, processed or produced;
(b)   the revenue generated;
(c)   the quantity of supplies or raw material used;
(d)   the profits generated by the licensee; this is probably the most difficult standard to use because, although conceptually attractive, it is very difficult to decide what deductions from revenue will be permitted.[6]

11.4 Non-monetary Consideration

In addition to payment by way of cash, the consideration payable to the transferor could include the following:

(a)   Equity shares issued by the licensee — the transferor will wish to determine what restrictions will be placed on the marketability of these shares, either as a result of securities regulations, regulations imposed by a stock exchange, or by the number of shares being actively traded in the open market. A thin market may prevent trades in a timely fashion.

(b)   Funding of continued research — as government funding shrinks, the need of universities for funding of continued research may prevail over the desire for royalties in the longer term.

(c)   Appointment to advisory boards — such appointments allow the inventor to maintain continued involvement in the development and marketing of the product and may give him or her prestige; conversely, the appointment may give prestige to the licensee by the inventor lending his or her name and reputation.

(d)   First rights — the transferor may have certain first rights granted by the licensee, such as a first right to all improvements, a right of first refusal to market the technology once it is developed, a first right to research or develop improvements, or to make, use or sell improvements. Some first rights are only for marketing rights of the subject technology after clinical or other tests are performed by the licensee.

---

[6]   For a further discussion see §2.5 of this text.

    (e)   Grant-back of improvements — a pooling of improvements through an "improvements club" allows all licensees to share improvements and know-how with each other.

    (f)   The settlement of outstanding litigation including a claim of infringement.

11.5 Release for Past Infringement

One consideration in a technology transfer agreement may be the release of the licensee for past infringements, which might be effective only upon a certain level of royalties or other performance levels being attained. The release may be for specifically stated infringements or may be a general release of all infringements by the licensee of specific intellectual property.

11.6 Duration of Period for Payment of Royalties

The period during which royalties are earned and, thus, are payable must not only satisfy the applicable antitrust rules but also good business practices — both often conclude that no payment should be required if no benefit is received.[7] Often, royalties are payable during the life of any patent that is a subject-matter of the licence, but this is not necessarily a good correlation between cost and benefit. Royalties should reflect the benefit received by the licensee and should correlate to a patent that is core to the transaction, rather than to all patents that are the subject of the licence.

11.7 Royalties Payable to Others

The technology transfer agreement should contemplate the licensee being required to pay a royalty to a third party, perhaps as a result of an underlying patent, a combination of many protected technologies into one product, or a claim for infringement producing a settlement that requires a royalty for continued use of the transferred technology.[8] Usually, the licensee should be entitled to deduct that third-party payment from the royalty payable to the transferor.

11.8 Interest on Overdue Payments

There should be a provision levying a pre-agreed reasonable interest rate on delayed payments. Some jurisdictions do not automatically provide for interest on amounts awarded in a court judgment; others allow for a rate that is lower than a commercial rate. A reasonable rate could reflect the fact that payment is in arrears and, thus, the licensee does not deserve or qualify for preferred rates, such as a bank's prime lending rate.

---

[7]   Unfortunately, antitrust rules are less flexible to compensate for changing economic demands than are good business practices.

[8]   See Chapter 16 of this text.

11.8.1 Other Consequences of Failure to Pay

The technology transfer agreement could go on to provide other consequences of a failure to pay, including termination. The local bankruptcy rules will have to be examined for any rules that may prevent termination for failure to pay if the licensee is in bankruptcy.[9]

11.9 Effect of Invalidity/Expiration of Intellectual Property Rights

The effect on payments if the subject intellectual property expires or is held to be invalid is discussed in §§7.14 and 11.3.1 of this text.

11.10 Periodic Reports

To satisfy the transferor that the proper royalty is being paid, the licensee will issue periodic reports, based on the same period used for calculating royalties. In addition to providing data to summarize the calculation of the royalty, the report could include details of competition encountered, complaints being made by customers about product quality, suggestions for modifications or additions to the offered products or services, forecasts of future sales (usually non-binding), marketing efforts made by the licensee, methods adopted to satisfy required standards of production and maintenance of confidentiality and compliance with field of use or other restrictions imposed by the technology transfer agreement.

11.10.1 Duty to Maintain Records

The licensee will be required to maintain records that will enable it to prepare these periodic reports. If accounting records are involved, the agreement should specify the generally accepted accounting principles to be adapted. The difference between generally accepted accounting principles of the relevant countries should be taken into account.

11.10.2 Right to Inspect

The transferor will want to inspect some, or all, of these records. In some cases, the transferor and licensee are competitors and this inspection could reveal confidential information that is not within the scope of the transferor's review. In such a case, an inspection by an independent entity, such as a firm of accountants, would be appropriate (chartered accountants in Canada or certified public accountants in the United States). If the scope of the inspection is beyond accounting matters, the transferor may wish to retain a firm that understands the nature of the subject technology transfer agreement. Some agreements specify that the independent company cannot act for competitors of the parties as well as not act for either party. How far back can the inspectors go in performing their

---

[9]   See, for example, s. 65 of the *Bankruptcy and Insolvency Act*, R.S.C. 1985, c. B-3.

review? Perhaps some period less than the statutory limitation period? The individuals making the inspection should be bound by secrecy obligations.

11.10.3 Frequency and Cost of Audit

The licensee does not want to be subject to frequent and vexatious audits. It may want to limit the frequency of audits to no more than one every 12-month period. The parties will wish to allocate the cost of the audit — many agreements allocate cost depending on whether errors are found. The size of the errors that determine the allocation of the cost should relate to the size of the transaction and should not be chosen arbitrarily. A $5,000 error threshold may be appropriate for an agreement producing royalties of $100,000 in the period audited (*i.e.*, 5 per cent) but may be entirely inappropriate if the royalties are expected to be $1,000,000 (*i.e.*, an 0.5 per cent error). The agreement could contemplate whether the error allowance is net of all errors, either in favour of the licensee or against the licensee, or the aggregate of errors before deducting those that are favourable to the licensee.

11.11 Withholding Taxes

Many countries require a licensee to deduct withholding tax on payments being remitted to foreign transferors. The technology transfer agreement might address whether the licensee must "gross up" the payment so that the transferor receives the full amount owing to it; in such a case, the right in the transferor's home country to obtain a tax credit should be taken into account. Whether the transferor is earning sufficient taxable income to gain full benefit of such a local credit is a relevant factor.[10]

11.12 Sales Taxes

In some jurisdictions, sales tax is considered to be included in the price for the goods or services, unless expressly stated to be in addition to such price, as is the case with the Canadian Goods and Services Tax.

11.13 Currency

In international transactions the currency of payment is relevant. Some countries require licensees to pay in the local currency (all too often those countries have a volatile currency exchange rate). The possibility of currency controls being imposed should also be of concern. If revenue is being earned in a currency other than the currency used for establishing royalties, the method of timing of the conversion will be relevant. Will that time be the time of receipt by the licensee or the time of payment by the licensee?

---

[10] See Chapter 12 of this text for further discussion.

11.14 Method of Payment

The negotiators will wish to take into account the time and place for payment, the method of effecting payment and the "clearing" relationship between the parties' bankers.

11.14.1 Payment Milestones

If the technology that is being transferred is not fully developed or proven, payments may depend on milestones being achieved.[11]

11.14.2 Security for Payment

If the licensee is not a solid financial entity or is located in a country where recovery by court action is not practically or economically available, the transferor may require some form of security for payment, such as a letter of credit. Conversely, the licensee may want the transferor's warranties of performance guarantees to be supported by some method of security. Some technology transfer agreements include a charge on the licensee's assets to secure payment; in such a case, registration under the local personal property security rules may be necessary.

---

[11] See Chapter 8 of this text for a discussion on customization and acceptance tests.

Chapter 12

TAXATION

A technology transfer agreement should not only satisfy the commercial goals of the parties. It should also ensure that the most advantageous tax consequences are achieved. For a cross-border transfer of technology, this means considering the domestic tax laws of two or more countries, as well as the applicable tax treaties. It can be a complicated exercise. However, it is important to at least have an appreciation of the tax consequences of exporting technology before starting to negotiate a technology transfer agreement.[1]

12.1 Moving Complexity

The process of determining the tax consequences of a technology transfer agreement reflects the complexity of the applicable taxation legislation and the treaties. Hardly can a person become expert in the tax treatment of a technology transfer agreement before the rules are changed as the taxing authorities perceive another loophole to be closed or another social policy to be implemented. Today's social policy is tomorrow's loophole. This chapter does not attempt to provide anything other than guides as to what basic principles should be raised by negotiators to a technology transfer agreement when meeting with their tax advisor.

Strategy: Obtain up-to-date tax advice from an expert for each territory involved.

12.2 Characterization of Payment

Payments under a technology transfer agreement will be treated either as a "capital" receipt or an "income" receipt. The manner of treatment required by generally accepted accounting principles does not necessarily determine treatment for tax purposes. The treatment under the domestic tax law in one country may differ from the treatment in another, and there may be a tax treaty that overrules both. The following sums up the issues for the parties to a technology transfer agreement.

The income tax consequences arising from a technology transfer often depend on three key factors. The first is the legal classification of the technology, for

---

[1] Shelley J. Kamin, "The Tax System and Technology Transfer Agreements" in M. Goudreau, G. Bisson, N. Lacasse and L. Perret, eds., *Exporting our Technology: International Protection and Transfers of Industrial Innovations* (Montreal: Wilson & Lafleur, 1995), p. 389, at 389.

example, whether it is the subject of a copyright or patent, or whether it is "know-how". The second is the form of the transfer, namely, whether the technology is being sold or assigned outright, or whether it is being licensed. The third factor is the method of payment, which is generally a lump sum or periodic royalties or both. A payment may be regarded as a lump sum payment, even though it is made by a series of instalments. It is important to keep these factors in mind when drafting a technology transfer agreement. Otherwise, the tax treatment of amounts paid under that agreement may not be the same as the parties had intended.[2]

Strategy: For licensing, know the tax treatment for each party to a technology transfer agreement.

12.2.1 Capital Versus Income

For tax purposes, payments characterized as "capital" are often treated more favourably than payments that are characterized as "income".[3] The tax treatment of receipt of the payment by the transferee, however, is not always the same as the tax treatment of the acquisition costs incurred by the other party making the same payment. Also, a payment that normally would be characterized as "capital" can lose that characterization for certain reasons. For example, in Canada, a payment that is based on production or usage will be treated as income, even though the same payment in another country may be treated as capital.[4] Additionally, even though a transaction in Canada would normally be treated as a capital one, it may be treated as giving rise to income for Canadian tax purposes on the basis of being a "venture in the nature of a trade" if it is one of a series of similar transactions.

Strategy: Watch for the other party's sensitivity to its tax treatment.

12.3 Tax Credits

In Canada, some types of expenditures qualify for special treatment. Some qualify as credits against tax paid (in contrast to being deductible against income only). Some qualify for actual payments from the government to a taxpayer who does not generate enough taxable income to benefit from a tax credit.

Strategy: In any strategic alliance, look for potential tax consequences to favourable tax programs encouraging social policies, such as research and development.

12.4 Applicable Taxing Authority in an International Transaction

Taxing authorities establish complex rules attempting to tax all the income earned within their country by domestic and foreign businesses. These rules will

---

[2] *Ibid.*

[3] See Catherine A. Brown, "Tax Aspects of a Transfer of Technology: The Asia-Pacific Rim," Canadian Tax Paper No. 87, pp. 388 ff., The Canadian Tax Foundation 1994. Helpful Discussion on Tax Treatment from a Canadian Point of View.

[4] See s. 12(1)(g) the *Income Tax Act*, R.S.C. 1985, c. 1 (5th Supp.).

reach strenuously to include a business or its income within its taxing jurisdiction. Thus, "transfer pricing" is a material issue, particularly if the parties are not dealing at arm's length.

Strategy: Each technology transfer relationship must be examined to determine its potential for bringing businesses within the scope of foreign taxation authority.

12.4.1 Withholding Tax and International Treaties

The Canadian and U.S. *Income Tax Acts* impose a duty on a domestic transferee of technology to withhold portions of payments made to a foreign transferor of that technology; this withholding can be as much as 25 per cent of the transfer consideration. In attempts to reduce the amount of withholding tax and to avoid double taxation (*i.e.*, taxation by the country requiring the withholding and taxation on the same payment by the country in which the transferor is sited), countries such as Canada and the United States enter into tax treaties. Canada and the United States entered into an Income Tax Convention signed September 26, 1980 and amended by Protocols signed as recently as June 15, 1995. This past Protocol reduces the maximum amount of withholding tax to 10 per cent. Some types of payments are subject to this 10 per cent withholding, some are exempt.

> The Treaty provides for the taxation of 13 general categories of income. These include income from real property, business profits, transportation, dividends, interest, royalties, gains from alienation, personal services, artists and athletes, pensions and annuities, government services, payments to students and other income. In a technology transfer arrangement, the relevant Treaty articles would depend on how the technology is transferred. . . . [A] typical technology transfer agreement might include all or any combination of the following: knowhow, trade secrets, patents and related technology, industrial designs, copyrights, trademarks, formulas, processes, models, prototypes, machinery or equipment, as well as a range of technical and professional services. Therefore 7 of these Treaty provisions will normally affect technology transfer arrangements: royalties (Article 12), business profits (Article 7) and, where applicable, the permanent establishment rules (Article 5), independent and dependent personal services (Articles 14 and 15), gains from the alienation of property (Article 13), and other income (Article 21).[5]

Strategies:

(1)   *The domestic tax law does not necessarily characterize a payment the same way the treaty does, so reference to both domestic rules and treaty rules will be necessary.*

(2)   *Each party to an international technology transfer agreement should determine the international tax consequences to the other party; do not assume that they "mirror" its domestic tax treatment.*

---

[5]   Catherine A. Brown, "The Canada–U.S. Tax Treaty: Its Impact on the Cross-Border Transfer of Technology" (unpublished), pp. 10–11.

12.4.2 Double Taxation

The Canada/U.S. Tax Treaty, often endeavouring — sometimes successfully, sometimes not — to avoid double taxation by allocating which country may tax the proceeds of a transaction under domestic law, requires the home country to provide a credit for the tax paid to the foreign country. Even with credits for tax paid in a foreign country, serious problems may be encountered if the transferor has no income and, therefore, cannot utilize the tax credit. Do not assume the tax credits will produce a neutral tax result.

12.4.3 Zero to 10 Per Cent in Seconds

The parties to a technology transfer agreement that is within the scope of the Canada/U.S. Tax Treaty will be anxious to determine if the applicable rate is 10 per cent or 0 per cent.[6] One solution to the problem may be "separate multi-stage agreements" which will separate out the payments for each type of technology that is within the scope of the technology transfer agreement. Be cautious, however, because there are no guidelines as to when, or how, contracts will be "linked" to determine which characterization will dominate.[7] Obviously, the taxing authorities will attempt to characterize an agreement that transfers different types of technology as substantially one that would trigger the maximum withholding tax.

> It may also prove cumbersome to separate out a portion between technology payments which will be subject to withholding and those which will not. This would occur, for example, even in the simple case where payment for the use of a patent is coupled with rental payments for the use of tangible property. The tax bureaucrat will be concerned first, about whether he can unbundle the payment; second, about the apportionment between exempt and non-exempt portions of the license fee and finally, about any documentation required to support the allocation, currently as well as on an annual basis. This may prove to be a substantial burden. As one author has pointed out, "if periodic valuation is necessary to support a taxpayer's allocation of royalties between technology and taxable intangibles such as trademark, it will impose an enormous system cost to both taxpayer and revenue authorities".[8]

Strategy: "Attempts by the licensee to allocate between the exempt and non-exempt royalty portions of the contract may also be met with some resistance by the licensor, whose obligation it is to withhold and remit. This may not be a . . . risk he or she is prepared to assume."[9]

This "substantial burden" may interfere unnecessarily with the global market for technology. Why should competitive technology developers in either Canada or the United States be placed at a disadvantage to competitors by tax rules?

---

[6]   *Ibid.*, p. 12
[7]   *Ibid.*, p. 37.
[8]   *Ibid.*, pp. 37 and 38 (footnotes omitted).
[9]   *Ibid.*, p. 38.

12.4.4 Sales Tax

Payments under any technology transfer may give rise to tax being levied under a sales tax, goods or services tax, or valued added tax regime. Some jurisdictions require very little "nexus" to demand payment of a sales tax. Often, the sales tax regime imposes responsibility on the transferee to collect the tax. The Canadian Goods and Services Tax provides that if the tax is not separately specified in an exigible transaction, the tax is considered to be included in the purchase price.[10]

Strategies:

    (1)   Watch for a sales tax being levied on a technology transfer.

    (2)   Allocate who bears responsibility for the sales tax. Do not assume that silence on the issue places the responsibility with the other side.

    (3)   Decide whether the tax is in addition to, or included in, the consideration paid on account of the transfer.

---

[10] See *Excise Tax Act*, R.S.C. 1985, c. E-15.

Part VI

TERM

Chapter 13

TERM AND TERMINATION

13.1 Introduction

The term of the project must have a definite beginning and end; sometimes the term may be renewed. It will be ended on the occurrence of specified material breaches of duty imposed on the defaulting party.

13.2 Specify Term

The commencement of the term of the rights granted does not always coincide with the date of execution of the agreement; in such cases the commencement date should be specifically stated. If the agreement causes the term to commence retroactively, avoid the possibility of an automatic default arising for failure to report or to pay royalties after the commencement date of the term but before the date of execution of the agreement. The agreement could have some specific provisions relating to the "pre-execution" term, the performance of which may be conditions precedent to the grant and continuance of the grant of permitted rights. If the technology is not yet proven or must be customized before the term commences, and the term of the licence will not commence until it is proven or customized, the negotiators should make sure the commencement of the term is finite and not susceptible to a dispute over the possibility that unauthorized activities have occurred outside the term.

13.2.1 Term Calculated on External Matters

Many patent licences provide that the term is for the life of a patent or for the life of the last patent of a group of patents to expire. This method of calculation may be used to avoid violations of an antitrust rule[1] while still providing the maximum term legally available. The licensee should examine the term of each patent, selecting only those patents that are material and calculating an appropriate term based on those patents rather than agreeing to pay royalties even though the remaining patents may be immaterial. The parties could provide a method of re-establishing royalties when material patents have expired.

---

[1] See Chapter 10.

13.3 Automatic Renewal

Although the parties may be reluctant to agree on a long initial term, they may accept a shorter term that is automatically renewed. For example, they could provide for a five-year term that will be automatically renewed for a further [three] successive [five-year] terms unless either party gives at least six months' notice to the other party of its desire for termination at the expiration of the current five-year term. Automatic renewals must be distinguished from "evergreen" contracts where there may be a basic term with an automatic extension for an indefinite term thereafter, terminable only after expiration of the basic term by one party giving the other party an appropriate notice. For example, a five-year project could be reviewed indefinitely and be terminable after the fifth year on five months' notice.

13.4 Events Giving Rise to Termination

These events include:

(a)   failure to attain specified performance requirements (this could terminate exclusivity or terminate all rights);

(b)   ceasing to do business;

(c)   breaching any provision of the agreement. Consider whether a particular breach can be remedied, and if so, whether time for a "cure" should be permitted before termination is effective. Some breaches, such as breach of secrecy obligations, cannot be cured; some can be cured promptly, such as payment of money, and some can be cured only with the expenditure of time and effort, such as improving product quality; and

(d)   bankruptcy.

13.4.1 Bankruptcy

If a licensee becomes bankrupt, under Canadian law the transferor cannot terminate the licence for failure to pay royalties that arose prior to the bankruptcy.[2] The effect of the transferor's bankruptcy must also be considered. The U.S. case, *Lubrizol Enterprises Inc. v. Richmond Metal Finishers Inc.*, established that a trustee in bankruptcy of the transferor could renounce licences granted by the bankrupt if they were "executory."[3] This produced unfair results, particularly when the licensee had made a material investment in the acquisition and exploitation of an exclusive licence. The U.S. *Bankruptcy Act* was amended to overcome some of the perceived unfairness.[4] It is not clear that a *Lubrizol*-type decision could be made in Canada; the two Bankruptcy Acts are very different.[5]

---

[2]   *Bankruptcy and Insolvency Act*, R.S.C. 1985, c. B-3; 1992 (en. 1992, c. 27, s. 30), s. 65.1.
[3]   756 F.2d 1043 (1985).
[4]   Section 356(n) of the U.S. *Bankruptcy Act*.
[5]   See also *Re Erin Features #1 Ltd.* (1991), 8 C.B.R. (3d) 205 (B.C.S.C.), and see the case comment by Gabor G.S. Takach and Ellen L. Hayes in (1993), 15 C.B.R. (3d) 66.

The U.S. curative legislation covers only the transferor becoming bankrupt and provides no remedy for an assignor of intellectual property rights that is receiving payment by way of royalties from an assignee in a relationship that, economically, is very similar to a licensee.

13.5 Terminating Agreement Versus Terminating Rights

Rather than terminating the agreement, it is preferable to terminate specific rights and obligations, leaving the balance of the provisions of the agreement in effect. Drafters who terminate the agreement often have to go to great lengths to specify what provisions survive. It is more helpful to the negotiators to a technology transfer agreement to specify what provisions terminate and then set out the consequences of termination.[6]

13.6 Consequences of Termination

The following are some of the consequences of termination that negotiators to a technology transfer could consider including in their agreement.

(a) The licensee ceases to use or exploit the licensed technology, including trademarks and logos.

(b) The licensee returns to the transferor all copies of confidential information and licensed products in its possession.

(c) After termination, if the licensee may sell the inventory on hand in the marketplace, the transferor might want to have the right to perform an audit of this inventory to determine what is there to be sold, to avoid continued production, particularly if it is software capable of easy continued reproduction. The transferor may wish to have the right to repurchase that inventory rather than permitting the licensee to sell it in the market-place. The right is especially appropriate if such a right to sell is permitted or required by the local legislation.

(d) The licensee pays all royalties earned pre-termination and (if it has the right to continue distribution) after termination, and

(e) The transferor has the right to audit the licensee's books and premises to satisfy itself that it has been paid in full and that the licensee has ceased to use, or otherwise exploit, the licensed technology.

---

[6] See Ronald B. Coolley, "Importance of Termination Clauses" in Les Nouvelles, the Journal of the Licensing Executives Society, Vol. XXV, No. 4, December 1990, p. 169.

Part VII

LIABILITY

Chapter 14

WARRANTIES

You wanted it to work?!

14.1 Allocation of Risk of Imperfection

Particularly with technology that does not have a well proven record, the extent of warranties granted will be the subject of serious negotiation. The licensee will want some assurance, or "warranty," that it will get at least the quality it expected; it often has good reason to be concerned about "untimeliness, inadequate productivity and questionable quality".[1] The transferor will want to limit its exposure to liability from what it considers to be unreasonable expectations by the licensee. The technology transfer agreement must record a mutually acceptable allocation of the risk of quality deficiencies.

14.2 Causes of Defects

Product liability can result from a defective design or defective information, defective manufacture or production, defective testing procedures, defective use, defective repair and defective user instructions or warnings.[2] Each of these possible defects should be considered in designing the technology transfer agreement.

14.3 Social Policy

In the 1800s the courts of the United Kingdom, Canada and the United States were each developing judicial social policy by establishing standards of quality that products could not fall below. They found it unconscionable for sellers to take money for products that were not merchantable or fit for the intended purpose. The courts were prepared to find liability for defective products based on negligence (a subdivision of the legal "tort" that imposes duties of care) or on contract based on implied warranties. This judicial social policy as it applies to

---

[1] Douglas E. Phillips, "When Software Fails: Emerging Standards of Vendor Liability Under Uniform Commercial Code" in American Bar Association, Section on Business Law, The Business Lawyer, November 1994, Vol. 50, p. 151, at 153 (hereinafter "Phillips, 'When Software Fails'").

[2] For further discussion see S.M. Waddams, *Products Liability* (Scarborough: Carswell, 1993), p. 38 (hereinafter "Waddams, *Products Liability*") and Woodley/World Intellectual Property Organization *Guide on the Licensing of Biotechnology* (Geneva: WIPO and LES, 1992), pp. 86–87.

the sale of goods has been enacted into statutory codes in many jurisdictions: in Alberta and many of the other Canadian common-law provinces as the *Sale of Goods Act*, based on the English *Sale of Goods Act* (now replaced by *The Unfair Contract Terms Act*);[3] in many U.S. states as the *Uniform Commercial Code Article 2*; and, for international contracts, in many countries by the adoption of the United Nations Convention on Contracts for the International Sale of Goods.[4]

14.3.1 Warranties Implied by Law may Depend on the Nature of the Transaction

Notwithstanding a position common to Canada and the United States that transactions considered to be unconscionable will not be enforced, the social policies concerning the remedies resulting from a supply of deficient goods, services and information have been handled differently from jurisdiction to jurisdiction. Most jurisdictions have enacted legislation that covers the sale of goods, but all too often this legislation is not sufficiently flexible to cover the licensing of technology, the supply of custom software or the provision of information. The types of technology transfer transactions can be broken into the sale of goods, the provision of services and the provision of information. Recognizing the demand produced by changes in technology, courts seemingly may stretch the facts, fitting them into one category or another, to allow the court to impose an appropriate remedy. For example, the task of classifying something as a "good" or a "service" can be very difficult. Software sold in a package at a retail store is likely to be considered as a "good" for the purposes of the sale of goods legislation. If, however, the same software is transmitted electronically, that transaction may no longer be a sale of a good but may now be classified as a provision of a service because there is no tangible component.[5]

14.3.2 Implied Warranties for the Sale of Goods

Many jurisdictions impose an obligation that the goods delivered must attain minimum levels of quality.

> The implied warranty is that the products would pass without objection in the trade under the contract description and are fit for the *ordinary* purpose to which

---

[3]   See Report on Sale of Goods, Ontario Law Reform Commission (hereinafter "Ontario Law Reform Commission Report"), Vol. 1 (1979) p. 7. See also Waddams, *Products Liability*, p. 9.

[4]   For example, for adoption of the United Nations Convention in Alberta, see the *International Conventions Implementation Act*, S.A. 1990, c. I-6.8, s. 2. See also Peter Winship, "Changing Contract Practices in the Light of the United Nations Sales Convention: A Guide for Practitioners," American Bar Association, Section on International Law and Practice, The International Lawyer, Fall 1995, Vol. 29, No. 3, p. 525 (hereinafter "Winship, 'Changing Contract Practices'").

[5]   See Chris Reid, *Limiting Risks in International Transactions: U.K. and EEC* (London: University of London, 1991), p. 5 (hereinafter "Reid, *Limiting Risks*").

such goods are used. The product need not be perfect. Breach of warranty turns on separating acceptable flaws from defects that go beyond the ordinary.[6]

These are often referred to as the warranties of "merchantability" and "fitness for a particular purpose". For many purposes other than for disclaimers, it is difficult to distinguish between these two warranties.[7]

A client of mine, a university professor who had a good sense of humour and who was marketing to other university professors who, he hoped, shared his humour, wrote,

> We strongly recommend that you test the program thoroughly before relying on its results. This disclaimer and limitation of liability that is included in this licence is absolutely sincere. Approach the program with scepticism. You should assume that it is a schizophrenic and bug-infested program and that it is completely unreliable until you have proven to yourself that the data sampled by your equipment in your environment is valid.

14.3.3 Provision of Services

A technology transfer agreement may include a provision of services; these services could include the customization or further development of technology, training and support.[8] The law may imply a warranty that the "service provider has the skill to complete the task" and that such skill will be applied with "reasonable care and diligence".[9] It is more questionable whether there is an implied warranty that a desired result will be achieved by the provider of services.[10] A disclaimer of these implied warranties requires different words than those used for implied warranties relating to the sale of goods; such a disclaimer may have to specifically disclaim negligence.[11] Drafting this type of disclaimer requires considerable creativity; such a disclaimer is "fundamentally at odds with the vendor's marketing goals of persuading the user that the [service] will meet all the user's needs. The marketing goal [may mandate] that the contracting goal remain unspoken" and, thus, ineffective.[12] It is questionable

---

[6]   Raymond T. Nimmer and Patricia A. Krauthaus, *Commercial Law of License Contracts*, September 9, 1993 (unpublished), p. 23 (hereinafter "Nimmer and Krauthaus, *Commercial Law*"), citing *Neilson Business Equipment Center, Inc. v. Italo Montelone, M.D.*, 524 A.2d 1172 (Del. 1987). See also *Australian Knitting Mills Ltd. v. Grant* (1933), 50 C.L.R. 387, at 418 (Aust. H. C.) adopted by the English House of Lords in *Henry Kendall & Sons (a firm) v. William Lillico & Sons Ltd., and others*, [1969] 2 A.C. 31, [1968] 2 All E.R. 444 (H.L.), for the comment "The condition that goods are of merchantable quality requires that they should be in such an actual state that a buyer fully acquainted with the facts and, therefore knowing what hidden defects exist, and not being limited to their apparent condition would buy them without abatement of the price . . . and without special terms." See also Alberta's *Sale of Goods Act*, R.S.A. 1980, c. S-2, s. 17, and Waddams, *Products Liability*, pp. 67 ff. and the Ontario Law Reform Commission Report, Vol. 1 at p. 193 ff.

[7]   See in Winship, "Changing Contract Practices", pp. 546–47.

[8]   Nimmer and Krauthaus, *Commerical Law*, p. 24.

[9]   *Ibid.*

[10] Waddams, *Products Liability*, p. 101.

[11] Nimmer and Krauthaus, *Commercial Law*, p. 26.

[12] Phillips "When Software Fails," p. 160.

whether "gross negligence" can be disclaimed, except, perhaps, in a negotiated contract between parties with equal bargaining power, who are not "consumers" under any legislation designed to protect consumers.[13]

14.3.4 Provision of Information

The relationship between an information provider and its customer will be examined by a court to determine if "there is an implied obligation imposed on the information provider to provide an accurate and complete result" or whether the emphasis is "more on the process by which the contract is performed," the former producing a higher duty of care than the latter.[14] An information provider may have a duty to provide accurate and complete information if

(a)   the information was provided in the course of "his business, profession or employment, or in any other transaction in which he has a pecuniary interest";

(b)   the recipient was justified in relying on that information and did rely on it;

(c)   the information provider "failed to exercise reasonable care of competence in obtaining or communicating the information"; and

(d)   there was a special relationship that justified a duty of reasonable care.[15]

A disclaimer for information provided "must refer specifically to either a disclaimer of negligence or a disclaimer of any responsibility for the accuracy of the information provided".[16]

14.3.5 Implied Warranty of Title and Implied Warranty Against Infringement

Under both the Sale of Goods legislation derived from the English *Sale of Goods Act* and the *Uniform Commercial Code* there is an implied warranty of title. In addition, in the *Uniform Commercial Code* there is an implied warranty against infringement, which implied warranty is not contained directly in the Sale of Goods legislation (it is not clear if the implied warranty of title includes an implied warranty against infringement). These implied warranties against infringement must be expressly disclaimed. The disclaimer must be reasonable to be effective in some jurisdictions and may be entirely ineffective in other jurisdictions.[17]

14.3.6 Implied Right to Reject

In both the Sale of Goods legislation and the *Uniform Commercial Code* there is an implied right for the buyer of goods to reject them after having an

---

[13]   See Ontario Law Reform Commission Report, p. 288.

[14]   Nimmer and Krauthaus, *Commercial Law*, p. 27.

[15]   Adapted from Nimmer, *ibid.*, pp. 29–30, who was quoting from the *Restatement of Torts (Second)* §552.

[16]   *Ibid.*, p. 30.

[17]   Reid, *Limiting Risks*, p. 4. Warranties against infringement are discussed further in Chapter 19, Section 19.3.

appropriate period of time to make an inspection to determine that the goods are of deficient quality.[18]

14.4 Implied Warranties and Duties as Guidelines

The negotiators to a technology transfer agreement might use the warranties implied by law as guidelines for their negotiated express warranties and then agree that these express warranties are the only ones that will govern their relationship. These negotiators could consider the following:

(a)   a warranty that the technology will perform substantially in accordance with stated specifications — perhaps the transferor's published specifications;[19]

(b)   a warranty that the technology will be fit for the licensee's expressly stated purposes;

(c)   if the contract contemplates customization or further development:

   (i)   detailed benchmarking and acceptance tests should be set out. "The acceptance test provision should define a clear and objective procedure for deciding when the supplier has satisfactorily completed performance."[20]

   (ii)   a warranty that the transferor's efforts will be representative of the "skill that it represents itself to have";[21] and that the transferor "will exercise that skill in a workmanlike and reasonably careful manner";[22]

   (iii) a warranty that the transferor's efforts will achieve a specified result;

(d)   if information, such as databases, are included in the technology transfer:

   (i)   a warranty that the information will cause the technology to obtain the intended result; or

   (ii)   a warranty that information will be accurate and complete; and

(e)   what defects attributable to one party give the other party the right to repudiate the contract rather than only the right to damages, or whether the right of repudiation is the only remedy.

14.5 Puffery and Salesmanship Versus Misrepresentation

Not all product descriptions (or representations) have the same legal effect.[23] Some statements are not intended to be relied on: they are merely "salesmanship

---

[18]   The right to reject is discussed further in Chapter 8.

[19]   Reid, *Limiting Risks*, p. 13.

[20]   *Ibid.*

[21]   Nimmer and Krauthaus, *Commercial Law*, p. 25.

[22]   *Ibid.*

[23]   Gerald H.L. Fridman, *Sale of Goods in Canada* (Scarborough: Thomson Canada Ltd., 1995), p. 149 (hereinafter "Fridman, *Sale of Goods*").

or puffery".[24] These "statements . . . are only intended to extol the virtues of the seller's goods and are not usually regarded by the ordinary, reasonable buyer as being of any [significance]".[25] It is a question of fact for each case whether a statement is meant to be binding on the parties.[26] It may depend on how central the feature described is to the transaction.[27] "The closer an alleged representation lies to the central features of the deal, the more likely a court will recognize an express warranty."[28]

14.5.1 Innocence Versus Fraudulent Representation

A statement about the features of the technology that misrepresents the true features could be made innocently or fraudulently. A misrepresentation made innocently that is not fundamental to the transaction may give rise to a claim for damages, particularly if the misrepresenting statement was made negligently. If a statement made by one party could be considered as essential or fundamental to the deal between the parties, it might entitle the other party to repudiate or "rescind" the contract and permit that party to ask the courts to place it in the position it would have been in if the contract had not existed.[29] If there is a fraudulent misrepresentation by one party, the other party may have the right to repudiate the contract or to claim damages.[30] This remedy made not always be as appealing as it initially looks; such a rescission may result in the licensee infringing the intellectual property rights to the technology that is the subject-matter of the licence since the rescission will result in the loss of the licence. Such a rescission may also disentitle the licensee to damages.

14.6 Conditions Versus Warranties

The statements that give rise to the right to treat the contract as at an end are sometimes referred to as "conditions"; statements that are not so essential or fundamental are then referred to as "warranties". Many *Sale of Goods Acts* are derived from the English *Sale of Goods Act* and use the word "condition" in reference to minimum product quality. They allow the buyer of deficient goods to choose between treating a contract as at an end (relying on a condition) or continuing the contract but seeking damages (relying on a warranty).[31] Under Article 2 of the U.S. *Uniform Commercial Code* (U.C.C.) "an express warranty is any affirmation, promise or description that 'becomes part of the basis of the bargain' of the parties".[32] Any disclaimer of implied warranties where a party is subject to

---

[24] Nimmer and Krauthaus, *Commercial Law*, p. 22, and see Fridman, *Sale of Goods*, p. 149.
[25] Fridman, *Sale of Goods*, pp. 149–50.
[26] *Ibid.*
[27] Nimmer and Krauthaus, *Commercial Law*, p. 22.
[28] *Ibid.*
[29] Fridman, *Sale of Goods*, pp. 157–58.
[30] *Ibid.*, p. 152.
[31] See, for example, the *Sale of Goods Act*, R.S.A. 1980, c. S-2, s. 14(1).
[32] Nimmer and Krauthaus, *Commercial Law*, p. 22.

any *Sale of Goods Act* derived from the English *Sale of Goods Act* should add the word "condition" to the U.C.C.'s standard word "warranty".

14.7 Outline of Matters to be Considered When Negotiating Express Warranties

The negotiators to a technology transfer agreement could use the requirements of the *Magnuson-Moss Warranty Act*[33] as a checklist for matters to be dealt with in the warranty clause:

(1)   the identity of all persons who are entitled to the benefit of the warranty;

(2)   a clear description of the covered product or components;

(3)   a statement of the remedy if there is a defect;

(4)   when the warranty period begins and its duration;

(5)   a step-by-step explanation of the procedures to obtain performance of any warranty obligation;

(6)   information about the availability of any informal dispute settlement mechanism;

(7)   any limitations on the duration of implied warranties; and

(8)   any exclusions or limitations on relief, such as incidental or consequential damages.[34]

14.7.1 Results Versus Processes

The types of warranties listed in §14.4 of this text illustrate the difference between warranties that emphasize the *result* and those that emphasize the *process*. This distinction should be kept in mind by the negotiators when designing the appropriate express warranties. A warranty that technology will perform or function in accordance with documented specifications is sometimes referred to as an "as-documented warranty".[35]

14.7.2 Conditions to Effectiveness of a Warranty

The effectiveness of an expressed contractual warranty may be subject to certain limitations. The warranty might

(a)   become invalid if the product is improperly used, maintained or repaired;

---

[33]   15 U.S.C. §§2301–2312.

[34]   Pegi A. Groundwater, "General Considerations in Drafting Software Licenses," a paper presented at the Licensing Executives Society Annual Meeting, October 26, 1992, pp. 3-34 and 3-35 (hereinafter "Groundwater 'General Considerations'").

[35]   American Bar Association, Section on Patent, Trademark and Copyright Law, Committee on Computer Programs, *Model Software License Provisions*, Committee Chair: D.C. Toedt III of Arnold, White & Durke, Houston, Texas, Section 602 (hereinafter "ABA Draft Model Software Agreement").

(b)   become invalid if it is modified or improperly combined in use with any other product;

(c)   become invalid if it is otherwise tampered with or damaged;

(d)   be effective only if the transferor is properly notified of the defect; or

(e)   be effective only if the defect was not caused by other technology or by an unauthorized combination with other technology.

The warranty may be restricted in time and may be effective only if the transferor is properly notified of the defect. In any event, the particulars of the condition to effectiveness should be reasonable and relevant to the specific technology.

14.7.3 Duration of Warranty

The negotiators should consider the duration of the warranty. Should it be less than the time period that would exist under the applicable limitation period? Sometimes it is very difficult to determine a limitation period. The technology transfer agreement could thus provide that the period for making a claim under the warranty is one year, commencing on delivery of the technology or some other mutually acceptable milestone being attained.[36] Some legislation that is designed to protect consumers will not allow a disclaimer of the implied warranties but will allow a limitation on the duration of the warranty.[37]

14.7.4 Scope of Warranty

The parties to a technology transfer agreement should agree on who will be protected by the warranty: the licensee, its sublicensees, its customers, and those who have no contractual relationship but who may be affected by the product, service or information. The agreement could also specify under what circumstances the warranty will extend to a particular class of persons.[38]

14.8 Know Where Your Warranties Are

In addition to appearing in a section of the agreement specifically dedicated to warranties, warranties can be found in:

(a)   technical specifications or other forms of description of the technology being transferred;

(b)   the negotiations leading up to execution of the definitive agreement, which could have been lengthy and may have included contradictory descriptions of the technology involved;[39]

---

[36]   D.C. Toedt III, ed., *Licensing Law Handbook 1987* (New York: Clark Boardman Co., Ltd., 1987), pp. 5-36 and 5-37 (hereinafter Toedt, "*Licensing Law Handbook 1987*").

[37]   For example, see the *Magnuson-Moss Warranty Act*, 15 U.S.C. §231, referred to in Toedt, *Licensing Law Handbook 1987*, p. 5-47.

[38]   Nimmer and Krauthaus, *Commercial Law*, p. 21.

[39]   To the author's consternation, in reviewing an agreement, all previous (and contradictory) descriptions were attached to the agreement as a substitute for expressly drafted warranties. There were great difficulties sorting out which ones would prevail in the event of a conflict.

(c)   promotional material, sales literature or product specification sheets;[40]

(d)   personal correspondence; or

(e)   oral communication.

An "entire agreement" clause that disclaims all representations or promises that are not included specifically in the agreement may be effective in narrowing down the scope of warranties. Yet, warranties could be included in schedules to the agreement, perhaps in a description of the features of the technology that may conflict with the warranties expressed in the "warranty clause". Warranties that are expressly made will override a general disclaimer of warranties.[41] A disclaimer must be unambiguous;[42] specific warranties will be favoured over general disclaimers.[43] Just before execution of the definitive agreement, the negotiators should, once more, review the agreement in its entirety, including all schedules, to make sure there are no stray warranties. All too often the description of the technology is drafted by someone other than the drafter of the warranty clause, and that person may inadvertently include descriptions that could be considered to be warranties.

14.9 Disclaimer of Implied Warranties

As stated earlier, in negotiated technology transfer agreements express warranties should be designed to property allocate risks between the parties and then all implied warranties could be disclaimed.

14.9.1 Licensing Strategies: Disclaiming Implied Warranties on the Sale of Goods

A disclaimer of implied warranties of the product quality of goods should do the following:

(a)   expressly disclaim the implied warranties; the express warranties are in addition to the implied warranties unless they are inconsistent;[44]

(b)   mention the word "merchantability" to disclaim the implied warranty of the merchantability for U.C.C. purposes;

(c)   make it clear that the acquiring party has notice and has agreed to accept the disclaimer;

(d)   be conspicuous; the U.C.C. states that the disclaimer must be conspicuous, and if it is in BLOCK CAPITALS it is deemed to be conspicuous for U.C.C. purposes. Consider breaking BLOCKS OF BLOCK CAPITALS into different parts to maintain the actual conspicuousness that may be required by other jurisdictions; and

(e)   use the words "conditions" and "warranties" in the disclaimer.

---

[40]   Groundwater "General Consultations," p. 3-62.

[41]   Nimmer and Krauthaus, *Commercial Law*, p. 22.

[42]   Fridman, *Sale of Goods*, p. 282.

[43]   Nimmer and Krauthaus, *Commercial Law*, p. 22.

[44]   Section 17(7) of the *Sale of Goods Act* , R.S.A. 1980, c. S-2, and see *Fording Coal Ltd. v. Harnischfeger Corp. Of Canada* (1991), 8 B.C.A.C. 25, 17 W.A.C. 250, 6 B.L.R. (2d) 157 (C.A.).

14.9.2 Unconscionability

Implied warranties cannot always be disclaimed. Legal systems "have long recognized the need to balance the freedom to contract with the need to protect the weaker party against over-reaching by the stronger party".[45] Some jurisdictions, therefore, have passed legislation that prevents disclaimers of implied warranties in "consumer transactions" and even in some commercial transactions. Even without enabling legislation, some courts will not enforce disclaimers of implied warranties where the parties do not have equal bargaining power and enforcement would be unconscionable.[46] The quality is measured not only in financial strength but also in technical expertise and market position. In some jurisdictions it may be "unconscionable" to disclaim warranties when the inherent risks are very high, particularly if they could result in death or personal injury.[47] Factors that a court may consider concerning the possibility of unconscionability or imposition of unreasonable terms include an examination of the negotiation process as to length of time in dealing, length of time for deliberations, the experience or astuteness of the parties, whether counsel reviewed the contract and whether the buyer was a reluctant purchaser.

14.10 Allocation of Risk

In product liability cases, the courts are forced to decide who shall be responsible for damages and to what extent. The negotiators of a technology transfer agreement do not have the benefit of hindsight, as does a court; they must endeavour to foresee who should bear the risks which are not only unknown in kind but also unknown as to the economic result. Some of the standards the courts use may provide useful guidelines to the negotiators to a technology transfer agreement.

(a)   Which party can better insure against the risk[48] or otherwise bear the loss?[49] It should not be assumed that this is the producer of the product; software developers may not be able to obtain product liability insurance at a reasonable cost due to the difficulty of assessing the risk.

(b)   Which party can better avoid risks being actually realized? For example, can an intermediate user recognize the defect and stop the use that otherwise would give rise to the risk?[50]

---

[45]   Ontario Law Reform Commission Report, p. 153.
[46]   See Waddams, *Products Liability*, p. 203. See also Toedt, *Licensing Law Handbook 1987*, p. 6-30.
[47]   See U.C.C. § 2-719(3).
[48]   See Waddams, *Products Liability*, p. 34. Also see Reid, *Limiting Risks*, p. 15.
[49]   See *ibid.*, p. 11. See also Ontario Law Reform Commission Report, p. 228 and Reid, *Limiting Risks*, p. 15.
[50]   See, for example, C.A. Wright, A.M. Linden and L.N. Klar, *Canadian Tort Law: Cases, Notes & Materials*, 9th ed. (Markham: Butterworths, 1990), pp. 16-19 – 16-20 (hereinafter "Wright and Linden, *Tort Law*"), quoting *Phillips v. Chrysler Corp. of Canada Ltd.*, [1962] O.R. 375, 32 D.L.R. (2d) 347 (H.C.J.) and *Haseldine v. C.A. Daw & Son Ltd.*, [1941] 2 K.B. 343, [1941] 3 All E.R. 156 (C.A.).

(c)   Which party can better determine or, perhaps, even control the scope of the risk? For example, one party may not have the ability even to foresee the type of use, which is often the case with many software licensors. This is not normally the case with producers of pharmaceutical products.

14.10.1 Pure Licences Versus Commercial Licences

A licence that grants only the right to exploit patented technology (a "pure" licence) merely allows the licensee freedom from a lawsuit.[51] In such case, the parties may agree that the licence involves no express warranties of quality of any sort. The more rights the agreement grants in addition to a pure licence of an intellectual property right, the more likely there will be "warranty and other performance obligations".[52]

14.10.2 Contract Versus Tort

In addition to "product" liability under contract, there can be liability under tort. Tort does not require the existence of a contractual relationship (or an extended contractual relationship as granted by some legislation) to make a claim for breach of express or implied warranties. To avoid injured parties being left without a remedy, the tort law in various jurisdictions developed product liability remedies independent of contractual remedies for product deficiencies; these remedies vary from jurisdiction to jurisdiction. In essence, there are three competing philosophies for the imposition of a duty and the resulting liability for breach of that duty. In order of increasing obligation and resulting liabilities they are:

(a)   liability for failure to take reasonable care in manufacturing or producing a product to avoid injury to a person who buys that product where there is not a reasonable possibility of intermediate examination;[53]

(b)   liability if the loss or damage results from the failure to use state-of-the-art measures to avoid a defect;[54] or

(c)   liability if it is merely proven that there is a defect in the product and that the product caused the injury ("strict liability").

Various jurisdictions have adopted variations of these types of product liability. Which one applies may depend on the nature of the product, including its inherent dangerousness and, sometimes, whether the use is by a commercial entity or by a consumer who is an individual.

---

[51]   Nimmer and Krauthaus, *Commercial Law*, p. 20.

[52]   *Ibid.*

[53]   This is based on *McAlister (or Donoghue) v. Stevenson*, [1932] A.C. 562, at 599, 101 L.J.P.C. 119 (H.L.); see also *MacPherson v. Buick Motor Co.*, 217 N.Y. 382.

[54]   See Reid, *Limiting Risks*, p. 9. Use of state-of-the-art measures may be a defence to certain types of product liability claims in England.

14.10.3 Duties

The technology transfer agreement could go on to specify

(a)   the duties of care imposed on each party. In many cases the manu-
facturer/producer will be required to prove it used all of the modern
methods available to make the product safe;[55]

(b)   the duties to warn users and, where appropriate "learned intermedi-
aries"[56] of inherent risks and damages. This duty can be described
as follows:

> The duty to warn is a continuing duty, requiring manufacturers to warn
> not only of dangers known at the time of sale, but also of dangers discov-
> ered after the product has been sold and delivered: . . . All warnings must
> be reasonably communicated, and must clearly describe any specific dan-
> gers that arise from the ordinary use of the product: . . .
>
> The rationale for the manufacturer's duty to warn can be traced to the
> "neighbour principle", which lies at the heart of the law of negligence,
> and was set down in its classic form by Lord Atkin in *Donoghue v.
> Stevenson.* . . . When manufacturers place products into the flow of com-
> merce, they create a relationship of reliance with consumers, who have
> far less knowledge than the manufacturers concerning the dangers inher-
> ent in the use of the products, and are therefore put at risk if the product is
> not safe. The duty to warn serves to correct the knowledge imbalance
> between manufacturers and consumers by alerting consumers to any dan-
> gers and allowing them to make informed decisions concerning the safe
> use of the product.[57]

If the consumer is being advised or assisted in the use of the product
by someone who can be described as a "learned intermediary," such
as a doctor in the case of breast implants, there is a duty on the manufacturer to warn that intermediary so that the intermediary can
behave in a "learned" fashion. Warning the learned intermediary can
be in addition, or in substitution,[58] to warning the consumer, depending on the circumstances.

(c)   the duties to provide a user manual designed and written to be under-
standable to the normal user; and

(d)   warnings to the users to have the product maintained only in accordance with the user manual and by an authorized service provider.

---

[55]   See Wright and Linden, *Tort Law*, p. 16-61, quoting Professor Plant in (1957), 24 Tenn. L. Rev. 938.
[56]   For example, see *Hollis v. Dow Corning Corp.* (1996), 14 B.C.L.R. (3d) 1, 129 D.L.R. (4th) 609,
[1996] 2 W.W.R. 77, 190 N.R. 241, 67 B.C.A.C. 1, 27 C.C.L.T. (2d) 1, 111 W.A.C. 1 (S.C.C.).
[57]   *Ibid.*, p. 618 (D.L.R.).
[58]   *Ibid.*, p. 622 (D.L.R.).

Chapter 15

LEGAL REMEDIES —
CONTRACT AND TORT

*Men's actions are so diverse and infinite that it is impossible to make
any general laws which may aptly meet with every particular and not
fail in some circumstances.[1]*

NATURE OF REMEDIES

15.1 Introduction

The purpose of this chapter is to set out the legal remedies that are available in the
event of a breach of a contractual or tortious duty. It is important that the negotiators
of a technology transfer agreement be aware of these remedies when allocating risks
of breaches of duties and deciding on the appropriate remedies.[2] The negotiators
must examine how these basic remedial principles have been applied in their jurisdictions. The remedies that are appropriate to any particular case may depend on the
nature of the breach. Breach of duties to deliver acceptable technology, to pay royalties when due, or to restrict competitive activities require different remedies.

15.2 Available Remedies

Before the parties negotiate an allocation of risk of liability arising out of a
breach of contractual or tortious duty, they should be aware of the various remedies that are available. Some of these are:

(a)   injunctions — an injunction is an order prohibiting a party from
engaging in specified conduct. Injunctions are granted in the discretion of the court; injunctions can be either granted for an interim
period or granted permanently. To obtain an injunction, the plaintiff
must be able to show that there is a serious issue to be tried, that its
claim is not frivolous or vexatious, that it has the rights it is claiming
to have and that its rights are being infringed in some fashion. Next,
the court will consider whether the defendant's conduct is causing
irreparable claim to the plaintiff. Irreparable harm is literally harm for

---

[1]   Lord Ellesmere in *Pearl of Oxford's Case* (1615), 1 Ret. Ch. 1, at 6.
[2]   Remedies for infringement of intellectual property rights will be discussed in Chapter 17.

which an award of money can provide no adequate recompense. In deciding whether to grant an interim injunction, a court will consider whether the balance of convenience in general favours the plaintiff or favours the preservation of the *status quo* until the final disposition of the action. The "balance of convenience" takes into account such issues as whether it would cause greater hardship to grant or refuse the injunction. Injunctions are appropriate where damages are not an adequate remedy because the wrong is continuing;

(b)   Anton Piller Order — this is a somewhat Draconian order derived from a case of that name that came before the House of Lords. It requires the defendant to open his or her doors to the plaintiff. The plaintiff may then search and seize offending material and pertinent books and records as a result of an order obtained without notice to the defendant. The purpose of such an order is to provide a quick and efficient means of recovering infringing material and of discovering the sources from which the material has been supplied and the persons to whom they are distributed before those concerned have had time to destroy or conceal them. The essence of the success of this remedy is surprise; the defendant does not have time to destroy the incriminating evidence. The grounds for such an order are an extremely strong *prima facie* case and very serious damage, potential or actual, to the applicant; there must be convincing, concrete, factual evidence that the defendants have in their possession such incriminating evidence. This order is often used in copyright infringement cases in countries, such as the United Kingdom and Canada, where the judicial decisions are influenced by the judicial House of Lords;

(c)   damages arising directly out of the breach of duty;

(d)   damages that are incidental to the breach;

(e)   damages that are consequential to the breach, including economic loss of profits;

(f)   punitive or exemplary damages;

(g)   aggravated damages;

(h)   costs — when authorized by law, the court can award costs against the losing party to compensate the successful party for its litigation costs;

(i)   interest — under the appropriate circumstances, the court can award interest on the damages that were assessed;

(j)   right to reject.

15.3 Direct Damages

The basic purpose of an award of damages "is to put the party complaining, so far as it can be done in money, in the position the party would have occupied if the wrong had not been done".[3] Under Canadian law, the plaintiff must establish

---

[3]   S.M. Wadams, "The General Principles of the Law of Damages", *Law of Remedies*, Special Lectures of the Law Society of Upper Canada, 1995, p. 15, at 15 (hereinafter "Waddam's 'General Principles'").

that it has suffered a loss and that the loss was caused by the defendant's wrong. The loss must not be too remote; it must be a loss that could reasonably have been contemplated by the parties on entering into the contract or that was reasonably foreseeable at the time of the occurrence of the tortious act. The Canadian courts are very reluctant to award damages for economic losses that are considered too remote. One component of direct or compensatory damages on a failure to deliver acceptable technology is the cost of obtaining acceptable substitute technology, if that is available.[4] If substitute technology is not available then the market value of the non-delivered technology valued as promised will have to be determined, and that value less the unpaid contract price will establish the quantum of damages.

15.4 Incidental Damages

The injured party may be able to recover damages that are incidental to curing the breach. These are out-of-pocket expenses; in the sale of goods context they include expenses incurred in the receipt, inspection and transportation of the goods, and expenses incurred in procuring substitute goods.[5] There may be a right to incidental damages, even if not specifically provided in applicable legislation, as a result of common law.[6]

15.5 Consequential Damages for Economic Loss

The Canadian courts have great difficulty in deciding what damages for economic loss are permitted. They are concerned about the remoteness of the economic losses and the possibility of opening a "floodgate" of lawsuits. In the United States, consequential damages are a matter of course.[7] From the point of view of the transferor of technology,

> incidental and consequential damages pose the greatest single threat that can flow from ineffective warranty disclaimers [and limitations on liability clauses]. One of the problems posed by such damages is that they bear no relationship to the cost of the [technology]. In addition, [the transferor] may have little or no idea of the nature of use and abuse to which customers [and licensees] may subject the [technology]. Under these circumstances, it is frequently difficult to form even a reasonably accurate estimate of potential damages.[8]

---

[4]   See the *Uniform Commercial Code*, §§2-708(1) and 2-706 (hereinafter U.C.C.), *per* Raymond T. Nimmer and Patricia A. Krauthaus, *Commercial Law of License Contracts*, September 9, 1993 (unpublished), p. 40 (hereinafter "Nimmer and Krauthaus, *Commercial Law*") and the *Sale of Goods Act*, R.S.A. 1980, c. S-2, s. 51.

[5]   U.C.C. §2-715 and D.C. Toedt III, ed., *Licensing Law Handbook 1987* (New York: Clark Boardman Co. Ltd.), p. 5-30 (hereinafter "Toedt, *Licensing Law Handbook 1987*").

[6]   Nimmer and Krauthaus, *Commercial Law*, p. 44, and see the Report on Sale of Goods, Ontario Law Reform Commission, Vol. 1 (1979), p. 420 (hereinafter "Ontario Law Reform Commission Report"). See also Waddams "General Principles," p. 9.

[7]   U.C.C., Article 2.

[8]   Toedt, *Licensing Law Handbook 1987*, p. 5-32, referring to software.

Indeed, the transferor could be liable for damages amounting to many times the amounts paid by the licensee and many times the profit the transferor could hope to derive from the technology transfer transaction;[9] all of this may occur without any "form of moral culpability" or negligence as a result of strict liability arising out of breach of warranty.[10]

15.6 Costs

In the United States, in suits based on contract or tort, costs incurred by the successful party are not normally recoverable from the losing party. In Canada, costs are recoverable, but the award usually covers only a portion of actual costs. A technology transfer agreement could provide that all costs incurred to enforce an agreement must be paid by the losing party; this clause should be designed to award costs where costs would not otherwise be awarded and to increase costs from the level normally awarded by a Canadian court to the full amount of costs incurred.

CONTRACTUAL LIMITATIONS ON LIABILITY

15.7 Pre-agreed Allocations of Risks

The negotiators to the technology transfer agreement should decide in advance what remedies would be available to each other for a breach of contractual or tortious duty owed by one party to the other. These remedies may very well be different than those available for an infringement of intellectual property rights or a breach of duty to maintain secrecy.

Strategies: The following are some pre-agreed allocations of losses arising from a breach:

    (1)   the fixing of a dollar amount for the maximum damages. This must be a reasonable pre-estimate of these damages; it should not be too high, as it may constitute a penalty, and not too low, as it may be set aside as unreasonable or unconscionable;[11]

    (2)   the pre-agreed estimate of damages shall exclude the application of all other remedies. If that is done, the negotiators might want to consider a back-up remedy in case that pre-agreed estimate is held to be invalid; and

    (3)   the software licence can provide that the pre-agreed estimate of damages shall equal the aggregate of the amounts paid by the licensee through the date of the breach (assuming that the licensor is the breaching party);

    (4)   the disclaimer of liability for incidental or consequential damages; and

    (5)   the disclaimer of punitive or exemplary damages.

---

[9]   Adapted from Ontario Law Reform Commission Report, p. 486.

[10] *Ibid.*, p. 46.

[11] See Toedt, *Licensing Law Handbook 1987*, pp. 6-31 and 6-32 and Pegi A. Groundwater, "General Considerations in Drafting Software Licenses," a paper presented at the Licensing Executives Society Annual Meeting, October 26, 1992.

15.8 Repair or Replace

Where equipment is provided with the technology transfer, a remedy for defects could be a requirement to repair or replace the defective components of the equipment. For many licensees, the important feature will not be that "there are no problems with the product, but that any problems that do occur will be corrected".[12] The warranty to repair or replace may permit a disclaimer of remedies for the implied warranties or merchantability or fitness for a particular purpose, but, perhaps, only to the extent that such repair or replacement, if made, will cure the defect.[13]

Strategies:

(1) *Always have a back-up remedy to cover the possibility that the "repair or replace" remedy fails its essential purpose[14] (or, as is referred to in some other jurisdictions, is "fundamentally breached").*

(2) *Consider stating in the agreement that the parties agree that equitable relief, such as restraining orders, is appropriate under the circumstances, in order to encourage the courts to exercise their discretion and grant these types of orders.*

(3) *Contractually provide for the recovery of full direct costs externally expended by the successful party to a lawsuit.*

SUIT FROM A THIRD PARTY

15.9 Risk of Third-party Law Suit

The allocation of risks between the parties will not affect the rights of third parties who are able to sue in tort (negligence and product liability).[15] The parties could agree which one of them is to assume:

(a) responsibility for third-party claims, perhaps allocated according to nature or quantum; and

(b) responsibility for insuring against third-party claims, perhaps with the insurer having no right to claim over against the other party.

An indemnity may have economic meaning only if it is backed up by insurance or some other form of security.

---

[12]   Toedt, *Licensing Law Handbook 1987*, p. 5-8.

[13]   *Ibid.*, p. 6-26.

[14]   *Ibid.*, p. 6-27.

[15]   See §14.10.2 of this text.

Chapter 16

INTELLECTUAL PROPERTY REMEDIES

16.1 Introduction

In this chapter, special remedies available as a result of infringement of intellectual property rights are reviewed. These remedies are specialized variations of the remedies for breach of contractual or tortious duty that were discussed in Chapter 15. These remedies will be of interest to negotiators of a technology transfer agreement as they allocate the risk that the transferred technology infringes rights possessed by others as well as the duty to prosecute infringers of the rights to the technology that is the subject-matter of the technology transfer agreement, together with the right to share in any resulting damages (awarded either in their favour or against them). The remedies vary depending on the type of intellectual property rights involved and the jurisdiction in which the judicial action is conducted. Remedies for infringement of intellectual property rights may be in addition to any contractual or tortious remedy that is concurrently available.

16.2 What Constitutes an Infringement?

For a discussion of the activities that constitute an infringement of intellectual property rights refer to Chapters 3 to 6 of this text.

PATENT INFRINGEMENT

16.3 Damages Provided by the U.S. Patent Act

Section 284 of the U.S. *Patent Act*[1] allows the following:

    (i)   damages adequate to compensate for the infringement, i.e., "computed so as to place the patentee in the position that it would have been in had the infringement not occurred",[2]

    (ii)   damages shall not be less than a "reasonable royalty for the use of the invention by the infringer" (note that this establishes a minimum; royalties are not the only standard of measuring damages.);

---

[1]   35 U.S.C.

[2]   Raymond T. Nimmer and Patricia A. Krauthaus, *Commercial Law of License Contracts*, September 9, 1993 (unpublished), p. 34 (hereinafter "Nimmer and Krauthaus, *Commercial Law*").

 (iii) the court may increase the damages up to three times the amount found or assessed (*i.e.*, trouble damages); and

 (iv) interest and costs as fixed by the court.

16.3.1 Loss of Profits

One method of determining damages is by the amount of lost profits that the patentee suffered. To establish lost profits, the patentee must prove what the profits would have been "but-for" the infringement.[3] The leading U.S. case of *Panduit Corp v. Stahlin Bros. Fibre Works*[4] sets out "four criteria, all of which the patentee must prove if the remedy is to apply, namely: (1) Demand for the patented product; (2) Absence of acceptable non-infringing substitutes; (3) Manufacturing and marketing capability to exploit the demand; and (4) The amount of profit he would have made".[5]

16.3.2 Royalties

Instead of loss of profits as the measure of damages, a fair royalty rate can be used to establish damages. The leading U.S. case, *Georgia-Pacific Corp. v. United States Plywood-Champion Papers, Inc.*,[6] sets out factors to be used by a court for establishing a fair royalty rate. Goldscheider[7] lists 13 of these factors:

1. royalty rates generally available to licensees of the holder of the infringed patent;

2. royalty rates paid by the infringer for comparable technology;

3. the nature and scope of licences giving rise to royalties used for comparison purposes, *e.g.*, do not compare royalties payable for exclusive licences to royalties payable for non-exclusive licences;

4. the practice of the patentee not to grant licences to anyone, instead keeping the technology for its own exclusive use;

5. the commercial relationship between the parties, *e.g.*, are they competitors?

6. the extent to which the infringer gained by marketing the infringing technology in conjunction with other products or services offered by the infringer, *e.g.*, "derivative or convoyed sales";[8]

7. the remaining duration of the patent and the duration of the "licence" to the infringer;

---

[3] Robert Goldscheider, "Litigation Backgrounder for Licensing", Les Nouvelles, Journal of the Licensing Executives Society, Vol. XXIX, No. 1, March 1994, p. 20, at 21 (hereinafter "Goldscheider 'Litigation Backgrounder'").

[4] 575 F.2d 1152, at 1156 (6th Cir. 1978).

[5] Goldscheider, "Litigation Backgrounder," p. 23.

[6] 318 F. Supp. 1116 (1970).

[7] Goldscheider, "Litigation Backgrounder," p. 23.

[8] *Ibid.* See also *Prism Hospital Software Inc. v. Hospital Medical Records Institute* (1994), 97 B.C.L.R. (2d) 201, [1994] 10 W.W.R. 305, 18 B.L.R. (2d) 1, 57 C.P.R. (3d) 129 (S.C.).

8. "the established profitability of the product made under the patent, its commercial success, and its current popularity";[9]
9. the nature and benefits derived from the patented inventions;
10. "the extent to which the infringer has made use of the [patented] invention and . . . the value of that use";[10]
11. the traditional profit margin;
12. the portion of the profit attributable to the infringing invention;
13. the amount that the patentee and the infringer would have agreed on
    (a) at the time the infringement commenced;
    (b) if both at had been reasonably and voluntarily trying to reach an agreement;
    (c) giving a reasonable profit margin to the infringer;
    (d) giving a reasonable reward to the patentee;[11]
    (e) considering the relative bargaining position of the parties;
    (f) the extent to which the infringement prevented the patentee from using or selling the invention; and
    (g) the market to be tapped.[12]

Goldscheider[13] suggests that three additional factors were added by a judge in his jury address in *Honeywell v. Minolta*:[14]

14. the relative bargaining positions of Honeywell and Minolta;
15. the extent to which the infringement prevented Honeywell from using or selling the invention; and
16. the market to be tapped.

16.4 The Canadian Patent Act and Damages

To be entitled to claim damages for patent infringement, a patent holder (or someone claiming under the patent holder) must show that the infringement actually caused the loss.[15] Section 55 of the Canadian *Patent Act*[16] outlines the remedies for infringement by stating that any person who infringes a patent is

    (a) liable to the patentee and to all persons claiming under the patentee for all damages sustained by the patentee or by any such person, after the grant of the patent, by reason of the infringement; and

---

9   Goldscheider "Litigation Backgrounder," p. 23.

10 *Ibid.*

11 The four factors, (a)–(d), are adapted from Goldscheider's list in the discussion of the *Georgia-Pacific* standards (p. 23).

12 The three factors, (e)–(g), are adapted from Goldscheider's comments on *Honeywell v. Minolta*, Civil Nos. 87-4847, 88-1624 (D.N.J. January 28, 1992) (p. 23).

13 At p. 23.

14 *Supra* note 12, p. 69.

15 George Francis Takach, *Patents: A Canadian compendium of law and practice* (Edmonton: Juriliber, 1993), p. 145, Section 10.34 (hereinafter "Takach, *Patents*").

16 *Patent Act*, R.S.C. 1985, c. P-4, s. 55 (rep. & sub. R.S.C. 1985, c. 33 (3rd Supp.), s. 21).

(b)   liable to pay reasonable compensation to the patentee and to all persons claiming under the patentee for any damages sustained by the patentee or by any such person by reason of any act on his part, after the application for the patent became open to the inspection of the public . . . and before the grant of the patent, that would have constituted an infringement of the patent if the patent had been granted on the day the application became open to the inspection of the public . . . .

16.4.1 Loss of Profits

If a Canadian court is having difficulty calculating the amount of the patentee's lost profits, the patent holder may be able to claim an amount equal to the net profits the infringer made from the infringement.[17] To this end, the patent holder may be able to claim for sales to all customers of the infringer, even to a customer who would not have purchased from the patent holder.[18] In addition, the patent holder may be able to claim for some loss of normal business, if it is proved that the loss was caused by the infringement.[19]

16.4.2 Royalties

Similar to the United States, royalties will be awarded in Canada where it is difficult to prove the loss of profits to the patent holder. The amount of royalties will be based on either (1) the amount the infringer is liable to pay under a licence agreement, or (2) in the absence of a licence agreement, an amount that is established as an equivalent market value for a licence of the subject-matter.[20]

16.4.3 Other Remedies

Other possible remedies for infringement are an interim injunction,[21] a final injunction, an order to deliver the infringing products and destroy them, interest, legal costs and the potential for punitive damages.[22]

---

[17] Takach, *Patents*, p. 145, Section 10.34(a), quoting *Collette v. Lasnier* (1886), 13 S.C.R. 563, at 576. This remedy is similar to an accounting of profits, which also may be available where there is a very close relationship between the infringer and the patent holder, such as that of principal and agent. See Takach, *Patents*, p. 147, Section 10.36.

[18] *Ibid.*, p. 146, Section 10.34(a), quoting *Electric Chain Co. v. Art Metal Works Inc.*, [1933] S.C.R. 581, at 589, [1933] 4 D.L.R. 21.

[19] *Ibid.*, p. 146, Section 10.34(c).

[20] *Ibid.*, p. 146, Section 10.34(b), quoting *Colonial Fastener Ltd. v. Lightning Fastener Co.*, [1937] S.C.R. 36, at 45, [1937] 1 D.L.R. 21.

[21] An interim injunction is used to stop an infringer from doing an activity before the case can get to court, whereas a final injunction is an order made by the court in the disposition of the case.

[22] The leading Canadian case on punitive damages is *Lubrizol Corp. v. Imperial Oil Ltd.* (1992), 45 C.P.R. (3d) 449 (Fed. C.A.), where the Court held that punitive damages may be awarded in cases of blatant infringement.

COPYRIGHT

16.5 The U.S. Position

The holder of copyright is entitled to recover the actual damages the holder has suffered as a result of the infringement, together with the profits of the infringer that were not included in those actual damages and, in any event, at the minimum statutory damages. Note that there is a dual award — the actual damages and the profits of the infringer. The recovery of actual damages is the normal standard for a breach of contract; the addition of the amount that the infringer's profits exceed those actual damages is intended to "prevent the infringer from unfairly benefitting from a wrongful act".[23] It is up to the infringer to establish the costs and, thus, make the proper deduction from revenues.[24]

16.5.1 Statutory Damages

The U.S. *Copyright Act* allows a copyright owner to elect, at any time before a final judgment is granted, to receive an amount not less than $250 and not more than $10,000 per action. The actual amount awarded will be at the discretion of the court[25] and may be varied depending on whether the infringer knew of the copyright and who has the burden of proving the infringement.[26]

16.6 The Canadian Position

A recent Canadian case, *Prism Hospital Software Inc. v. Hospital Medical Records Institute*, sets out the various remedies available on infringement of copyright.[27] In that case, Prism Hospital, the plaintiff, licensed its software to Hospital Medical Records Institute, the defendant, for distribution to Canadian hospitals, permitting the defendant to modify the software. Not being satisfied with its role as a distributor, the defendant released its own software in place of the plaintiff's software. The "replacement" software copied substantial portions of the plaintiff's software, errors and all. The Court stated that the remedies "given should be tailored to attempt to place Prism back in the position [it] would have been in but for the breaches of contract and copyright".[28] The orders granted by the Court in the *Prism* case included:

(i)   a declaration that the defendant's software was an infringing work;

(ii)   an injunction prohibiting further copying of the plaintiff's work and *of the infringing work*;

---

[23]   Nimmer and Krauthaus, *Commercial Law,* p. 33.

[24]   *Ibid.*, pp. 33 –34.

[25]   U.S. *Copyright Act,* 17 U.S.C. §504(1).

[26]   If the infringement was wilful and the copyright owner had the burden of proving this, and does so, the award may be as high as $50,000. If the infringer did not know of the copyright, the award may be as low as $100. See the U.S. *Copyright Act,* 17 U.S.C. §504(2).

[27]   (1994), 97 B.C.L.R. (2d) 201, [1994] 10 W.W.R. 305, 18 B.L.R. (2d)1, 57 C.P.R. (3d) 129.

[28]   *Ibid.*, at 154 (B.L.R.).

(iii)   withdrawal of the defendant's software from the installed sites;

(iv)   delivery up to the plaintiff of all infringing copies in the defendant's possession, except as necessary to provide continued maintenance during the transitional period;

(v)   delivery up to the plaintiff of all necessary information to permit conversion of all user's data to the plaintiff's software;

(vi)   costs associated with changing the user sites from the defendant's software to the plaintiff's software; and

(vii) immediate cessation of the marketing of the defendant's software.

The injunction permitted the defendant to maintain the software during the transitional period.

16.6.1 Canadian Compensatory Damages for Infringement of Copyright

Section 35 of the *Canadian Copyright Act*[29] is very similar to section 504 of the U.S. *Copyright Act*, with the exception of statutory damages. It provides:

> 35(1) Where any person infringes the copyright in any work that is protected under this Act, the person is liable to pay such damages to the owner of the right infringed as he may have suffered due to the infringement, and in addition thereto such part of the profits that the infringer has made from the infringement as the court may decide to be just and proper.

The Court in the *Prism* case notes that the "damages described are cumulative not alternative".[30] The "burden of proof is on the plaintiff to show what its losses are".[31]

TRADEMARKS

16.7 Introduction

As mentioned in Chapter 5, trademarks are within both federal and provincial/ state jurisdiction. This section on remedies will be restricted to remedies under the Canadian and U.S. *Trademark Acts*.[32]

16.8 Canadian Remedies

The remedies for infringement of a Canadian trademark are Anton Piller relief, interim and permanent injunctions, damages, accounting for profits, delivery up or disposal of infringement materials and prohibition of importation of products bearing an infringing trademark.[33] In Canada, the plaintiff can have compensa-

---

[29]   R.S.C. 1985, c. C-42.

[30]   *Prism, supra* note 27, at 158 (B.L.R.).

[31]   *Ibid.*, at 157.

[32]   *Trade-marks Act*, R.S.C. 1985, c. I-13, (hereinafter *Trade-marks Act* (Canada)) and U.S. *Trade-mark Act*, 15 U.S.C.

[33]   *Trade-marks Act* (Canada), s. 53 (rep. & sub. S.C. 1993, c. 44, s. 234).

tion only for the loss the plaintiff sustained or an accounting of profits earned by the defendant, but not both.[34] The plaintiff is not to be better off because of the infringement; the plaintiff is only to be restored to the same position it would have been in if the wrong had not occurred.[35]

16.9 U.S. Remedies

The U.S. *Trademark Act* provides that the plaintiff shall be entitled, subject to certain provisions and subject to principles of equity,[36]

> to recover (1) defendant's profits, (2) any damages sustained by the plaintiff, and (3) the costs of the action. The court shall assess such profits and damages or cause the same to be assessed under its direction. In assessing profits, the plaintiff shall be required to prove defendant's sales only; defendant must prove all elements of cost or deduction claimed. In assessing damages, the court may enter judgement according to the circumstances of the case, for any sum above the amount found as actual damages, not exceeding three times such amount. If the court shall find that the amount of recovery based on profits is either inadequate or excessive the court may, in its discretion, enter judgement for such sum as the court shall find to be just, according to the circumstances of the case. Such sum in either of the above circumstances shall constitute compensation and not a penalty. The court in exceptional cases may award reasonable attorney fees to the prevailing party. In certain provisions the court must enter judgement for three times such profit or damages, whichever is greater, together with reasonable attorney's fee.

TRADE SECRETS

16.10 No Single Law

In both Canada and the United States, no single piece of legislation covers trade secrecy.[37] In the United States, many states have adopted some version of the *Uniform Trade Secrets Act*, which separately provide remedies appropriate for those states. None of the common-law provinces of Canada has passed any legislation relating to trade secrets. The remedies, therefore, will vary depending on the locality.

16.10.1 Contract Law versus Trade Secrecy Law versus Trust Law

In trade secrecy cases, the courts have drawn on three areas of the law. They will impose remedies arising out of any contract between the parties, they may rely on a separate duty of trade secrecy or they may find a fiduciary duty and apply trust law.[38] In some states, these areas of the law provide mutually exclusive

---

[34] David J.A. Cairns, *The Remedies For Trademark Infringement* (Toronto: Carswell, 1988), p. 144.

[35] *Ibid.*

[36] Section 35, 15 U.S.C. §1117.

[37] See Chapter 6 of this text.

[38] See the difficulty that the Supreme Court of Canada had in the *Lac Minerals* case. The judges disagreed about the appropriate causes of action and remedies. See *International Corona Resources v. LAC Minerals Ltd.*, [1989] 2 S.C.R. 574, 69 O.R. (2d) 287, 36 O.A.C. 57, 61 D.L.R. (4th) 14, 101 N.R. 239, 44 B.L.R. 1, 26 C.P.R. (3d) 97, 35 E.T.R. 1, 6 R.P.R. (2d) 1.

remedies. The remedies available in trade secrecy cases, in principle, mirror those available under contract or tort laws.

(a)   injunctions — the injunction could be designed to prevent a continued use or disclosure of the trade secret and even to extend to the production of the resulting product by any process and not just the secret process.[39] The duration of the injunction may be the time "it would have taken defendant to independently develop or reverse engineer the technology";[40]

(b)   damages equal to the loss suffered by the plaintiff;[41]

(c)   damages equal to the profits unjustly received by the defendant;[42]

(d)   a combination of damages lost by the plaintiff and new profits unjustly received by the defendant (which is comparable to the standard of damages allowed for copyright infringement).[43] A Canadian court is unlikely to allow such a double recovery;

(e)   a reasonable royalty rate — particularly valuable when the first two approaches will not produce a "logical amount of damages"[44] drawing analogy to patent cases. Litigation Backgrounder favours the reasonable royalty standard and provides the following guideline:

> In calculating what a fair licensing price would have been had the parties agreed, the trier of fact should consider such factors as the resulting and foreseeable changes in the parties' competitive posture; the prices past purchasers or licensees may have paid; the total value of the secret to the plaintiff, including the plaintiff's development costs and the importance of the secret to the plaintiff's business; the nature and extent of the use the defendant intended for the secret; and finally whatever other unique factors in the particular case which might have affected the parties' agreement, such as the ready availability of alternative processes.[45]

TIME LIMITATIONS ON REMEDIES

16.11 Take Action in Time

All remedies available to a patent, copyright, trademark or trade secret holder are subject to limitations relating to the passage of time. These limitations may be a

---

[39]   See *General Electric Co. v. Chien Min-Sung*, 843 F. Supp. 776 (D. Mass. 1994).

[40]   See American Bar Asociation, Section on the Intellectual Property Law, *Annual Report* 1994–95, p. 343 (hereinafter "ABA *Annual Report*, 94/95").

[41]   See Goldscheider "Litigation Backgrounder", p. 28.

[42]   *Ibid.*

[43]   The *Restatement of Law (Third)*, Unfair Competition, Preliminary drafts 1 to 3 indicated that the plaintiff should be entitled only to the greater of the two numbers and not to both of the two numbers. The *Uniform Trade Secrets Act*, however, provides that "a plaintiff can recover both damages for the actual loss as well as unjust enrichment, so long as the unjust enrichment loss is not taken into account in computing damages for actual loss". See ABA *Annual Report*, 94/95, p. 352.

[44]   Goldscheider "Litigation Backgrounder," p. 28.

[45]   *Ibid.*, quoting from *University Computing Co. v. Lykes-Youngstown Corp.*, 504 F.2d 519 (5th Cir. 1974).

result of statutory provision[46] or a result of common-law principles.[47] For example, the holder may be "estopped," or, in other words, prevented, from using a certain remedy because the holder knew the infringer was committing the activity and did nothing about it, or the holder may possibly be limited by "laches" because the holder waited too long to take the action.

NEGOTIATION ISSUES

16.12 Allocate Risks of Product Failure

When allocating which party bears the risk of infringement of third-party intellectual property rights, consider:

(a) Implied warranties of title/against infringement — Under both the *Sale of Goods* legislation and the *Uniform Commercial Code (U.C.C.)*, there are implied warranties of title, *i.e.*, the seller of a good implies it has the right to pass title of that good to the buyer. Additionally, in the *U.C.C.* but not in the *Sale of Goods* legislation, there is an implied warranty against infringement. Can a warranty against infringement be implied either from the common law or from the use of the word "title"?

Strategies:

(1) Out of prudence, a negotiated technology transfer agreement should provide express warranties of title/against infringement appropriate for the transaction and should expressly disclaim any implied warranties.

(2) In Canada, a prudent negotiator should not assume that a warranty of "title" does not include a warranty against "infringement".

(b) Express warranties of title/against infringement — It may be beyond the knowledge of many parties whether there has been an infringement on their part. In the case of copyright, was the creator truly employed? Was the relationship within any statutory work-for-hire rules? Is there any possibility of joint ownership? Did the creator include only original work or include something copied from another source? Instead of providing an express warranty that there is no infringement, the parties might provide a warranty that the party has no knowledge of an infringement and include a separate covenant imposing full responsibility on one party for defence of infringement and any damage suffered. Thus, the party is not

---

[46] Most jurisdictions maintain a *Statute of Limitations* that governs the time within which an action can be commenced. See, for example, the analysis of the Alberta *Limitations of Actions Act*, R.S.A. 1980, c. L-15, in *Lubrizol v. Imperial Oil, supra* note 22, at 475.

[47] See *Cadbury Schweppes Inc. v. FBI Foods Ltd.* (1994), 1 B.C.L.R. (3d) 258, [1995] 4 W.W.R. 104, 59 C.P.R. (3d) 129 (S.C.); additional reasons (1994), 93 B.C.L.R. (2d) 318, [1994] 8 W.W.R. 727 (S.C.), where the Court held that the owner of a trade secret for "Clamato Juice" was not entitled to an injuction due to the passage of time, but was still in time to claim other remedies.

providing a warranty that it cannot verify, and is avoiding a suggestion that such a warranty was fundamental to the transaction and was fraudulently given.[48]

(c)   Scope of Warranty and Defence/Indemnity Obligation — Some of the factors that negotiators to a technology transfer agreement might consider when allocating risk of infringement are:

    (i)   territorial restrictions on the indemnity; even if the licence is world-wide, should the indemnity be effective only for the jurisdictions where the bulk of the commerce is expected?

    (ii)   which party receives the greatest benefit from the exclusivity granted or retained by the technology transfer agreement. If the technology transfer is exclusive, that party may be the licensee; if the technology transfer is non-exclusive, that party may be the transferor.

(d)   The allocation of risk of infringement if the licensee has been granted a licence only in one of many fields of use, and other fields of use have been reserved to the transferor or its licensees.

(e)   Which party should bear the risk of a patent issuing after the agreement has been signed, the details of the patent application not having been previously disclosed (either as a result of issuance or as a result of disclosure under the 18-month rule).[49]

(f)   Will the transferor have the right to modify or replace the allegedly infringing technology with non-infringing material? What criteria will be used for the functional and performance specifications of the substituted technology to make sure that the qualities of the transferred technology are maintained?

(g)   Will either party have the right to enter into a licence to obtain continued use of the infringing material; can that licence be obtained only when infringement has been established, or when the claim is first made or somewhere in between, perhaps based on an infringement opinion from qualified legal counsel?

(h)   Who will have the right to conduct the defence and who will have the right to settle? Consider the following:

    (i)   who will decide the merits and costs of a settlement?

    (ii)   the economics of replacing or modifying the allegedly infringing technology so that it becomes non-infringing but has substantially similar capabilities to the allegedly infringing technology.

    (iii) the economics and uncertainties of litigation;

    (iv)   potential non-litigious methods of settlement of any such claim;

---

[48]   For example, see American Bar Association, Section on Patent, Trademark and Copyright, Committee on Computer Programs, *Draft Model Software License Provisions*, Committee Chair: D.C. Toedt III of Arnold, White & Durke, Houston, Texas, Article 7.

[49]   See §3.16.1 of this text.

(v)   the seriousness of the alleged infringement;

(vi) the strength of the patent infringed;

(vii) the importance of the patent infringed to the business of each of the parties;

(viii) the expected costs of the proceedings;

(ix) the difficulty of obtaining the necessary evidence to support the proceedings; and

(x)   the risk of any third-party infringer making a serious challenge to the validity of a patent or patent claim.[50]

(i)   Do the royalties continue after infringement is alleged, but before infringement is proven?

(j)   Which party will maintain documents in anticipation of litigation, in accordance with pre-agreed specifications of quality and type?[51]

(k) What conditions, if any, apply to protection offered against infringement?

    (i)   prompt notification[52] (Is there really an essential correlation between prompt notification and right to an indemnity?);

    (ii) the indemnitor has the right to have conduct of the action;

    (iii) the indemnitor has the sole right to settle; and

    (iv) infringement did not result from misuse or a combination of uses that separately were non-infringing.

(l)   What limitations on exposure to liability will be pre-agreed?

---

[50] See also ABA *Annual Report*, 94/95, p. 389, for patent litigation strategies.

[51] See ABA *Annual Report*, 94/95, p. 389.

[52] American Intellectual Property Law Association, 1994, 1995, "A Guide to Patent Law Harmonization: Towards a More Inventor-friendly Worldwide Patent System", p. 122 E.

Chapter 17

DISPUTE RESOLUTION

Currently, much creative experimentation is taking place with the aim of improving dispute resolution processes. The experimentation embraces innovative dispute resolution methods, new models, new models of dispute resolution, and variations and combinations of these methods and models.[1]

17.1 Introduction

Most parties to a technology transfer agreement are familiar with the traditional methods of dispute resolution: court proceedings and arbitration. As a result of concern over the cost and effectiveness of these traditional procedures, there is a movement to find alternative methods. These methods range from some form of negotiation, to the use of a mediator/facilitator, to some form of adjudicator.[2] The distinction between the separate methods is becoming blurred as parties try to combine the processes for their particular purposes, but always with the intent of producing a better result than could come from a normal court proceeding. Article 2022 of the North American Free Trade Agreement (NAFTA) provides that Canada, Mexico and the United States "shall, to the maximum extent possible, encourage and facilitate the use of arbitration and other means of alternative dispute resolution for the settlement of international and commercial disputes between private parties of the free trade area".

17.2 The Court Process

Court proceedings are attractive because they involve well-tested evidentiary rules and principles intended to produce just results. Since the cost of the courtrooms, reporters and judges is paid by the government, this method of dispute resolution is often the least costly of the alternatives (but occasionally excluding the cost of the result). Court proceedings often produce surprises including:

---

[1]   Alberta Law Reform Institute, "Civil Litigation: The Judicial Mini-Trial," Dispute Resolution Special Series, Discussion Paper No. 1, August 1993, p. 1 (hereinafter "Judicial Mini-Trial").

[2]   Tom Arnold, *A Vocabulary of ADR Procedures, Introduction to Patenting & Licensing*, Licensing Executive Society (U.S.A. and Canada), Inc., 1995 Manual (hereinafter "Arnold *Vocabulary*"), pp. 1–2. This material also appears in the manual *Technology Transfer 1996*, Licensing Executives Society (U.S.A. and Canada).

(a)   the expense of lawyers and expert witnesses in protracted court motions, discoveries, trial and appeals;

(b)   the allocation of business resources from revenue-producing efforts to the court proceedings;

(c)   the stress the court process puts on key witnesses who are also trying to carry on normal family/business activities;

(d)   the failure to establish at trial facts that previously were thought to be obvious;

(e)   the decisions of some juries; and

(f)   the fallibility of some judges, which may or may not result from inability to comprehend the factual/legal issues.[3]

17.3 Insert an Arbitration Clause

Instead of automatically inserting an arbitration clause, the negotiators to a technology transfer agreement might consider the broad spectrum of alternatives available to them. Alternative dispute resolution has produced not only a multitude of dispute resolution centres but also libraries of material on the topic. This chapter will merely try to acquaint the reader with some of the alternatives.

17.4 Progressive Management Involvement

If the parties have a similar management structure, it is often appropriate to require progressive management involvement before a dispute is referred to arbitration or court proceedings. The American Bar Association Draft Model Software Agreement[4] designates the three levels of management required to deal with a dispute and provides a time period for each level of management to deal with the dispute before the dispute moves on to the next level.[5] The levels of management and the time period could vary depending on the subject-matter of the dispute involved.

17.5 Negotiations in Good Faith

If progressive management involvement is not appropriate, the agreement could provide for an obligation to negotiate in good faith before the parties move to adjudication. Since "good faith" is often debatable, the agreement could either provide a short time period or permit any party to refer the matter to adjudication if it feels that "the good faith" negotiations are not proceeding to its satisfaction.

---

[3]   Adapted from Judicial Mini-Trial, p. 13.

[4]   American Bar Association, Section on Patent, Trademark and Copyright Law, Committee on Computer Programs, *Draft Model Software License Provisions*, Committee Chair: D.C. Toedt III of Arnold, White & Durke, Houston, Texas (hereinafter "ABA Draft Model Software Agreement").

[5]   ABA Draft Model Software Agreement, Section 1021.

17.6 Injunctive Relief

If immediate action to stop an activity that could have highly injurious results is necessary, the agreement could provide that the requirement to negotiate does not preclude the right to apply for an injunction or similar relief. If the arbitrators have the ability to grant injunctive relief that will be enforceable under the local law, the agreement could give the arbitrators the power to grant that relief. Interim injunctions as well as permanent injunctions must be contemplated. The availability of interim relief can be particularly valuable in many intellectual property contexts in order to stop irreparable harm to the interests of the owner of an intellectual property right. It is not uncommon, for example, to seek interim injunctive relief to prevent the marketing of a product that allegedly infringes a patent or a trademark, to prevent disclosure of trade secrets or to prevent destruction of evidence establishing that an intellectual property right is being infringed or assisting in quantifying damage done by infringing actions. In these cases, the lack of interim relief can cause damage that cannot be rectified or adequately compensated by subsequent determination on the merits of the dispute.[6]

17.7 Wise Counsel[7]

As an adjunct to good faith negotiations, some agreements contemplate referring specified issues to a panel consisting of "wise" individuals employed by the parties. The facts and arguments are placed informally before this panel. If the panel agrees, their decision will be binding on all parties. If the panel does not agree, the dispute can be referred to mediation or some form of adjudication. Instead of using a panel of individuals drawn from the parties, there could be a neutral and, perhaps, expert fact-finder, or someone who assumes the role of an ombudsman.

17.8 Mediation

Mediation works best when it is voluntarily selected by parties who want to resolve the dispute and to continue to do business together.[8] Mediation is a non-adjudicative process that facilitates settlement negotiations. The mediator acts as a facilitator and takes a very pro-active role in trying to facilitate communications between the parties, often shuttling back and forth between the parties who are occupying separate rooms.[9] Mediation allows the parties to maintain control over the proceedings by using a mediator of their choice with appropriate privacy in a process that encourages enhanced negotiations carried on in an informal atmosphere.[10] "Justice is not the mediator's primary

---

6   "Consultation document prepared by the International Bureau, Proposed WIPO Supplementary Emergency Interim Relief Rules," World Intellectual Property Organization, April 19, 1996.
7   See Arnold, *Vocabulary*, pp. 4–8.
8   *Ibid.*, p. 12.
9   *Ibid.*, pp. 10 –14.
10   Joanne Goss, "An Introduction to Alternative Dispute Resolution", Alberta Law Review, Vol. XXXIV, No. 1, October 1995, p. 1, at 9.

goal";[11] facilitating communication between the parties with the intent of producing a mutually acceptable resolution is the common goal.[12] Mediation is a "safe procedure"[13] that often produces timely and cost-effective results. Mediation is not effective

    (a)   if there is a severe power imbalance between the parties;

    (b)   where a party is in need of a legal precedent;

    (c)   where an individual in charge of the dispute resolution for one party wants to avoid ultimate responsibility and, thus, personally needs a decision from a mutual third party;

    (d)   where the parties distrust each other or there is no need for a continued relationship.[14]

17.9 Mediation and Arbitration (MED-ARB)

MED-ARB stands for some combination of mediation and arbitration.[15] If mediation fails, the technology transfer agreement could provide for an automatic transfer of the issue to arbitration, either before the individual(s) who served as mediator(s) or before new arbitrators who have not been exposed to the frank and full discussions that mediation is intended to encourage.

17.10 Private Mini-trials

There are two types of mini-trials — private and judicial. Private mini-trials involve presentation of facts and argument to the individuals who represent the parties and have the authority to settle. This procedure may be useful when the proceedings have progressed far enough to expose the majority of legal and factual issues, usually as a result of the discovery process in an adjudicative proceeding. The parties must be "committed to resolving the dispute with a minimum of expense, delay and disruption".[16] The neutral advisor in a private mini-trial usually does not take a pro-active role, as a mediator does, but can take on any role requested by the parties.[17]

> For settlement to occur, the persons present must have the authority to settle. In a private mini-trial, the case is presented to the parties themselves (the "principals") who receive "a crash course on the subject of the dispute". The principals "are responsible for hearing the presentations and making decisions for each party". The persons selected must have "positions of organizational authority sufficient to allow them to make unilateral decisions regarding the disputes". Furthermore, they must not have been "personally or closely involved" in any part of the dispute. They must

---

[11]   Arnold, *Vocabulary*, p. 11.

[12]   *Ibid.*

[13]   *Ibid.*

[14]   *Ibid.*, p. 14.

[15]   *Ibid.*, p. 17.

[16]   Judicial Mini-Trial, p. 16, quoting Edelman and Carr, "The 'Mini-Trial:' An Alternative Dispute Resolution Procedure" (1987), 42 The Arbitration Journal 7, at 11.

[17]   See Judicial Mini-Trial, pp. 2–3, for a list of possible roles that can be taken.

also "be prepared for some amount of second-guessing upon successful conclusion of a mini-trial" and "be of sufficient stature to withstand" pressures from within the organization. In addition to the qualities already identified, they "must possess the temperament and skills to negotiate a settlement fair and reasonable to both parties based on both the facts presented and on their background knowledge".[18]

17.11 Judicial Mini-trials

Instead of presenting the case to the parties, as is done in a private mini-trial, in a judicial mini-trial the case is presented to a judge or to someone acting like a judge, who is a neutral, "characteristically expert in the subject area . . . who initially presides over the proceedings and hears evidence partially in a passive role like a judge though also cross-examining points and commenting on evidence and arguments here and there to put them in perspective, and who presents a conclusion without prior private conversation with any party or party representative (on this point different from mediation)".[19] Like the private mini-trial, the intent is to produce a negotiated settlement. One of the greatest strengths of the mini-trial, in contrast to traditional court proceedings, is the flexibility it offers to the parties.[20] Like mediation and the private mini-trial, the judicial mini-trial is not appropriate where there is no relationship to be preserved[21] or where the case involves "unsettled or novel questions of law — especially if the unresolved legal issue involves the establishment of important legal precedent — 'the credibility of witnesses, multiple parties', unusually 'factually complex, lengthy, or factually contested cases', multiple party disputes, and cases that are 'potentially tainted by fraud'".[22]

> The judicial mini-trial can be conceptualized, philosophically, either as an "advanced negotiation technique" or as "expedited litigation". The resolution of the litigation will have been expedited if settlement is achieved. Short of settlement, the mini-trial process may help counsel to clarify and narrow the issues, eliminate some, and thus shorten the length of the trial that does take place. Participating in the mini-trial process will give the lawyers a headstart on their preparation to present and argue the case at trial, thereby promoting "more efficient use of legal time than may occur during the drawn-out preparation that takes place over many years in the typical big case."[23]

If the judicial mini-trial does not produce a settlement, the trial will come before a different judge than the one who participated in the judicial mini-trial,[24] though the neutral could become a mediator if that is appropriate.[25]

---

18 Judicial Mini-Trial, pp. 27–28 (footnotes omitted).
19 Arnold, *Vocabulary*, p. 38. See also Judicial Mini-Trial, p. 6.
20 Judicial Mini-Trial, p. 17.
21 *Ibid.*, p. 18.
22 *Ibid.*, p. 19 (footnotes omitted).
23 *Ibid.*, p. 5.
24 *Ibid.*, p. 33.
25 Arnold, *Vocabulary*, p. 39.

17.12 Arbitration

Arbitration is a form of adjudication that produces a binding win-lose result. Some arbitration is referred to as non-binding, but that type of arbitration is merely a variety of mediation. Arbitration has much of the formality and inflexibility of a court proceeding (both are virtues under the right circumstances). There are, however, many varieties of arbitration and the negotiators to a technology transfer agreement should not casually accept any arbitration clause or treat it as irrelevant legal boilerplate. Some arbitration rules specify three arbitrators if the parties do not designate a specific number; some specify a single arbitrator. Some rules of arbitration permit arbitrators who are not independent. Some rules require detailed decisions, others require no decision unless otherwise specified.[26] A negotiator should be aware of the rules that will apply to arbitration arising out of their agreement. Tom Arnold provides an annotated set of rules that the drafters of technology transfer agreements should consider. Some of these rules are:

(a)   the number of arbitrators to be involved, the experience required of each, and how they are selected;

(b)   all disputes will be referred to arbitration;

(c)   contrast a dispute arising out of the due payment of royalties with a dispute over the rejection of technology based on functional defects;

(d)   should the different topics be referred to different types of arbitration with different adjudicators being preferred?

(e)   time and place of arbitration; language to be used and availability of experienced interpreters;

(f)   the necessity for reasons, taking into account the delay and increased costs that result from reasons being required;

(g)   the procedural rules to be followed;

(h)   payment of costs; and

(i)   the enforceability of the arbitrator's award through the court system in the local country (which is particularly important in less developed countries).[27]

17.13 Baseball Arbitration

Derived from arbitration used to settle pay disputes with baseball players, baseball arbitration requires the parties to write out their proposed settlement and to present it to the arbitrator before proceeding to arbitration. At the completion of the arbitration, the arbitrators will be required to open the sealed proposals for the first time and to select one of the proposals.[28]

---

[26]   Tom Arnold, "Arbitration? Here Are Real Recommendations" in Les Nouvelles, Journal of the Licensing Executive Society, Vol. XXVII, No. 1, March 1993, p. 24, at 24.

[27]   For an excellent checklist of matters to be considered see Tom Arnold's 32-point checklist in *Vocabulary*, p. 29.

[28]   Arnold, *Vocabulary*, p. 25.

17.14 Mediation And Last Offer Arbitration (MEDALOA)

This is a combination of Mediation And Last Offer Arbitration (a variety of baseball arbitration). In essence, the parties proceed through mediation and, if the mediation fails, they proceed to arbitration. In simple cases the mediator moves immediately to "baseball arbitration" and selects only one of the proposed settlement offers. In more complex cases, the dispute goes through the more traditional arbitration procedure but the arbitrator is still restricted to one of the proposed offers.[29]

17.15 Availability

Before selecting any one of many variations of dispute resolution, the negotiators to the technology transfer agreement must consider the availability and enforceability of the dispute resolution mechanisms under the local law.

---

[29] *Ibid.*, p. 26.

Part VIII

LEGALESE

Chapter 18

PRELIMINARY MATTERS AND DRAFTING STYLE[*]

The agreement should be precise and concise, using business language without ambiguity.

18.1 Licences are Contracts

Technology transfer agreements are contracts and the general principles for the drafting and interpretation of contracts apply. Unlike many contracts, however, the relationship also must contemplate a flexible, vibrant and changing business relationship. The certainty that lawyers prefer is often not available in these agreements. In the end, it must be recognized that "agreements to agree" are not enforceable, so the need for business flexibility must be balanced with the legal need for enforceability.

18.2 Parties

The parties to the technology transfer agreement must be clearly and correctly identified. Because different companies may be incorporated in different jurisdictions with the same names, it is recommended to state each company's name as well as its place of incorporation, perhaps including the location of its head office. Upon identifying any party that has any material relationship with the United States, examine the nature of the party, the transaction and the subject technology to see where they fit in the U.S. Anti-Trust I.P. Guidelines.[1]

18.2.1 Divisions

A division of a company is not a legal entity; the company itself should be party to the agreement with the use of the technology restricted to the appropriate division. The agreement could contemplate the division disappearing in a corporate reorganization and might use a functional description for the division (for example, if the technology is an innovative herbicide, describe the part of the company's business that manufactures and sells fertilizer for use on agricultural lands). The agreement could also contemplate the company itself being acquired or merged with another company.[2]

---

[*] This material is derived from the author's work, "Dreadful Drafting, The Do's and Don'ts of Licensing Agreements."

[1] See Chapter 10 of this text.

[2] See Chapter 7 of this text.

18.2.2 Partnerships

If one party is a partnership, the agreement could state the names of the current partners, and the party signing the agreement should provide a warranty of authority to bind the partnership. In some jurisdictions partnerships must be registered and their registration details could be inserted in the agreement.

18.2.3 Determining the Nature of Business Entities Involved

In some countries it is more difficult to determine the nature of business entity and who has what corporate authority. This has been a significant problem in the countries formerly comprising the U.S.S.R. Local advice may be necessary.

18.3 Effective Date

Because several agreements relating to the same subject-matter could be entered into as the relationship of the parties develops, the first page of the agreement could contain a reference date or refer to an effective date. If the word processor that is used requires "footers" for later determining the location of the document on the computer, a date for each draft can be inserted in the footer for ease of reference.

18.4 Place of Signing

Frequently, agreements will specify where they are signed. This may influence the choice of law, and, thus, the application of local laws, as well as imposition of sales and other taxes.

18.5 Recitals

Recitals are useful for setting out the background to the agreement and for establishing some initial definitions. Recitals can be used to assist a reader in understanding the intention of the parties, their prior relationship, if any, and what each party expects to contribute to, and receive out of, the relationship established by the agreement. No substantive part of the agreement (*i.e.*, a commitment by either party) should appear in the Recitals if they are placed physically (as is often the case in Canada) before the statement "IT IS AGREED" (or however worded). Recitals are particularly powerful assists to the business reader, especially if the agreement moves immediately from the Recitals to the essential terms (*e.g.*, the grant clause), with definitions and the usual boiler-plate clauses located at the end of the agreement. The definitions can be placed in an appendix for ease of access. Mayers and Brunsvold recommend that the contract opener set out a header "which identifies the parties and assigns the agreement an effective date . . . a set of 'recitals', and a formalistic transition clause such as 'NOW THEREFORE the parties agree as follows'"[3], rather than have the formal "IT IS AGREED" clause follow the recitals in the traditional Canadian way.

---

[3]   Harry R. Mayers and Brian G. Brunsvold, *Drafting Patent License Agreements*, 3rd ed. (Washington D.C.: The Bureau of National Affairs, Inc., 1994), p. 13.

18.6 Benefits Derived from Definitions

Those who negotiate a technology transfer agreement will not necessarily be the same as those persons who will be responsible for its execution and management, since, among other reasons, personnel in enterprises change over a period of time. It is essential, therefore, that the technology transfer agreement reflect definitely and accurately the intention of the parties, and avoid, to the greatest extent possible, ambiguity and misunderstandings. Language is a rich source of possible misunderstandings, particularly in the context of international agreements, since different nuances in the meaning of words in the same language used in different regions of the world are common, and the meaning of concepts differs between languages. For these reasons, a technology transfer agreement commonly contains definitions of key terms in relation to which misunderstandings must be avoided at all costs.[4]

18.6.1 Use Definitions to Isolate Issues

Definitions allow the drafter of the technology transfer agreement to isolate issues for the reader. Definitions reduce the verbiage and the accompanying complexity and, thus, help the drafter to "achieve clarity and consistency without burdensome repetition".[5]

Strategy: Use definitions to achieve clarity.

18.6.2 Expansive Definitions

Some definitions do not truly define the meaning (*i.e.*, confine the meaning of the defined word to certain specifics).[6] Instead, some definitions of the word expand the normal meaning, for example, "*Software* means the computer program and user manual." Sometimes the definition does not define the word at all but only adds a specific meaning to its ordinary meaning. For example, "*Software* includes the user manual." "Software" is not a term that is defined at all by this definition (does it mean executable code, source code, annotations, flow charts?); this definition, instead of adding certainty, has added an unexpected component (*i.e.*, the "user manual"). Sometimes an expansive "definition" is appropriate; more often it gives rise to confusion.

Strategy: Whenever possible, design definitions to limit and not to expand the meaning.

---

4   General Considerations Concerning Licensing, *Guide on the Licensing of Buy-Out Technology*, World Intellectual Property Organization, Chapter 4, p. 39, at 41–42. Some might suggest that lawyers speak a different language than most businesspeople and this has the same cultural impact as travelling from one country to another.

5   See Robert C. Dick, *Legal Drafting in Plain English*, 3rd ed., (Scarborough: Carswell, 1995), p. 77 (hereinafter "Dick, *Legal Drafting*"), quoting from R. Dickerson, *The Fundamentals of Legal Drafting* (Boston and Toronto: Little, Brown & Co., 1965), p. 98. Dick provides a helpful discussion of the various types of definitions.

6   David Mellinkoff, *Legal Writing: Sense & Nonsense* (St. Paul, Minn.: West Publishing Co., 1982), p. 26 (hereinafter "Mellinkoff, *Legal Writing*").

18.6.3 Forced Definitions

Some definitions are more than expansions of meanings; they give meanings that have no correlation to the normal meaning of the word that is being used, for example, "Software means a user manual." Anyone reading the technology transfer agreement and encountering the word "software" might be misled or, at a minimum, very frustrated each time that he or she has to translate the common meaning to the forced meaning. Forced definitions are found even in patent applications.

Strategies:

(1)   *A reader of any document should check the definition section carefully to arrive at the intended meaning and should watch for forced meanings that disguise the business intent.*

(2)   *Better yet, do not use nor permit others to use forced definitions in negotiated technology transfer agreements.*

18.6.4 Sources of Definitions

The use of definitions that have been used previously and, perhaps, even discussed in judicial decisions can assist in acheiving clarity and precision. Definitions can be found:

(a)   in legal dictionaries;

(b)   in specialized manuals;[7] and

(c)   in published precedents.[8]

Strategy: Use previously interpreted definitions.

18.6.5 Unless the Context Otherwise Requires

Drafters often write "in this Article 2, the following words shall have the following meanings, *unless the context otherwise requires*". The last five words negatively influence the definition section. Each time a defined word appears, the reader will be required to decide whether the definition applies or whether the "context" of the agreement here, or in any other place, requires another meaning. The goal of the use of definitions is to increase precision and ease of reading and analysis.

Strategies:

(1)   *The words "unless the context otherwise requires" reduce precision and make the agreement more difficult to read.*

(2)   *Drafting laziness should not detract from precision.*

---

[7]   For example, Robert P. Bigelow, *Computer Terminology: Judicial and Administrative Definitions*, Computer Law Association, 1993; the *1993-94 Licensing Law Handbook;* and "Samples of Selected Definitions of Biotechnology Terms Occurring in License Agreements", Chapter 6 of the *Guide on the Licensing of Biotechnology*, Woodley/World Intellectual Property Organization (Geneva: WIPO and LES, 1992), p. 97.

[8]   For example, The ABA Draft Model Software Licenses and the AIPLA Software Licensing Compendium.

18.7 Coupled (Tripled?) Synonyms

The traditional drafting style suffers from the long-standing use of strings of synonyms.[9] We often see the use of well-worn phrases such as "releases, relinquishes, quits and forever discharges". Some strings of synonyms always seem to appear together; some writers seem to feel incomplete without all the words being there.[10] Sometimes strings of synonyms are used by drafters who are insecure about the meaning of the individual word, and, as a result of their insecurity, they include them all.[11] Some strings of synonyms can be reduced to one or two words without changing the legal meaning. Long-established precedents should be rewritten to keep the meat and throw out the filler.

Strategy: Eliminate redundant words — less is more.

18.7.1 Long, Long Sentences

Some writers seem to like long sentences — in some cases, 500 words or more without a period. These long, long sentences significantly increase the risk of errors in typing and in proofreading. Errors are lost in the mass of words.

Strategies:
(1)   Avoid verbose, sloppy writing that may produce surprising results.
(2)   Carefully proofread long, long sentences.

18.8 Plain Language

Increasingly, clients are demanding "simple" documents.[12] Too often this results in legal principles being discarded with the legal language. As Mellinkoff notes in "Rule 5" of his superb book on drafting:

> Rule 5: WRITE LAW SIMPLY. DO NOT PUFF, MANGLE OR HIDE.
>
> The only thing about legal writing that is both unique and necessary is law. To simplify legal writing, first get the law right. You can't simplify by omitting what the law requires or including what the law forbids. The better you know the law, the easier to decide what law ought to go in, and what is overkill or window dressing.[13]

---

[9]   See Dick, *Legal Drafting*, p. 126.
[10]   Mellinkoff, *Legal Writing*, p. 126, states: "The explanations for wordiness in legal writing do not justify keeping it that way."
[11]   Dick, *Legal Drafting*, suggests, at p. 127, that this insecurity may result from inadequate training. This is true to some extent, but many adequately trained and skilled drafters still suffer from this insecurity.
[12]   So are many legislators. See, for example, the EC Directive on Unfair Terms in Consumer Contracts (Directive 93/13) which
>   imposes an obligation that all contract terms must be drafted in plain intelligible language which, amongst other things, may require suppliers of goods distributed throughout Europe to draft contracts in the national languages of each state or, perhaps, to prepare separate contracts for use in each state. Investment in translations of contractual terms may be a simple step in the direction of compliance with the Directive.
[13]   Mellinkoff, *Legal Writing*, p. 101.

18.8.1 Inclusive Language

As a result of the plain language movement, document drafters increasingly are endeavouring to use inclusive language.[14] With modern word processors, documents can be customized. For example, if all parties are female, the feminine gender could be used throughout, instead of using the masculine gender and relying on a phrase saying that the masculine gender includes the feminine gender. Unfortunately, writing in genderless English is very difficult[15] and sometimes obscures plain language rather than creating it. The use of "you" and "we" in documents may help.

18.9 Visual Appeal

With improved laser printers and libraries of available fonts, documents can be made visually attractive as well as comprehensible. Visual appeal may overcome a reader's initial negative reaction to a complex document.

18.9.1 Block Capitals

Many agreements use block capitals for every defined word. For example, "TRANSFEROR" and "TRANSFEREE". These capitalized words frequently BLOCK communication flow; a feature that should be retained for emphasis has been squandered on a defined word.[16] The use of initial upper-case letters serves the purpose of distinguishing defined words.

Strategy: Do not use BLOCK letters for defined words; they BLOCK the communication flow.

18.10 Marketing

The marketing process does not stop once the drafter of the technology transfer agreement puts pen to paper (or fingers to keyboard). The document should continue to market the technology being offered, not serve as a hindrance to the marketing and negotiating process.

Strategy: Market! Market! Market!

---

[14]   Beware of the mischievous typographical error; one document provided "words importing the masculine gender shall include the feminine and *neutered* gender". The word "neutered" might apply to my "Garfield" sized ex-tomcat, but it would seem to have little other application.

[15]   See Dick, *Legal Drafting*, p. 165.

[16]   The use of BLOCK CAPITALS is a breach of Netiquette — it is equivalent to shouting or "flaming".

Chapter 19

LEGAL RULES AND PROCEDURES

19.1 Introduction

The legal boiler-plate in a technology transfer agreement often seems tedious and endless. There is a tendency to overlook the importance of the rules that innocently sit at the back of the agreement because they do not directly deal with business issues. The boiler-plate, however, may materially alter the position of the parties. The governing law clause may introduce unexpected social policy; the entire agreement clause may exclude promises that one party had expected. This boiler-plate may also provide standard warranties and some legal rules.

19.2 Governing Law and Forum

The branch of law known as "conflict of laws" applies if there is any element of a contract that involves a foreign party. In this context, "foreign party" often refers to a party from another province, another state or another country.[1] A "conflict" may arise if the parties are from different jurisdictions, or the contract is made or is to be performed in a foreign jurisdiction. The conflict of law rules resolve three questions: (1) Which jurisdiction's courts will be entitled to adjudicate on the issue? (2) Which jurisdiction's laws will apply? and (3) Will a foreign award be recognized in each party's home jurisdiction?[2] For example, in an electronic transaction, the transferor could be in Calgary, the licensee in Houston and the technology in London. Will the contract law of Alberta or Texas apply? Will the intellectual property rules of Canada, the United States, or the United Kingdom govern? These conflict of law questions are the subject of statute and common law, and each must be examined to determine how the law applies to the particular facts. Usually, the parties are able to select which jurisdiction will provide the governing laws. A party should not necessarily assume that its own law or judicial system is best. An effective restraining order may be available only from the defaulting party's home jurisdiction.[3] When choosing the jurisdiction whose laws will govern consider the following:

---

[1]   See Dicey and Morris, *The Conflict of Laws*, 12th ed. (London: Sweet & Maxwell, 1993), Vol. 1, p. 3.

[2]   *Ibid.*, p. 4.

[3]   Pegi A. Groundwater, "General Considerations in Drafting Software Licenses," a paper presented at the Licensing Executives Society Annual Meeting, October 26, 1992.

(a)   the selected jurisdiction should have "ample precedents" on the matters in question;[4]

(b)   the agreement should exclude the governing law's "conflict" rules; parties adopting a governing law usually intend to adopt a law that applies to parties domiciled in the same jurisdiction, carrying on activities only in that jurisdiction;

(c)   the parties should review the selected law to determine whether it favours the transferor or the licensee;

(d)   "important idiosyncrasies" in the law of the chosen jurisdiction must be examined, such as the required method of disclaiming implied warranties. For example, not all jurisdictions require "CAPITALS" as required by the *Uniform Commercial Code*. Some jurisdictions have unusual rules relating to penalties or to "consumer" rights;[5] and

(e)   the effect on a world-wide marketing plan if the law of different jurisdictions are applied to the same standard form contract.[6]

When deciding on the appropriate jurisdiction that will provide the judicial forum for determining the legal issues, consider the following:

(a)   the availability of experts who can testify about rules if the forum is not in the same jurisdiction that provides the governing law rules;

(b)   the relationship of each party to the selected jurisdiction;

(c)   the ability of the aggrieved party to effectively enforce the award in the defaulting party's home jurisdiction;

(d)   whether, in the selected jurisdiction, there is a choice of courts (*e.g.*, federal versus state), and, if so, the benefits offered by each court system as contrasted with the disadvantages.

19.3 Standard Warranties

In addition to warranties about product quality, title and against infringement,[7] warranties of authority and against material adverse facts are appropriate, including:

(a)   a warranty of valid corporate subsistence;

(b)   a warranty of power and authority to enter into the agreement;

(c)   a warranty that the execution and performance of the agreement will not contravene any other subsisting agreement;

(d)   a warranty that there is no "kick back" payable as a result of the execution of the agreement; and

(e)   a warranty that there is no existing fact (including bankruptcy) that would prevent the party from fulfilling its obligations under the agreement.[8]

---

[4]   *Software Licensing Compendium* (Boston: American Intellectual Property Law Association, 1992), Vol. 1, p. 129.

[5]   *Ibid.*

[6]   *Ibid.*

[7]   See Chapters 14, 15 and 16 of this text.

[8]   American Bar Association, Section on Patent, Trademark and Copyright Law, Committee on Computer Programs, *Model Software License Provisions*, Committee Chair: D.C. Toedt III of Arnold, White & Durke, Houston, Texas, para. 1051.2

19.4 Survival

If the agreement terminates (rather than the project), some clauses should survive the termination.[9] These include confidentiality obligations and restrictive covenants as well as the obligation to pay amounts then due. Promises made before execution of the agreement should also "survive".

19.5 Assignability

If an agreement is characterized as a "personal services" contract, it is usually not assignable. Otherwise, the agreement usually is assignable. Rather than having assignability determined by often conflicting rules of the common law, the agreement should establish the assignability rules. Some agreements prohibit assignment under any circumstances; some permit assignment with the consent of the other parties; some merely request notice to be given to the other party once the assignment has occurred. If assignment requires consent, the agreement should provide the guidelines for approval or rejection of a proposed assignment. Some agreements require the assignor to provide details of the financial, production and marketing capabilities of the assignee, and whether the assignee is a competitor of the non-assigning party.

19.6 Entire Agreement

The transferor and the licensee may have had lengthy negotiations; the transferor may have promoted its technology by using all sorts of superlatives. The agreement could exclude all that puffery by combining an "entire agreement" clause with a limited and narrow warranty. This clause states that the only promises that will be binding will be those actually written in the agreement and that all others are excluded. The transferor wants this clause to provide certainty to its obligations. The licensee will want to make sure all representations and warranties are included in the agreement and should not rely on any "gentlemen's" or side agreements.

CONCLUSION

A successful licensing arrangement is virtually assured (assuming the technology has merit) if the negotiations leading up to the licence are full and frank, if the licence agreement is well drafted for the particular purpose and if the developer works at maintaining a continuing relationship of support for its customer.

---

[9]   See Chapter 13 of this text.

Appendix A

CHECKLIST FOR INTERNATIONAL LICENSING AGREEMENTS

*This Licence Checklist is based in part on the LES Patent Licence
Checklist and the LES Health Committee Checklist*

1. PARTIES AND BACKGROUND

1.1 Parties
    a. Identification
    b. Capacity or corporate authority, names and addresses
    c. Partnership titles, names and addresses of partners
    d. Legal capacity of foreign firms

1.2 Effective Date of Agreement or Reference Date

1.3 Place Where Agreement is Made

1.4 Background/Recitals
    a. Licensed subject-matter
    b. Prior relationship between parties
    c. What each party will contribute
    d. Statement of expectations

2. DEFINITIONS

3. GRANT OF RIGHTS

3.1 Subject Matter of
    a. Patents
    b. Trademark
    c. Copyright
    d. Industrial design
    e. Chip design
    f. Know-how
    g. Trade secret

3.2 Exclusivity
    a. Exclusive

      i.   First refusal for other exclusive territories
      ii. Duration of first refusal right
      iii. Matching offers of third party ("hard" first refusal)
      iv. Matching offer of licensor before third party offers solicited ("soft" first refusal)
   b. Non-exclusive

3.3   Scope of Grant
   a. Make
   b. Use
   c. Sell
   d. Dispose
   e. Copy
   f. Modify
   g. Distribute
   h. Display
   i. Bundle

3.4   Field of Use
   a. Limited uses
   b. Solely in specified combination
   c. Style or size of product
   d. Sale or use limited to prescribed customers
   e. Sale or use through specified trade channels

3.5   Quantity Limitations
   a. Maximum
      i.   Fixed number
      ii. Percent of industry sales
      iii. Percent of licensor's sales

3.6   Price Limitations (watch restraint of trade implications)

3.7   Tying Arrangements (watch restraint of trade implications)

3.8   Territory
   a. Exclusive
   b. Limited exclusive
   c. Non-exclusive

3.9   Transferability
   a. Non-transferable
   b. Transferable
   c. Transferable to affiliates

3.10 Additional Grants
   a. Affiliates — different locations
   b. Replacement (for equipment specific licence)
   c. Relocation (for site licence)

3.11 Most Favourable Terms and Conditions
    a. Scope of clause
       i.   All terms generally
       ii. Royalty terms only
    b. Application of more favourable terms
       i.   Automatically
       ii. At licensee's option
    c. Original licensee entitled to
       i.   Notification of later licence
       ii. Copy of later licence

3.12 Special Aspects Concerning Patents
    a. Maintenance in force of patent
    b. Duty to pay renewal fees
    c. Option of licensee to acquire patents

3.13 Where Licensed Patent Invalid
    a. Right to terminate
    b. Effect on royalty payments
    c. Liability of licensor to licensee
       i.   Limited to duty to co-operate
       ii. Arbitrary amount (*e.g.*, not exceeding licence fee)
       iii. Not in excess of compensation received from licensee

3.14 Sublicences
    a. Prohibited
    b. Permitted
       i.   Affiliates
          A. If dealing as if at arm's length
          B. Royalties guaranteed by licensee
          C. Compliance guaranteed by licensee
          D. Sharing of royalties
             (1) Lump sum payments
             (2) Running royalties
          E. Reporting of sublicence being granted
          F. Form of sublicence
          G. Effect of termination of licence
             (1) Termination of sublicence
             (2) Right of licensor to assume sublicence
             (3) Obligation of licensor to assume sublicence

3.15 Improvements
    a. Definitions of "improvement"
    b. By licensor — licensor to licensee
       i.   Inclusion in licence
          A. Automatic
          B. At option of licensee

        C. At option of licensor
    ii.   Exclusive
        A. Royalty free
        B. Compensation
    iii. Non-exclusive
        A. Royalty free
        B. Compensation
    iv. Except out improvements made under special contract to third parties
  c. By licensee — "grant-back" licence to licensor
    i.   Exclusive
        A. Royalty free
        B. Compensation
    ii.   Non-exclusive
        A. Royalty free
        B. Compensation
  d. Sublicence of improvements
    i.   By parties jointly
    ii.   Joint ownership maintained
  e. Allocation of patent prosecution expenses
  f. Improvements developed by other licensee
  g. Related matters
  h. Invention agreements with key employees
  i. Duration of licence re improvements

4.   SPECIAL ASPECTS CONCERNING PATENTS

4.1   Patent Marking
  a. Form of notice
    i.   As specified by statute
    ii.   As specified in agreement
    iii. As specified by licensor during term of agreement
  b. Position of notice on products

4.2   Prosecution of Licensed Application
  a. Responsibility for prosecution
    i.   Direction of prosecution
    ii.   Expenses of prosecution
  b. Effect of non-allowance of claims on royalty payments

4.3   Foreign Exploitation by Licensee
  a. Licence under foreign patents
    i.   Responsibility for patent costs
    ii.   Sublicensing rights
  b. Authority to export
  c. Prohibition of exports

4.4   Option to Purchase Patent

a. Outright option
b. First right to purchase

5.   SPECIAL ASPECTS CONCERNING TRADE SECRETS

5.1   Furnishing of Information

5.2   Technical Information
a. Specifications
b. Delivery
c. Form, language and system of measurement
d. Produced by third parties
e. Missing information

5.3   Quality Control

5.4   Trademark Notifications

6.   SPECIAL ASPECTS CONCERNING CONFIDENTIAL INFORMATION

6.1   Definition of "Confidential Information"

6.2   Duration of Obligation

6.3   Exceptions — Permitted Disclosure
a. Public domain
b. Developed independently
c. Acquired from third party
d. In licensee's possession
e. Government authorities
f. Court and arbitration proceedings
g. Auditors
h. Bankers
i. Joint venturers

6.4   Duties of Care

6.5   Restrictions on Use

6.6   Disclosure to Employees and Others having a "Need-to-Know"

6.7   Disclosure to Subsidiaries, Affiliates or Associates and Approved Research Institutions

6.8   Disclosure to Subcontractors

6.9   Disclosure to Promote Sale

6.10 Previous Agreements

6.11 Indemnification for Breach

b. At licensee's plant site

11.2 Training Personnel — Licensor
a. Number

11.3 Trainees — Licensee
a. Number and qualifications
b. How chosen
c. Substitutions for unsatisfactory trainees
d. Accreditation of training

11.4 Duration of Training

11.5 Language of Training Seminars

11.6 Living and Working Conditions for Licensor's Personnel in Licensee's Country
a. Living conditions for licensor's/licensee's personnel
b. Costs
c. Safe departure, etc.
d. Working conditions at licensee's plant site
e. Phone and fax, etc.
f. Hours of work
g. Holidays
h. Access to site and all relevant data

11.7 Other Services
a. Design and engineering services
b. Technological consulting services
c. Repairs and maintenance services
d. Marketing and commercial services
e. Planning research and development service
f. Additional services
g. Changes in services
h. Fees for services
i. Furnishing advisory services
    i. Time limitations
    ii. Compensation for licensor
j. Responsibility for damages and injuries by acts of licensor
k. Employment of licensor or retention as consultant

12. SUPPLY OF RAW MATERIALS, COMPONENTS, SPARE PARTS, EQUIPMENT, ETC.

12.1 Purchase of Equipment from Licensor

12.2 Option to Purchase
a. From licensee

b. From licensor

12.3 Purchase in Licensee's Country

12.4 Assurances of Source of Supply
   a. Stated preference
   b. Favoured nation
   c. Non–discrimination
   d. Purchase from alternative sources

12.5 Quality of Materials

12.6 Price
   a. Market price
   b. Price at which licensor sells to other licensees
   c. No less favourable, etc.

12.7 Exclusion of Items from Contract Price in Licensing Agreement

12.8 Delivery of Equipment
   a. Dates and effect of delay
   b. Manner of shipment
   c. Responsibilities of licensor
   d. Responsibilities of licensee
   e. Passage of title
   f. Assignment of warranty
   g. Confirmation of delivery
   h. Payment dependent upon receipt of confirmation
   i. Risk

13. EXPLOITATION OF LICENSED TECHNOLOGY

13.1 Duty to Exploit
   a. Fill demand only
   b. Create demand also
   c. Payment of minimum royalty as satisfaction of duty

13.2 Specific Obligations
   a. Production facilities
      i.   Time of completion
      ii. Capacity
   b. Production and sales
      i.   Time of commencement
      ii. Product standards
      iii. Minimum units
   c. Advertising
      i.   Approval by licensor
      ii. Minimum budget
   d. Servicing

15.5 Royalties for Different Components of Licenced Technologies — Separate Pricing or Pricing as a Whole
   a. Patent
   b. Trademarks
   c. Copyright
   d. Trade Secrets

15.6 Variable Consideration
   a. Rate
      i. Flat sum per unit
      ii. Flat percentage of gross or net sales
      iii. Rate decreases or increases with increasing sales
      iv. Differential
      v. Temporarily low
      vi. Flat sum per year
      vii. Flat sum for paid-up licence
      viii. Dollar amount ceiling on annual payments
      ix. Dollar amount ceiling on aggregate payment
      x. Lower royalties if licensee opts to make a lump-sum payment
      xi. Annual or aggregate dollar amount ceiling on royalties to apply if licensee opts to make a lump-sum payment
      xii. Payment until a certain number of units are sold, then an increase or decrease in initial rate (or a fully-paid licence)
   b. Base
      i. Number of units
         A. Manufactured, sold or processed
         B. All units or patented only
         C. Definition of "sold"
         D. One payment per unit
      ii. Supplies or raw materials used
         A. Volume basis
         B. Cost basis
      iii. Use compensation received by licensee
      iv. Net sales of licensee
         A. All articles or patented only
         B. Definition of "sold"
         C. Definition of "net sales"
         D. Effect of credit losses
         E. Sales to affiliates
      v. Profits of licensee

15.7 Royalties for Combination Products
   a. Any royalty relief
   b. Simple algebraic reduction
   c. Subject to floor rate

15.8 Royalties to Continue Past Patent Expiry during Period of Regulatory Exclusivity

15.9 Nationality of Parties
    a. Foreign licensee/sublicensee to be responsible for withholding taxes
    b. Licensee to pay all royalties at full rate regardless of where the "sales" take place
    c. Licensee to provide licensor with certificate for withholding tax paid

15.10 Royalty Payment
    a. Payment mandatory
       i.   In advance of each royalty period
       ii. At end of each royalty period
    b. Payment optional
       i.   To retain exclusiveness
       ii. To maintain licence
    c. In satisfaction of duty to exploit
    d. Carry over of payments from one period to another

15.11 Related Matters
    a. Allowance for royalties payable to others
    b. Exemption on sales to other licensees
    c. Interest on overdue payments
    d. Effect of termination on obligation to pay accrued royalties

16. SETTLEMENT OF PAYMENT

16.1 Reporting
    a. Frequency
    b. Content of royalty reports

16.2 Maintenance and Inspection of Records
    a. Duty to maintain records
    b. Account for progress
    c. Right of licensor to inspect
       i.   Financial records
       ii.   Production records
       iii. Inventory on hand
       iv. Measures implemented to maintain secrecy, quality control, etc.
    d. Inspection by licensor
    e. Inspection by independent auditor
       i.   Method of selection of auditor
       ii.   Pre-agreement on satisfactory auditors
    f. Time limitation
    g. Information confidential

16.3 Cost of Audit

16.4 Withholding of Taxes

16.5 Designation of Currency of Obligation and Payment
    a. Currency of the obligation
        i.   Local currency
        ii. Foreign currency
    b. Currency of the payment
        i.   Local currency
        ii. Local currency — restricted circumstances
        iii. Foreign currency
    c. Rate of exchange
        i.   Source
        ii. Date for determination

16.6 Foreign Exchange Controls

16.7 Designation of Instrumentalities for Remittance and Receipt of Payment

16.8 Payment
    a. Time and place for payment
    b. Method of payment
        i.   Effect of new or changed laws
        ii. Effect of change in exchange control law
    c. Late payments
    d. Interest
    e. Termination

16.9 Payment Milestones — Conditions Precedent to Payment
    a. Execution of agreement
    b. Approval of implementation of documentation (*i.e.*, documents detailing steps re supply and installation)
    c. Factory test completed
    d. Technology delivered to site
    e. Installation completed
    f. Preliminary acceptance
    g. Final acceptance

16.10 Security for Payment
    a. Letters of credit
        i.   Transferrable
        ii. Revocable
        iii. Irrevocable
        iv. Confirmed
    b. Stand-by letters of credit
    c. Performance guarantee
    d. Forfeit financing
    e. Failure of guarantee
        i.   Liquidated damages

    ii.   Guarantee of liquidated damages

  f. Payment documents

16.11 Certification of Net Selling Price

17. RELEASE FOR PAST INFRINGEMENTS

17.1 Licensor/Licensee's Customers

17.2 Absolute

17.3 Conditional
    a. On continuance of agreement
    b. On payment of prescribed sum

17.4 Specific or General Release

18. SUBLICENSING AND SUBCONTRACTING

18.1 To Third Persons
    a. Prohibited
    b. Permitted

18.2 To Associates
    a. Prohibited
    b. Permitted

18.3 To Government Agencies or Institutions
    a. Prohibited
    b. Permitted
    c. Back in rights of government

18.4 Terms and Duration

18.5 Licensor Reserves Right to Examine Each Assignee and Withhold Consent
    a. Unreasonably
    b. Within reason

18.6 Copy to Licensor

18.7 Rights and Liabilities of Licensor Regarding Royalties

19. ACCEPTANCE TESTS

19.1 Performance of Tests
    a. Time period within which acceptance tests must be conducted
    b. Notification to licensor of intention to conduct test
    c. Rights and obligations of licensor
        i.   To attend at testing
        ii.   Right to conduct or to participate in testing
        iii. Obligation of licensor to provide advisor or to conduct tests

d. Tests to be conducted
e. Records of test results
f. Raw materials, components or machinery, etc. obtained from source other than licensor
   i. Licensee to supply
   ii. Allowance for pre-test by licensor to ensure these meet with specifications
g. Performance test criteria
   i. Quantity of output
   ii. Quality of output
h. Acceptance test condition precedent to payment
i. Test almost passed
   i. Partial payment
   ii. No payment
j. Test not passed due to licensor's fault
   i. Extension period given to licensor to attempt to remedy
   ii. Where remedied — penalty for delay or no penalty
   iii. Where not remedied — penalty or non-payment of retention amount
k. Test not passed due to licensee's fault
   i. Payment without penalty
l. Where test not run within time set due to delays caused by licensee
m. Payment of retention amount without requirement of test
n. Allowance for interruption of tests by *force majeure*

19.2 Failure to Meet Performance Guarantee
a. Modifications at licensor's cost
b. Costs shared
c. Departure from operating conditions – modifications by licensee
d. Failure resulting from engineering not part of technology
e. Failure resulting from design information provided by licensee
f. Failure resulting from raw materials supplied by licensee

19.3 Repetition of Tests

19.4 Delay in Commencement — Extension

19.5 Warranty

19.6 Fulfilment of Performance Guarantee

19.7 Deemed Fulfilment of Performance Guarantee

20. WARRANTIES OF QUALITY

20.1 Merchantability

20.2 Fitness for Purpose

20.3 Conformity with Specifications

20.4 Commercial Utility

20.5 No Warranty

20.6 Disclaimer of Further Warranties
  a. Implied warranties under Canadian legislation (*e.g.*, Alberta *Sale of Goods Act*)
    i. Merchantability
    ii. Fitness for a particular purpose
  b. Implied warranties under foreign legislation (*e.g.*, *Uniform Commercial Code* — U.S.A.)
  c. Implied warranties under U.N. Convention on International Sale of Goods
  d. Warranty that technology will meet licensee's requirements
  e. Warranty that operation will be continuous or error free

20.7 Conditions Precedent and Effectiveness of Warranties

20.8 Guarantee of Equipment Capacity

20.9 Agreement by Licensee Not to Represent to Third Parties that any Warranty is given by the Licensor

21. PERMITS

21.1 Duties of Licensee
  a. Obtain all necessary government approvals within licensee's country
  b. Make all necessary declarations for importing anything into licensee's country
  c. Obtain all necessary permits and visas required by government in licensee's country
  d. Comply with all laws and regulations in licensee's country relating to use of technology being transferred

21.2 Duties of Licensor
  a. Obtain all necessary government approvals within licensor's country
  b. Obtain all necessary permits and visas required by government in licensor's country
  c. Allocation of costs
  d. Obtain permits condition precedent to agreement

22. INSURANCE

22.1 Personal Injury

22.2 Property Damage

22.3 General

    a. Workers' compensation
    b. Employer's liability
    c. Professional liability
    d. Automobile liability
    e. Licensee as additional named insured

22.4 Placement
    a. Amount
    b. Acceptable insurer

23. SAFETY MEASURES

23.1 Duties of Licensor Relating to
    a. Design
    b. Initial training
    c. Supervision
    d. Provision of information for safe operation and handling

23.2 Duties of Licensee Relating to
    a. Engineering
    b. Installation
    c. Process operation
    d. Maintenance
    e. Modifications
    f. Training
    g. Supervision
    h. Establishment of safety and security check systems

23.3 Safety Tests
    a. Initial testing
    b. Periodic inspections

23.4 Development of Emergency Plan

23.5 Accident Investigation and Reporting

24. ENVIRONMENTAL MATTERS

24.1 Liability of Licensor for Environmental Damage
    a. To licensee
       i.   Full liability
       ii. Limited liability
       iii. No liability
    b. To third parties

24.2 Representations and Warranties by Licensor

24.3 Disclosure
    a. Right of licensee to conduct environmental inspection at licensor's plant

b. No liability if full disclosure and right to inspect

24.4 Insurance

25. ACKNOWLEDGMENT OF VALIDITY

25.1 Scope of Clauses
    a. All operations generally
    b. Only operations within licence

25.2 Duration
    a. Term of licence
    b. Term of patents

26. ADMISSION OF INFRINGEMENT

26.1 Scope of Clause
    a. General admission
    b. Specific to identified devices/processes/portions (of copyrighted work)

27. ENFORCEMENT OF LICENSED PATENT

27.1 Right or Obligation of
    a. Licensor
    b. Licensee
    c. Parties jointly

27.2 Allocation of Expenses and Recoveries

27.3 Inaction or Default by One Party
    a. Enforcement by other party
    b. Termination of agreement by other party

27.4 Invalidity of Licensed Patent

28. WARRANTIES OF TITLE, INFRINGEMENT

28.1 Patents and Patent Applications
    a. Validity of patent
    b. Non-infringement

28.2 Ownership of Technology and Right to Licence
    a. Non-infringement
    b. No subsisting or further licences

28.3 Duty to Notify of Claims

28.4 Duty of Licensor to Defend where Action Brought Against Licensee

28.5 Defense of Action
    a. Responsibility for conduct of defence

      iii. Initial period subject to renewal
   c. Option to cancel
      i.   At any time on notice
      ii. Within an initial period
      iii. After a stated period

32. TERMINATION

32.1 By Licensor
   a. Any default of licensee
   b. Bankruptcy or insolvency of licensee
   c. Ceases to carry on business
   d. Non-payment of royalties
   e. Non-payment of minimum royalties
   f. Failure to render royalty and production reports
   g. Failure to exploit
   h. Failure to safeguard confidential information

32.2 By Licensee
   a. Any default of licensor
   b. Licensor not owner of rights
   c. Failure to enforce patents
   d. Patent invalid

32.3 By Either Licensor or Licensee

32.4 Manner of Effecting
   a. Notice of default
   b. Period to remedy
   c. Notice of termination

33. POST-TERMINATION

33.1 Product on Hand
   a. Right of licensee to sell
   b. Rights of licensor to purchase
   c. Limitation in time or units

33.2 Payment of Royalties
   a. Accrued royalties
   b. Royalties on authorized post-termination sales
   c. Examination of licensee's records

33.3 Dealing with Confidential Information
   a. Return of confidential information in tangible form
   b. Destruction of confidential information in tangible form (*e.g.*, on computer)
   c. Continued maintenance of secrecy of confidential information

38.3 When Effective

39. MISCELLANEOUS CLAUSES

   a. Waiver
   b. Governing law
   c. Severability of provisions
   d. Appointment of representative
   e. Language
   f. Original and translations
   g. Governing version
   h. Currency
   i. Further assurances
   j. Enurement
   k. Schedules
   l. Modifications or amendments
   m. Written modifications only
   n. Entire agreement
   o. Counterpart signing
   p. Effective date
   q. Execution

SELECTED BIBLIOGRAPHY

Agmon, Jonathan, Stacey Helpern and David Parker. *The Federal Trademark Dilution Act of 1995*. http://www.ll.georgetowm.edu/lc/internic/trademarks/dilut1.html.

Andrews, William P., Jr. "Limiting Risks in International Transactions: Current Legal Issues in the United States Domestic Transactions for Computer Goods and the Unsigned Services." A paper presented to the World Computer Law Congress, 1991.

Arnold, Tom. *A Vocabulary of ADR Procedures, Introduction to Patenting & Licensing*. Licensing Executive Society (U.S.A. and Canada), Inc., 1995 Manual. Also in *Technology Transfer 1996*. Licensing Executives Society (U.S.A. and Canada).

————. "Arbitration? Here Are Real Recommendations." Les Nouvelles, Journal of the Licensing Executive Society, Vol. XXVII, No. 1, March 1993, p. 24.

————. "100 Factors Involving in Pricing the Technology Licensing." Licensing Law Library. *1988 Licensing Law Handbook*. New York: Clark Boardman Co., Ltd..

August, Casey P. and Derek K.W. Smith. "Software Expression (SSO), Interfaces, and Reverse Assembly," Canadian Intellectual Property Rev., Vol. 10, No. 3, 1994, p. 679.

Bartlett, John. *Familiar Quotations: A Collection of Passages, Phrases and Proverbs Traced to Their Sources in Ancient and Modern Literature*. 16th ed. Edited by Justin Kaplan. Boston: Little, Brown, 1992.

Bender, David and Diana Jarvis. "Multimedia Licensing." An address to the Licensing Executive Society (U.S.A. and Canada) 1994 Annual Meeting, Advanced Software Licensing Issues Seminar, Thursday, October 20, 1994.

Blecher, Melvin. "Legal Standards for Inventorship." Foley and Lardner, home page http:biotechlaw.ari.net.

Branscomb, Lewis M. "Building Capacity to Create, Share, and Use Technology: Civil and Military Models." An Entrepreneurial Approach to the Commercialization of Technology. March 7 and 8, Edmonton, Alberta, Canada. Workshop sponsored by PACT (Partnership/Alberta for the Commercialization of Technology) (Unpublished).

Brown, Catherine A. "Tax Aspects of a Transfer of Technology: The Asia-Pacific Rim." Canadian Tax Paper No. 87. The Canadian Tax Foundation 1994.

————. "The Canada-U.S. Tax Treaty: Its Impact on the Cross-Border Transfer of Technology." (Unpublished).

Brunsvold, Brian G. and Dennis P. O'Reilly. "Implied Licenses." Licensing Executive Society (U.S.A. and Canada) 1993 Annual Meeting. (Unpublished).

Burnside, Michael. "Intellectual Property as a Non-Tariff Barrier." Presented to the Canadian Bar Association, September 26, 1990 at its annual meeting in London, England.

Burshtein, Sheldon. "Surfing the Internet: Canadian Intellectual Property Issues." Presented at the 1996 McGill University Meredith Lectures, May, 1996.

Cairns, David J.A. *The Remedies For Trademark Infringement*. Toronto: Carswell, 1988.

Chesler, Lawrence. "Specifications, Acceptance Testing, Acceptance Procedures and Risk Allocations in Agreements for Complex Systems: The Vendor's Perspective." The Computer Law Association Bulletin, Vol. 6, No. 1, 1991.

Classen, H. Ward, Marc R. Paul and Gary D. Sprague. "Increasing Corporate Competitiveness By Utilizing Independent Contractors." The Computer Law Association Bulletin, Vol. 11, No. 1, 1996, p. 3.

Coolley, Ronald B. "Drafting a Granting Clause." Les Nouvelles, Journal of the Licensing Executive Society, Vol. XXVII, No. 4, December 1992, p. 12.

————. "Importance of Termination Clauses." Les Nouvelles, Journal of the Licensing Executive Society, Vol. XXV, No. 4, December 1990, p. 169.

————. "Recent Developments in Emerging Issues in Licensing." The Licensing Journal, Vol. 14, No. 86, p. 7

Coats, William S. and David M. Barkan, "Multimedia Licensing Issues." Presented in "Evolving Strategies in Evolving Industries" 1994 Licensing Executive Society Winter Meeting, February 16, 1994.

Crispen, John and Terry Marsh. "Preparing for the Future — Implement a Grant-Back." Presentation at the Licensing Executive Society (Canada) 1994 Annual Meeting.

Dicey and Morris, *The Conflict of Laws*. 12th ed. London: Sweet & Maxwell, 1993.

Dick, Robert C. *Legal Drafting in Plain English*. 3rd ed. Scarborough: Carswell, 1995.

Dickerson, R. *The Fundamentals of Legal Drafting*. Boston and Toronto: Little, Brown & Co., 1965.

Drysdale, John and Michael Silverleaf. *Passing off Law and Practice*. 2nd ed. London: Butterworths, 1995.

Fridman, Gerald H.L. *Sale of Goods in Canada*. Scarborough: Thomson Canada Ltd., 1995.

Goldscheider, Robert. *Companion to Licensing Negotiations, Licensing Law Handbook*. New York: Clark Boardman Callaghan, 1993-94.

————. "Litigation Backgrounder for Licensing." Les Nouvelles, Journal of the Licensing Executive Society, Vol. XXIX, No. 1, March 1994, p. 20.

Goss, Joanne. "An Introduction to Alternative Dispute Resolution." Alberta Law Rev., Vol. XXXIV, No. 1, October 1995, p. 1.

Goudreau M., G. Bisson, N. Lacasse and L. Perret, eds., *Exporting Our Technology: International Protection and Transfers of Industrial Innovations.* Montreal: Wilson & Lafleur, 1995.

Granados, Patricia D. "How to prove that you are an Inventor or were the first to Invent." Foley and Lardner, home page http://biotechlaw.ari.net.

Groundwater, Pegi A. "General Considerations in Drafting Software Licenses." A paper presented at the Licensing Executive Society Annual Meeting, October 26, 1992.

Henderson, D.G. "Patent Licensing: Problems from the Impression of the English Language." Ottawa L. Rev., Vol. 4, 1970, p. 62.

Hughes, Roger T. *Hughes on Copyright and Industrial Design.* Rev. ed. Markham: Butterworths, 1984.

————. *Hughes on Trademarks.* Rev. ed. Vancouver: Butterworths Canada Ltd. (loose-leaf).

Jones, Phillip B.C. "Overview of United States Patent Law." Foley and Lardner, home page http://biotechlaw.ari.net.

Kamin, Shelley J. "The Tax System and Technology Transfer Agreements" in M. Goudreau, G. Bisson, N. Lacasse and L. Perret, eds. *Exporting Our Technology: International Protection and Transfers of Industrial Innovations.* Montreal: Wilson & Lafleur, 1995, p. 389.

Kaufman, Kenneth M. "Legal and Business Issues for On-Line Publishers and Content Providers." *The Internet and Business: A Lawyer's Guide to the Emerging Legal Issues.* Edited by Joseph F. Ruh, Jr. The Computer Law Association, Current Issues Publications Series, 1996, p. 107.

Legal Analysis to Support Proposed Examination Guidelines for Computer-implemented Inventions. October 3, 1995. Patent and Trademark Office, United States Department of Commerce.

MacLaren, Terrence F. *Intellectual Property: Worldwide Trade Secrets Law.* Edited by Terrence F. MacLaren. Rev. ed. New York: Clark Boardman Callaghan, 1995.

Mayers, Harry R. and Brian G. Brunsvold. *Drafting Patent License Agreements.* 3rd ed. Washington, D.C.: BNA Books, 1994.

McCabe, Philip J. "Reverse Engineering of Computer Software: A Trap for the Unwary?" The Computer Law Association Bulletin, Vol. 9, No. 2, 1994, p. 4.

McGavock, Daniel M., David A. Haas and Michael P. Patin. "Factors Affecting Royalty Rates." Les Nouvelles, Journal of the Licensing Executive Society, Vol. XXVII, No. 2, June 1992, p. 107.

Meadows, James E. "Ownership Issues Presented in Independent Consultant Engagements: Applying the 'Work for Hire' Doctrine to Computer Programmers." The Computer Law Association Bulletin, Vol. 2, No. 2, 1992, p. 24.

Melincoe, Alan H. "Locked out licensees." "Intellectual Property." http://www.portal.com/~recorder/melon.html.

Mellinkoff, David. *Legal Writing: Sense & Nonsense.* St. Paul, Minn.: West Publishing Co., 1982.

Milgrim, R.M. *Milgrim on Licensing.* Rev. ed. New York: Matthew Binder, 1995.

Nimmer, Raymond T. and Patricia A. Krauthaus. *Commercial Law of License Contracts.* September 9, 1993. (Unpublished).

Nolan, Sandra M. "Resolving Inventorship." Blast, Bulletin of Law/Science and Technology, American Bar Association Section of Science and Technology, No. 95, October 1995, p. 5.

Oppedahl, Carl. "Patent Marking of Systems." Santa Clara Computer and High Technology Law Journal, Vol. 11, No. 2, 1995, p. 205. On the Internet at http: //www.patents.com/lrl.htm.

Peterson, Gale R. "Trade Secrets In an Information Age." Houston L. Rev., Vol. 32, No. 2, 1995.

Phillips, Douglas E. "When Software Fails: Emerging Standards of Vendor Liability Under Uniform Commercial Code." American Bar Association, Section on Business Law, The Business Lawyer, Vol. 50, November 1994, p. 151.

Preston, John T. "Success Factors in Technology Development." An Entrepreneurial Approach to the Commercialization of Technology. March 7 and 8, Edmonton, Alberta, Canada. Workshop sponsored by PACT (Partnership/Alberta for the Commercialization of Technology) (Unpublished).

Radcliffe, Mark. "Key Issues for User of Multimedia." Les Nouvelles, Journal of the Licensing Executive Society, Vol. XXX, No. 2, June 1995, p. 93.

Ramsay, John T., in *Intellectual Property: Worldwide Trade Secrets Law.* Edited by Terrence F. MacLaren. Rev. ed. New York: Clark Boardman Callaghan, 1995.

Reichman, Jerome H. "GATT, TRIPS and NAFTA, the TRIPS component of the GATT's Uruguay Round: Competitive Prospects for Intellectual Property Owners in an Integrated World Market." Fordham Intellectual Property, Media and Entertainment Law Journal, Vol. 14, No. 1, Summer 1993, p. 1. Also printed in M. Goudreau, G. Bisson,

N. Lacasse and L. Perret, eds., *Exporting Our Technology: International Protection and Transfers of Industrial Innovations.* Montreal: Wilson & Lafleur, 1995.

————. "Intellectual Property In International Trade and the GATT" in M. Goudreau, G. Bisson, N. Lacasse and L. Perret, eds., *Exporting Our Technology: International Protection and Transfers of Industrial Innovations.* Montreal: Wilson & Lafleur, 1995, p. 3.

Reid, Chris. *Limiting Risks in International Transactions: U.K. and EEC.* London: University of London, 1991, p. 5.

Roberts, R.J. "Technology Transfer Agreements and North American Competition." M. Goudreau, G. Bisson, N. Lacasse and L. Perret, eds., *Exporting Our Technology: International Protection and Transfers of Industrial Innovations.* Montreal: Wilson & Lafleur, 1995. Also in Intellectual Property Journal, Vol. 9, No. 3, December 1995, p. 247.

Scott, Michael D. and James L. Talbott. "Multimedia: What is it, Why is it Important and What do I need to Know About It?" The Computer Law Association Bulletin, Vol. 8, No. 3, 1995, p. 14.

Seidel, Arthur H., Steven J. Meyers and Nancy Rubner-Frandsen. *What the General Practitioner Should Know about Trademarks and Copyrights.* 6th ed. Philadelphia: American Law Institute-American Bar Association Committee on Continuing Professional Education.

Shiftley, Charles W. and Bradley J. Hulbert. "'Best Efforts' May Not Be the Best Advice." Les Nouvelles, Journal of the Licensing Executive Society, Vol. XXVII, No. 1, March 1992, p. 37.

Sommer, Evelyn M. "Patent and Technology License Agreements Explained." The Licensing Journal, August 1993.

Sookman, Barry B. *Computer Law: Acquiring and protecting information technology.* Toronto: Carswell, 1989.

Sullivan, Patrick H. "Royalty Rates Conform to 'Industry Norm'." Les Nouvelles, Journal of the Licensing Executive Society, Vol. XXIX, No. 3, September 1994, p. 140.

Takach, George Francis. *Patents: A Canadian compendium of law and practice.* Edmonton: Juriliber, 1993.

Tamaro, Normand. *The Annotated Copyright Act.* Scarborough: Carswell, 1995.

Tapscott, Don. *The Digital Economy: Promise and Peril in the Age of Networked Intelligence.* McGraw-Hill, 1966.

Terry, Kathleen R. "Anti-trust and Technology Licensing." Journal of the Association of University Technology Managers, Vol. VII, 1995, p. 83.

Teter, Timothy S. "Merger and the Machines: An Analysis of the Pro-compatibility Trend in Computer Software Copyright." Standford L. Rev., Vol. 45, April 1993, p. 1061.

Todara, John C. "Potential Changes in U.S. Patent Laws: The Publication of Patent Applications." Canadian Intellectual Property Rev., Vol. 12, No. 2, August 1996, p. 227.

Toedt, D.C., III, ed. *1987 Licensing Law Handbook.* New York: Clark Boardman Co., Ltd., 1987.

Tramposch, Albert. "Harmonization of Industrial Property Laws." M. Goudreau, G. Bisson, N. Lacasse and L. Perret, eds., *Exporting Our Technology: International Protection and Transfers of Industrial Innovations.* Montreal: Wilson & Lafleur, 1995, p. 101.

Trebilcock, Michael J. *The Common Law of Restraint of Trade, A Legal and Economic Analysis.* Toronto: The Carswell Co. Ltd., 1986.

Vavor, David "What is a Trade Secret." *Trade Secrets.* Edited by Roger T. Hughes. Toronto: Law Society of Upper Canada, 1990. Papers presented at a conference held at Osgoode Hall, November 24, 1989.

Waddams, S.M. "The General Principles of the Law of Damages." *Law of Remedies*, Special Lectures of the Law Society of Upper Canada, 1995, p. 15.

————. *Products Liability.* Scarborough: Carswell, 1993.

Winship, Peter. "Changing Contract Practices in the Light of the United Nations Sales Convention: A Guide for Practitioners." American Bar Association, Section on International Law and Practice. The International Lawyer, Vol. 29, No. 3, Fall 1995, p. 525.

Woodley, John H. "Taking Care of Trade Secrets: Controlling and Exploiting Trade Secrets in Law and Practice." *Trade Secrets.* Edited by Roger T. Hughes. Toronto: Law Society of Upper Canada, 1990. Papers presented at a conference held at Osgoode Hall, November 24, 1989.

Woodley/World Intellectual Property Organization. *Guide on the Licensing of Biotechnology.* Geneva: WIPO and LES, 1992.

Wright, C.A., A.M. Linden and L.N. Klar. *Canadian Tort Law: Cases, Notes & Materials.* 9th ed. Markham: Butterworths, 1990.

Yoches, E. Robert. "Strategies for Patent Protection." *Corporate Counsel's Guide to Intellectual Property.* Chesterland, Ohio: Business Laws, Inc., 1996, p. 1.205.

INDEX

(references are to section numbers)

M

N

P